CONTENTS

FIGURES

TABLES

PREFACE

This book is based upon my experiences as a research student, practitioner and teacher. The difficulties I faced in understanding research as a student, my discoveries about what was applicable and inapplicable in the field as a practitioner, and my development of the ability to communicate difficult concepts in simple language without sacrificing technicality and accuracy as a teacher have become the basis of this book.

Research methodology is taught as a supporting subject in several ways in many academic disciplines such as health, education, psychology, social work, nursing, public health, library studies and marketing research. The core philosophical base for this book comes from my conviction that, although these disciplines vary in content, their broad approach to a research inquiry is similar. This book, therefore, is addressed to these academic disciplines.

It is true that some disciplines place greater emphasis on quantitative research, and some on qualitative research. My own approach to research is a combination of both. Firstly, the objective decides whether a study should be carried out adopting a qualitative or a quantitative approach. Secondly, in real life most research is a combination of both methods. In a study, some aspects may be qualitative, and others quantitative. This book, therefore, has been written to provide theoretical information in an operational manner about methods, procedures and techniques that are applicable to both approaches, though heavily slanted towards quantitative research.

Research as a subject is taught at different levels. The book is designed specifically for students who are newcomers to research, and who may have a psychological barrier with regard to the subject. I have therefore not assumed any previous knowledge on the part of the reader; I have omitted detailed discussion of aspects that may be inappropriate for beginners; I have used many flow charts and examples to communicate concepts; and areas covered in the book follow a 'simple to complex' approach in terms of their discussion.

The structure of this book, which is based on the model developed during my teaching career, is designed to be practical. The text of the book is therefore organised around the operational steps in the research process. All the information needed to take a particular step is provided in one place. Each chapter is devoted to a particular aspect of that step (see figure below). For example, 'Formulating a research problem' is the first operational step in the research process. For this you need to know how to review literature, formulate a research problem, deal with variables and their measurement, and construct hypotheses. Hence, under this step, there are four chapters. The information they provide will enable you to formulate a problem that is researchable. These chapters are titled: 'Reviewing the literature', 'Formulating a research problem', 'Identifying variables', and 'Constructing hypotheses'. Similarly, for the operational step III, 'Constructing an instrument for data collection' the chapters titled 'Selecting a method of data collection', 'Collecting data using attitudinal scales', and 'Establishing the validity and reliability of a research instrument' will provide sufficient information for you to develop an instrument for data collection for your study. At each step, a smorgasbord of methods, models and procedures is provided so the most appropriate one can be selected.

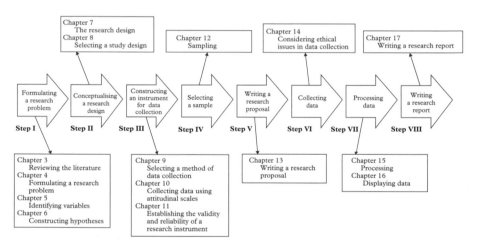

It is my belief that a sound knowledge of research methodology is essential for undertaking a valid study. Up to the process of data collection to answer your research questions, a knowledge of research methods is crucial. Statistics and computers play a significant role in research but their application is mainly after the data has been collected. To me, statistics are useful in confirming or contradicting conclusions drawn from analysed data, in providing an indication of the magnitude of the relationship between two or more variables under study, in helping to establish causality, and in ascertaining the level of confidence that can be placed in your findings. A computer's application is primarily in data analysis, the calculation of statistics, word processing and the graphic presentation of data, where it saves time and makes it easier for you. This book does not include statistics or information about computers.

The second edition of the book incorporates some of the suggestions received from reviewers and colleagues. A new chapter has been added: Chapter 18 'Research methodology and practice evaluation'. This chapter explores the links between research methodology and intervention/program evaluation, and provides information about different aspects of evaluation research. Chapter 9 'Selecting a method of data collection' has been expanded to incorporate, in greater depth, commonly used qualitative methods of data collection. There is now more in-depth discussion of research paradigms. There was a suggestion to change the placement of Chapter 13, 'Writing a research proposal' and bring it forward as some academic departments expect students to start developing their research proposals quite early; however, I decided against it because of its logical current placement. Additions have also been made in many other chapters to provide a balanced picture. In places the language has been changed to enhance flow and ease in reading.

I am grateful to a number of people who have helped me in the writing of this book. I am immensely thankful to Dr Norma Watson, who has put enormous effort into editing this book and in providing valuable comments on its contents. I would not have been able to complete the task without her unqualified help.

My students have taught me how to teach research. This book is an outcome of the feedback I have received from them over the years. How, and at what stage, a concept should be taught, I have learnt from my students. I thankfully acknowledge their contribution to this book.

I also thank Dr Denis Ladbrook, who has reviewed some of the chapters of the first edition and given valuable suggestions, Dr Deenaz Damania, a long-time friend and an expert in qualitative research, for her inspiration and comments, and Valerie Marlborough for her excellent copy editing of this edition.

Ranjit Kumar

CHAPTER
one

Research: a way of thinking

Research: a way of examining your practice

Research is undertaken within most professions. More than a set of skills, research is a way of thinking: examining critically the various aspects of your day-to-day professional work; understanding and formulating guiding principles that govern a particular procedure; and developing and testing new theories for the enhancement of your practice. It is a habit of questioning what you do, and a systematic examination of the observed information to find answers, with a view to instituting appropriate changes for a more effective professional service. Let us take some disciplines as examples.

Suppose you are working in the field of health. You may be a front-line service provider, supervisor or health administrator/planner. You may be in a hospital or working as an out reach community health worker. You may be a nurse, doctor, occupational therapist, physiotherapist, social worker or other paramedic. In any of these positions, some of the following questions may come to your mind:

* How many patients do I see every day?
* What are some of the most common conditions prevalent among my patients?
* What are the causes of these conditions?
* Why do some people have a particular condition whereas others do not?
* What are the health needs of the community?
* Why do some people use the service while others do not?
* What do people think about the service?
* How satisfied are patients with the service?
* How effective is the service?
* How can the service be improved?

You can add many other questions to this list. At times it may be possible to ignore these questions because of the level at which you work, at other times you may make an effort to find answers on your own initiative, or, sometimes, you may be required to obtain answers for effective administration and planning.

Let us take another discipline: business studies. Assume you work in the area of marketing. Again, you can work at different levels: as a salesperson, sales manager or sales promotion executive. The list of questions that may come to your mind can be endless. The types of question and the need to find answers to them will vary with the level at which you work in the organisation. You may just want to find out the monthly fluctuation in the sale of a particular product, or you may be asked to develop an R & D strategic plan to compete for a greater share of the market for the products produced by your company. Besides these, there could be many other questions for which you require answers. For example:

* What is the best strategy to promote the sale of a particular product?
* How many salespersons do I need?
* What is the effect of a particular advertising campaign on the sale of this product?

- How satisfied are the consumers with this product?
- How much are consumers prepared to spend on this item?
- What do consumers like or dislike about this product?
- What type of packaging do consumers prefer for this product?
- What training do the salespersons need to promote the sale of this product?
- What are the attributes of a good salesperson?

To take a different example, let us assume that you work as a psychologist, counsellor or social worker. While engaging in the helping process you may ask yourself (or someone else can ask) the following questions:

- What are my clients' most common presenting problems?
- What are their most common underlying problems?
- What is the socioeconomic background of my clients?
- Why am I successful in certain cases and not in others?
- What resources are available in the community to help a client with a particular need?
- What intervention strategies are appropriate for this problem?
- How satisfied are my clients with my services?

As a supervisor, administrator or manager of an agency, again different questions relating to efficient and effective service may come to your mind. For example:

- How many people are coming to my agency?
- What are the socioeconomic-demographic characteristics of my clients?
- How many cases in a day can a worker effectively handle?
- Why do some people use the service while others do not?
- How effective is the service?
- What are the most common needs of clients who come to this agency?
- What are the strengths and weaknesses of the service?
- How satisfied are the clients with the service?
- How can I improve this service for my clients?

As a professional you might be interested in finding answers to theoretical questions, such as:

- Which is the most effective intervention for a particular problem?
- What causes X or what are the effects of Y?
- What is the relationship between two phenomena?
- How do I measure the self-esteem of my clients?
- How do I ascertain the validity of my questionnaire?
- What is the pattern of program adoption in the community?
- Which is the best way of finding out community attitudes towards an issue?
- Which is the best way to find out the effectiveness of a particular treatment?
- How can I select an unbiased sample?
- What is the best way to find out about the level of marriage satisfaction among my clients?

In this age of consumerism you cannot afford to ignore the consumers of a service. Consumers have the right to ask questions about the quality and effectiveness of the service they are receiving and you, as a service provider, have an obligation to answer their questions. Some of the questions that a consumer may ask are:

- How effective is the service that I am receiving?
- Am I getting value for money?
- How well-trained are the service providers?

Most professions that are in the human service industry would lend themselves to the questions raised above and you as a service provider should be well prepared to answer them. Research is one of the ways to help you to answer such questions objectively.

Applications of research

Very little research in the field is pure in nature. That is, very few people do research in research methodology *per se*. Most research is applied research, which has wide application in many disciplines. Every profession uses research methods in varying amounts in many areas. They use the methods and procedures developed by research methodologists in order to increase understanding in their own profession and to advance the professional knowledge base. It is through the application of research methodology that they strengthen and advance their own profession. Examine your own field. You will find that its professional practice follows procedures and practices tested and developed by others over a long period of time. It is in this testing process that you need research skills, the development of which fall in the category of pure research. As a matter of fact, the validity of your findings entirely depends upon the soundness of the research methodology adopted.

Research techniques applied entirely in nature are used primarily for professional consolidation, understanding, development and advancement.

As just mentioned, the questions that can be raised about any profession where you directly or indirectly provide a service—health (nursing, occupational therapy, physiotherapy, community health, health promotion, public health), education, town planning, library studies, psychology, business studies, social work—can be considered from four different perspectives:

1 the service provider;
2 the service administrator, manager and/or planner;
3 the service consumer; and
4 the professional.

These perspectives are summarised in Figure 1.1. It is impossible to list all the issues in every discipline but this framework can be applied to most disciplines and situations in the humanities and the social sciences to identify, from the viewpoint of the above perspectives, the possible issues in your own academic field.

Figure 1.1 Applications of research

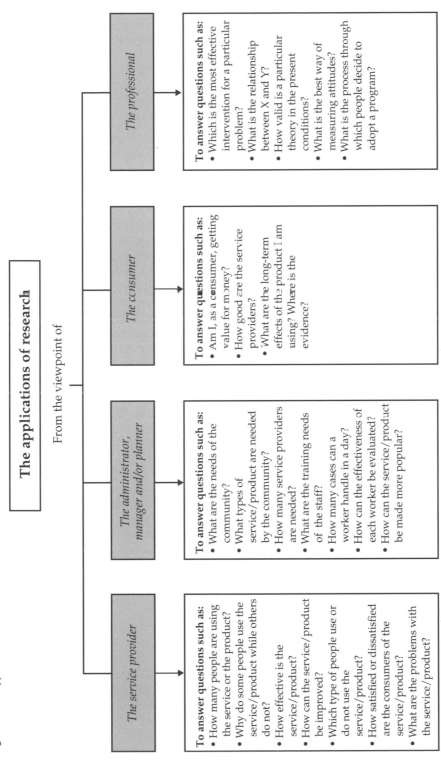

The applications of research

From the viewpoint of

The service provider

To answer questions such as:
• How many people are using the service or the product?
• Why do some people use the service/product while others do not?
• How effective is the service/product?
• How can the service/product be improved?
• Which type of people use or do not use the service/product?
• How satisfied or dissatisfied are the consumers of the service/product?
• What are the problems with the service/product?

The administrator, manager and/or planner

To answer questions such as:
• What are the needs of the community?
• What types of service/product are needed by the community?
• How many service providers are needed?
• What are the training needs of the staff?
• How many cases can a worker handle in a day?
• How can the effectiveness of each worker be evaluated?
• How can the service/product be made more popular?

The consumer

To answer questions such as:
• Am I, as a consumer, getting value for money?
• How good are the service providers?
• What are the long-term effects of the product I am using? Where is the evidence?

The professional

To answer questions such as:
• Which is the most effective intervention for a particular problem?
• What is the relationship between X and Y?
• How valid is a particular theory in the present conditions?
• What is the best way of measuring attitudes?
• What is the process through which people decide to adopt a program?

Definitions of research

There are several ways of obtaining answers to your professional questions. These methods range from the fairly informal, based upon clinical impressions, to the strictly scientific, adhering to the conventional expectations of scientific procedures. *Research is one of the ways to find answers to your questions.* When you say that you are undertaking a research study to find out answers to a question, you are implying that the process:

1. is being undertaken within a framework of a set of philosophies;
2. uses procedures, methods and techniques that have been tested for their validity and reliability;
3. is designed to be unbiased and objective.

Your philosophical orientation may stem from one of the several paradigms and approaches in research—positivist, interpretive, phenomenolist, action or participatory, feminist, qualitative, quantitative—and the academic discipline in which you have been trained. The concept of 'validity' can be applied to any aspect of the research process. It ensures that in a research study correct procedures have been applied to find answers to a question. 'Reliability' refers to the quality of a measurement procedure that provides repeatability and accuracy. 'Unbiased and objective' means that you have taken each step in an unbiased manner and drawn each conclusion to the best of your ability and without introducing your own vested interest. The author makes a distinction between bias and subjectivity. Subjectivity is an integral part of your way of thinking that is conditioned by your educational background, discipline, philosophy, experience and skills. Bias, on the other hand, is a deliberate attempt to either conceal or highlight something. For example, a psychologist may look at a piece of information differently from the way in which an anthropologist or a historian looks at it.

Adherence to the three criteria mentioned above enables the process to be called 'research'. Therefore, when you say you are undertaking a research study to find the answer to a question, this implies that the method(s) you are adopting fulfils these expectations (discussed later in the chapter).

However, the degree to which these criteria are expected to be fulfilled varies from discipline to discipline and so the meaning of 'research' differs from one academic discipline to another. For example, the expectations of the research process are markedly different between the physical and the social sciences. In the physical sciences a research endeavour is expected to be strictly controlled at each step, whereas in the social sciences rigid control cannot be enforced and sometimes is not even demanded.

Within the social sciences the level of control required also varies markedly from one discipline to another, as social scientists differ over the need for the research process to meet the above expectations. Despite these differences among disciplines, their broad approach to inquiry is similar. The research model in this book is based upon this broad approach.

As beginners in research you should understand that research is not all technical, complex, statistics and computers. It can be a very simple activity designed to provide answers to very simple questions relating to day-to-day activities. On the other hand, research procedures can also be employed to

formulate intricate theories or laws that govern our lives. The difference between research and non-research activity is, as mentioned, in the way we find
answers: the process must meet certain requirements to be called research. To
identify these requirements let us examine some definitions of research.

> The word *research* is composed of two syllables, *re* and *search*. The dictionary
> defines the former as a prefix meaning again, anew or over again and the latter as
> a verb meaning to examine closely and carefully, to test and try, or to probe.
> Together they form a noun describing a careful, systematic, patient study and
> investigation in some field of knowledge, undertaken to establish facts or
> principles (Grinnell 1993: 4).

Grinnell further adds: 'research is a structured inquiry that utilises acceptable
scientific methodology to solve problems and creates new knowledge that is
generally applicable.' (1993: 4)

Lundberg (1942) draws a parallel between the social research process,
which is considered scientific, and the process that we use in our daily lives.
According to him:

> Scientific methods consist of systematic observation, classification and inter-
> pretation of data. Now, obviously, this process is one in which nearly all people
> engage in the course of their daily lives. The main difference between our day-to-
> day generalisations and the conclusions usually recognised as scientific method
> lies in the degree of formality, rigorousness, verifiability and general validity of the
> latter (Lundberg 1942: 5).

Burns (1994: 2) defines research as 'a systematic investigation to find
answers to a problem'.

According to Kerlinger (1986: 10), 'scientific research is a systematic,
controlled empirical and critical investigation of propositions about the
presumed relationships about various phenomena'. Bulmer (1977: 5) states:
'Nevertheless sociological research, as research, is primarily committed to
establishing systematic, reliable and valid knowledge about the social world'.

Characteristics of research

From these definitions it is clear that research is a process for collecting,
analysing and interpreting information to answer questions. But to qualify
as research, the process must have certain characteristics: it must, as far as
possible, be controlled, rigorous, systematic, valid and verifiable, empirical,
and critical.

Let us briefly examine these characteristics to understand what they
mean.

- **Controlled**—in real life there are many factors that affect an outcome.
  A particular event is seldom the result of a one-to-one relationship. Some
  relationships are more complex than others. Most outcomes are a sequel
  to the interplay of a multiplicity of relationships and interacting factors.
  In a study of cause-and-effect relationships it is important to be able to
  link the effect(s) with the cause(s) and vice versa. In the study of
  causation, the establishment of this linkage is essential; however, in
  practice, particularly in the social sciences, it is extremely difficult—and
  often impossible—to make the link.

The concept of control implies that, in exploring causality in relation to two variables, you set up your study in a way that minimises the effects of other factors affecting the relationship. This can be achieved to a large extent in the physical sciences, as most of the research is done in a laboratory. However, in the social sciences it is extremely difficult as research is carried out on issues relating to human beings living in society, where such controls are impossible. Therefore, in the social sciences, as you cannot control external factors, you attempt to quantify their impact.

- **Rigorous**—you must be scrupulous in ensuring that the procedures followed to find answers to questions are relevant, appropriate and justified. Again, the degree of rigour varies markedly between the physical and the social sciences and within the social sciences.
- **Systematic**—this implies that the procedures adopted to undertake an investigation follow a certain logical sequence. The different steps cannot be taken in a haphazard way. Some procedures must follow others.
- **Valid and verifiable**—this concept implies that whatever you conclude on the basis of your findings is correct and can be verified by you and others.
- **Empirical**—this means that any conclusions drawn are based upon hard evidence gathered from information collected from real-life experiences or observations.
- **Critical**—critical scrutiny of the procedures used and the methods employed is crucial to a research inquiry. The process of investigation must be foolproof and free from any drawbacks. The process adopted and the procedures used must be able to withstand critical scrutiny.

For a process to be called research, it is imperative that it has the above characteristics.

Types of research

Research can be classified from three perspectives (Figure 1.2):

1 *application* of the research study;
2 *objectives in undertaking* the research;
3 *inquiry mode* employed.

These three classifications are not mutually exclusive—that is, a research study classified from the viewpoint of 'application' can also be classified from the perspectives of 'objectives' and 'inquiry mode employed'. For example, a research project may be classified as pure or applied research (from the perspective of application), as descriptive, correlational, explanatory or exploratory (from the perspective of objectives) and as qualitative or quantitative (from the perspective of the inquiry mode employed).

Figure 1.2   Types of research

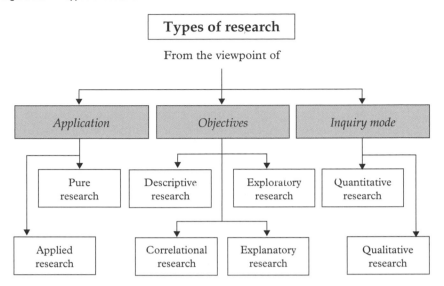

Application

If you examine a research endeavour from the perspective of its application, there are two broad categories: pure research and applied research. In the social sciences, according to Bailey (1978: 17):

> Pure research involves developing and testing theories and hypotheses that are intellectually challenging to the researcher but may or may not have practical application at the present time or in the future. Thus such work often involves the testing of hypotheses containing very abstract and specialised concepts.

Pure research is also concerned with the development, examination, verification and refinement of research methods, procedures, techniques and tools that form the body of research methodology. Examples of pure research include developing a sampling technique that can be applied to a particular situation; developing a methodology to assess the validity of a procedure; developing an instrument, say, to measure the stress level in people; and finding the best way of measuring people's attitudes. The knowledge produced through pure research is sought in order to add to the existing body of knowledge of research methods.

Most of the research in the social sciences is applied. In other words the research techniques, procedures and methods that form the body of research methodology are applied to the collection of information about various aspects of a situation, issue, problem or phenomenon so that information gathered can be used in other ways—such as for policy formulation, administration and the enhancement of understanding of a phenomenon.

Objectives

If you examine a research study from the perspective of its objectives, broadly a research endeavour can be classified as descriptive, correlational, explanatory or exploratory.

A study classified as *descriptive research* attempts to describe systematically a situation, problem, phenomenon, service or program, or provides information about, say, the living conditions of a community, or describes attitudes towards an issue. For example, it may attempt to describe the types of service provided by an organisation, the administrative structure of an organisation, the living conditions of Aboriginal people in the outback, the needs of a community, what it means to go through a divorce, how a child feels living in a house with domestic violence, or the attitudes of employees towards management. The main purpose of such studies is to describe what is prevalent with respect to the issue/problem under study.

The main emphasis in a *correlational research* study is to discover or establish the existence of a relationship/association/interdependence between two or more aspects of a situation. What is the impact of an advertising campaign on the sale of a product? What is the relationship between stressful living and the incidence of heart attack? What is the relationship between fertility and mortality? What is the relationship between technology and unemployment? What is the effect of a health service on the control of a disease, or the home environment on educational achievement? These studies examine whether there is a relationship between two or more aspects of a situation or phenomenon and, therefore, are called correlational studies.

Explanatory research attempts to clarify why and how there is a relationship between two aspects of a situation or phenomenon. This type of research attempts to explain, for example, why stressful living results in heart attacks; why a decline in mortality is followed by fertility decline; or how the home environment affects children's level of academic achievement.

The fourth type of research, from the viewpoint of the objectives of a study, is called *exploratory research*. This is when a study is undertaken with the objective either to explore an area where little is known or to investigate the possibilities of undertaking a particular research study. When a study is carried out to determine its feasibility it is also called a *feasibility study* or a *pilot study*. It is usually carried out when a researcher wants to explore areas about which s/he has little or no knowledge. A small-scale study is undertaken to decide if it is worth carrying out a detailed investigation. On the basis of the assessment made during the exploratory study, a full study may eventuate. Exploratory studies are also conducted to develop, refine and/or test measurement tools and procedures. Table 1.1 shows types of research study from the viewpoint of objectives.

Although, theoretically, a research study can be classified in one of the above perspectives, in practice most studies are a combination of the first three categories; that is, they contain elements of descriptive, correlational and explanatory research. In this book the guidelines suggested for writing a research report encourage you to integrate these aspects.

Table 1.1 Types of research studies from the viewpoint of objectives

Examples	Aim	Main theme	Type of research
• Socioeconomic characteristics of residents of a community • Attitudes of students towards quality of teaching • Types of service provided by an agency • Needs of a community • Sale of a product • Attitudes of nurses towards death and dying • Attitudes of workers towards management • Number of people living in a community • Problems faced by new immigrants • Extent of occupational mobility among immigrants • Consumers' likes and dislikes with regard to a product • Effects of living in a house with domestic violence • Strategies put in place by a company to increase productivity of workers	**To describe what is prevalent regarding:** • a group of people • a community • a phenomenon • a situation • a program • an outcome	**To describe what is prevalent**	**Descriptive research**
• Impact of a program • Relationship between stressful living and incidence of heart attacks • Impact of technology on employment • Impact of maternal and child health services on infant mortality • Effectiveness of a marriage counselling service on extent of marital problems • Impact of an advertising campaign on sale of a product • Impact of incentives on productivity of workers • Effectiveness of an immunisation program in controlling infectious disease	**To establish or explore:** • a relationship • an association • an interdependence	**To ascertain if there is a relationship**	**Correlational research**
• Why does stressful living result in heart attacks? • How does technology create unemployment/employment? • How do maternal and child health services affect infant mortality? • Why do some people have a positive attitude towards an issue while others do not? • Why does a particular intervention work for some people and not for others? • Why do some people use a product while others do not? • Why do some people migrate to another country while others do not? • Why do some people adopt a program while others do not?	**To explain:** • *why* a relationship, assoc-ation or intercependence exists • *why* a particular event occurs	**To explain why the relationship is formed**	**Explanatory research**

Inquiry mode

The third perspective in our typology of research concerns the process you adopt to find answers to your research questions. Broadly, there are two approaches to inquiry:

1 the *structured* approach;
2 the *unstructured* approach.

The structured approach to inquiry is usually classified as *quantitative research* and unstructured as *qualitative research*. In the structured approach everything that forms the research process—objectives, design, sample, and the questions that you plan to ask of respondents—is predetermined. The unstructured approach, by contrast, allows flexibility in all these aspects of the process. The structured approach is more appropriate to determine the *extent* of a problem, issue or phenomenon; the unstructured, to explore its *nature*. Both approaches have their place in research. Both have their strengths and weaknesses. Therefore, you should not 'lock' yourself into solely quantitative or qualitative research. The choice of a structured or unstructured approach, and of a quantitative or qualitative mode of inquiry, should depend upon:

• **Aim of your inquiry**—exploration, confirmation or quantification.
• **Use of the findings**—policy formulation or process understanding.

The distinction between quantitative and qualitative research, in addition to the structured/unstructured process of inquiry, is also dependent upon some other considerations which are briefly presented in Table 2.1 on page 17.

The study is classified as qualitative if the purpose of the study is primarily to describe a situation, phenomenon, problem or event; the information is gathered through the use of variables measured on nominal or ordinal scales (qualitative measurement scales); and if analysis is done *to establish the variation* in the situation, phenomenon or problem *without quantifying it*. The description of an observed situation, the historical enumeration of events, an account of the different opinions people have about an issue, and a description of the living conditions of a community are examples of qualitative research.

On the other hand, the study is classified as a quantitative study if you want to *quantify the variation* in a phenomenon, situation, problem or issue; if information is gathered using predominantly quantitative variables; and if the analysis is geared to ascertain the *magnitude of the variation*. Examples of quantitative aspects of a research study are: How many people have a particular problem? How many people hold a particular attitude?

The use of statistics is *not* an integral part of a quantitative study. The main function of statistics is to act as a test to confirm or contradict the conclusions that you have drawn on the basis of your understanding of analysed data. Statistics, among other things, help you to quantify the magnitude of an association or relationship, provide an indication of the confidence you can place in your findings and help you to isolate the effect of different variables.

It is strongly recommended that you do not lock yourself into becoming either solely a quantitative or solely a qualitative researcher. It is true that there are disciplines that lend themselves predominantly either to qualitative or to quantitative research. For example, such disciplines as anthropology, history and sociology are more inclined towards qualitative research, whereas psychology, epidemiology, education, economics, public health and marketing are more inclined towards quantitative research. However, this does not mean that an economist or a psychologist never uses the qualitative approach, or that an anthropologist never uses quantitative information. There is increasing recognition by most disciplines in the social sciences that both types of research are important for a good research study. The research problem itself should determine whether the study is carried out using quantitative or qualitative methodologies.

Both qualitative and quantitative approaches have their strengths and weaknesses, and advantages and disadvantages. 'Neither one is markedly superior to the other in all respects' (Ackroyd & Hughes 1992: 30). The measurement and analysis of the variables about which information is obtained in a research study are dependent upon the purpose of the study. In many studies you need to combine both qualitative and quantitative approaches. For example, suppose you want to find out the types of service available to victims of domestic violence in a city and the extent of their utilisation. Types of service is the qualitative aspect of the study as finding out about them entails description of the services. The extent of utilisation of the services is the quantitative aspect as it involves estimating the number of people who use the services and calculating other indicators that reflect the extent of utilisation.

Paradigms of research

There are two main paradigms that form the basis of research in the social sciences. It is beyond the scope of this book to go into any detail about these. The crucial question that divides the two is whether the methodology of the physical sciences can be applied to the study of social phenomena. The paradigm that is rooted in the physical sciences is called the systematic, scientific or positivist approach. The opposite paradigm has come to be known as the qualitative, ethnographic, ecological or naturalistic approach. The advocates of the two opposing sides have developed their own values, terminology, methods and techniques to understand social phenomena. However, since the mid-1960s there has been a growing recognition that both paradigms have their place. The research purpose should determine the mode of inquiry, hence the paradigm. To indiscriminately apply one approach to all the research problems can be misleading and inappropriate.

A positivist paradigm lends itself to both quantitative and qualitative research. You can conduct qualitative research within the positivist paradigm. However, the author makes a distinction between qualitative data on the one hand and qualitative research on the other as the first is confined to the measurement of variables and the second to a use of methodology.

The author believes that no matter what paradigm the researcher works within, s/he should adhere to certain values regarding the control of bias, and the maintenance of objectivity in terms of both the research process itself and the conclusions drawn. It is the application of these values to the process of information gathering, analysis and interpretation that enables it to be called a research process.

SUMMARY

There are several ways of collecting and understanding information and finding answers to your questions—research is one way. The difference between research and other ways of obtaining answers to your questions is that in a process that is classified as research, you work within a framework of a set of philosophies, use methods that have been tested for validity and reliability, and attempt to be unbiased and objective.

Research has many applications. You need to have research skills to be an effective service provider, administrator/manager or planner. As a professional who has a responsibility to enhance professional knowledge, research skills are essential.

The typology of research can be looked at from three perspectives: application, objectives and the inquiry process. From the point of view of the application of research, there is applied and pure research. Most of the research undertaken in the social sciences is applied, the findings being designed either for use in understanding a phenomenon/issue or to bring change in a program/situation. Pure research is academic in nature and is undertaken in order to gain knowledge about phenomena that may or may not have application in the near future, and to develop new techniques and procedures that form the body of research methodology. A research study can be carried out with four objectives: to describe a situation, phenomenon, problem or issue (descriptive research); to establish or explore a relationship between two or more variables (correlational research); to explain why certain things happen the way they do (explanatory research); and to examine the feasibility of conducting a study (exploratory research). From the point of view of the mode of inquiry, there are two types of research: quantitative and qualitative. The main objective of a qualitative study is to describe the variation in a phenomenon, situation or attitude, whereas quantitative research, in addition, helps you to quantify the variation.

There are two main paradigms that form the basis of social science research: positivist and naturalist. The crucial question that divides the two is whether the methodology of research in the physical sciences can be applied to research in the social sciences.

CHAPTER
two

The research
process: a quick
glance

But much advantage will occur if men of science become their own epistemologists, and show to the world by critical exposition in non-technical terms the results and methods of their constructive work, that more than mere instinct is involved in it: the community has indeed a right to expect as much as this (Poincaré 1952: xii).

The research process: an eight-step model

Research methodology is taught as a supporting subject in several ways in many academic disciplines at various levels by people committed to a variety of research paradigms. Though paradigms vary in their contents and substance, their broad approach to inquiry, in the author's opinion, is similar. Such ideas have also been expressed by Festinger and Katz, who in the foreword of their book *Research Methods in Behavioral Sciences* say that 'Although the basic logic of scientific methodology is the same in all fields, its specific techniques and approaches will vary, depending upon the subject matter' (1966: vi). Therefore, the model developed here is generic in nature and can be applied to a number of disciplines in the social sciences. It is based upon a practical and step-by-step approach to a research inquiry and each step provides a smorgasbord of methods, models and procedures.

Suppose you want to go out for a drive. Before you start, you must decide where you want to go and then which route to take. If you know the route, you do not need to consult a street directory but, if you do not, you need to use one. Your problem is compounded if there is more than one route. You need to decide which one to take. The research process is very similar to undertaking a journey. As with your drive, for a research journey there are also two important decisions to make. The first is to decide *what you want to find out about* or, in other words, what research questions you want to find answers to. Having decided upon your research questions or problems, you then need to think *how to go about finding their answers*. The path to finding answers to your research questions constitutes research methodology. Just as there are posts along the way to your travel destination, so there are practical steps through which you must pass in your research journey in order to find the answers to your research questions (Figure 2.1). The sequence of these steps is not absolute. With experience you can change it. At each operational step in the research process you are required to choose from a multiplicity of methods, procedures and models of research methodology which will help you to best achieve your objectives. This is where your knowledge base of research methodology plays a crucial role.

The aim of this book is to provide you with knowledge that will enable you to select the most appropriate methods and procedures. The strength of this book lies in anchoring the theoretical knowledge to the posts of the research journey. A smorgasbord choice at each operation step aims to provide, at a beginner's level, knowledge of methods and procedures used both by qualitative and quantitative researchers, though the book is more inclined towards the quantitative way of thinking.

Figure 2.1   The research journey—touch each post and select methods and procedures appropriate for your journey

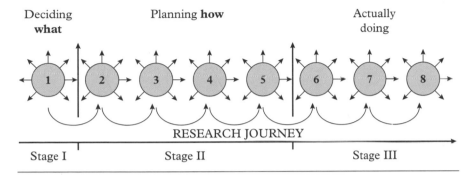

Quantitative and qualitative research methodologies differ in the philosophy that underpins their mode of inquiry as well as, to some extent, in methods, models and procedures used. Though the research process is broadly the same in both, quantitative and qualitative research are differentiated in terms of the methods of data collection, the procedures adopted for data processing and analysis, and the style of communication of the findings. If your research problem lends itself to a qualitative mode of inquiry, you are more likely to use the *unstructured interview* or *observation* as your method of data collection. When analysing data in qualitative research you go through the process of identifying themes and describing what you have found out during your interviews or observation rather than subjecting your data to statistical procedures. Table 2.1 summarises the differences between qualitative and quantitative research.

Table 2.1   Differences between qualitative and quantitative research

Difference with respect to:	*Quantitative research*	*Qualitative research*
Underpinning philosophy	Rationalism: 'That human beings achieve knowledge because of their capacity to reason' (Bernard 1994: 2)	Empiricism: 'The only knowledge that human beings acquire is from sensory experiences' (Bernard 1994: 2)
Approach to inquiry	Structured/rigid/predetermined methodology	Unstructured/flexible/open methodology
Main purpose of investigation	To quantify extent of variation in a phenomenon, situation, issue etc.	To describe variation in a phenomenon, situation, issue etc.

(Continued on next page)

Table 2.1—*Continued*

Difference with respect to:	Quantitative research	Qualitative research
Measurement of variables	Emphasis on some form of either measurement or classification of variables	Emphasis on description of variables
Sample size	Emphasis on greater sample size	Fewer cases
Focus of inquiry	Narrows focus in terms of extent of inquiry, but assembles required information from a greater number of respondents	Covers multiple issues but assembles required information from fewer respondents
Dominant research value	Reliability and objectivity (value-free)	Authenticity but does not claim to be value-free
Dominant research topic	Explains prevalence, incidence, extent, nature of issues, opinions and attitude; discovers regularities and formulates theories	Explores experiences, meanings, perceptions and feelings
Analysis of data	Subjects variables to frequency distributions, cross-tabulations or other statistical procedures	Subjects responses, narratives or observation data to identification of themes and describes these
Communication of findings	Organisation more analytical in nature, drawing inferences and conclusions, and testing magnitude and strength of a relationship	Organisation more descriptive and narrative in nature

Since, at a number of steps of the research process the choice of methods and procedures is influenced by quantitative/qualitative distinction, the methods and procedures discussed in some chapters are differentiated; however, I have tried to keep this distinction to the minimum as the model is applicable to both. Note that this book is for beginners. There is not enough space to cover extensively the applicability and use of each method, model and procedure. I have elaborated on those associated with quantitative research more than on those linked to qualitative research. For a deeper understanding of a method or procedure relating to either, you may wish to consult other books identified in the text.

Figure 2.2 shows the proposed model. The tasks identified in *arrows* are the operational steps you need to follow in order to conduct a study, quantitative or qualitative. Topics identified in *rectangles* are the required theoretical knowledge needed to carry out these steps. The tasks identified in *circles* are the intermediary steps that you need to complete to go from one step to another. It is important for a beginner to work through these steps in the proposed sequence, though with experience you do not need to follow the sequence.

Figure 2.2   The research process

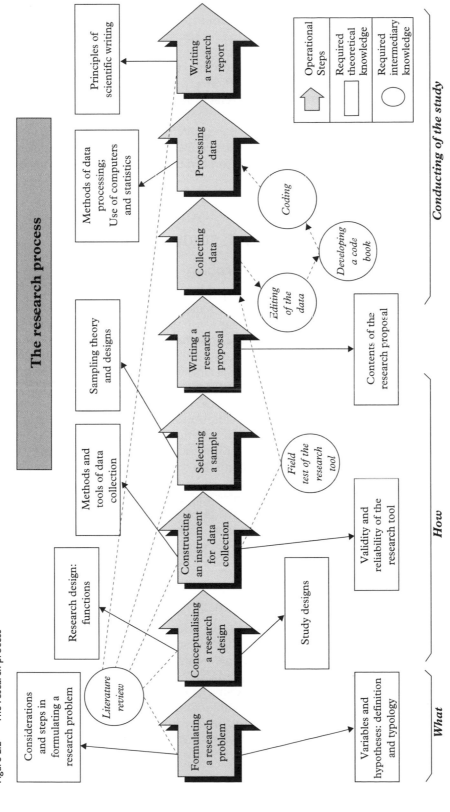

This book is written around the theoretical knowledge required to undertake each operational step and follows the same sequential progression as is needed to undertake a research investigation. For each operational step, the required theoretical knowledge is further organised, in different chapters, around the operational step to which, in the author's opinion, it is most logically related (Figure 2.3). Again, for a beginner, it is important to study this diagram to relate the theoretical knowledge to the operational steps.

The following sections of this chapter provide a quick glance at the whole process to acquaint you with the various tasks you need to undertake to carry out your study, thus giving you some idea of what the research journey involves.

Steps in planning a research study

Step I: formulating a research problem

Formulating a research problem is the first and most important step in the research process. A research problem identifies your destination: it should tell you, your research supervisor and your readers *what* you intend to research. The more specific and clear you are the better, as everything that follows in the research process—study design, measurement procedures, sampling strategy, frame of analysis and the style of writing of your dissertation or report—is greatly influenced by the way in which you formulate your research problem. Hence, you should give it considerable and careful thought at this stage. The main function of formulating a research problem is to decide *what* you want to find out *about*. Chapter 4 deals in detail with various aspects of formulating a research problem.

It is extremely important to evaluate the research problem in the light of the financial resources at your disposal, the time available, and your own and your research supervisor's expertise and knowledge in the field of study. It is equally important to identify any gaps in your knowledge of relevant disciplines, such as statistics required for analysis. Also, ask yourself whether you have sufficient knowledge about computers and software if you plan to use them.

Step II: conceptualising a research design

An extremely important feature of research is the use of appropriate methods. Research involves systematic, controlled, valid and rigorous exploration and description of what is not known and establishment of associations and causation that permit the accurate prediction of outcomes under a given set of conditions. It also involves identifying gaps in knowledge, verification of what is already known, and identification of past errors and limitations. The strength of *what* you find largely rests on *how* it was found.

The main function of a research design is to explain *how* you will find answers to your research questions. The research design sets out the logic

Figure 2.3   The chapters in the book in relation to the operational steps

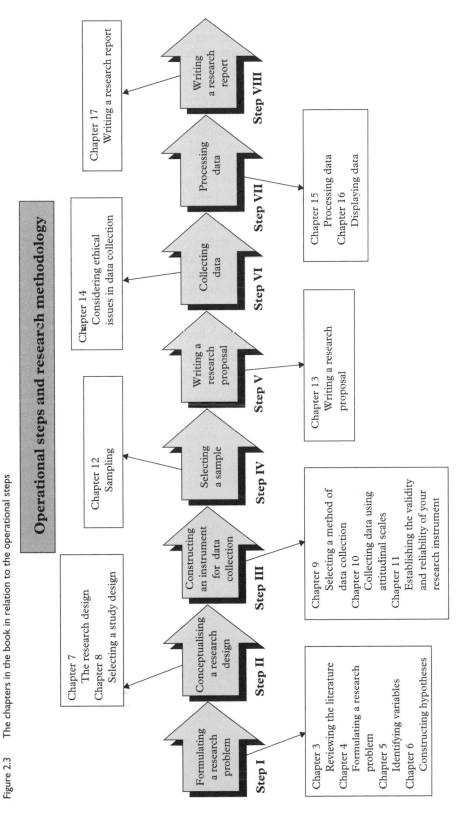

of your inquiry. A research design should include the following: the study design *per se* and the logistical arrangements that you propose to undertake, the measurement procedures, the sampling strategy, the frame of analysis and the time-frame. For any investigation, the selection of an appropriate research design is crucial in enabling you to arrive at valid findings, comparisons and conclusions. A faulty design results in misleading findings and is therefore tantamount to wasting human and financial resources. In scientific circles, the strength of an empirical investigation is primarily evaluated in the light of the research design adopted. When selecting a research design it is important to ensure that it is *valid, workable* and *manageable*. Chapter 7 provides details about research design.

There is an enormous variety of study designs and you need to be acquainted with some of the most common ones. Chapter 8 explains some of these designs. Select or develop the design that is most suited to your study. You must have strong reasons for selecting a particular design; you must be able to justify your selection; and you should be aware of its strengths, weaknesses and limitations. In addition, you will need to explain the logistical details needed to implement the suggested design.

Step III: constructing an instrument for data collection

Anything that becomes a means of collecting information for your study is called a 'research tool' or a 'research instrument'. For example, observation forms, interview schedules, questionnaires and interview guides are all classified as research tools.

The construction of a research tool is the first 'practical' step in carrying out a study. You will need to decide how you are going to collect data for the proposed study and then construct a research instrument for data collection. Chapter 9 details the various methods of data collection and Chapter 10 deals with methods for collecting data using attitudinal scales.

If you are planning to collect data specifically for your study (primary data), you need to either construct a research instrument or select an already constructed one. The process of developing a research instrument is also discussed in Chapter 9. The concepts of validity and reliability in relation to a research instrument are discussed in Chapter 11.

If you are using secondary data (information already collected for other purposes), develop a form to extract the required data. In order to determine what information is required, go through the same process as described for primary data above.

Field testing, also known as pre-testing, a research tool is an integral part of instrument construction. As a rule, the field test should not be carried out on the sample of your study but on a similar population.

If you are planning to use a computer for data analysis, you may wish to provide space for coding the data on the research instrument.

Step IV: selecting a sample

The accuracy of your findings largely depends upon the way you select your sample. The basic objective of any sampling design is to minimise, within the limitation of cost, the gap between the values obtained from your sample and those prevalent in the population.

The underlying premise in sampling is that, if a relatively small number of units is selected, it can provide—with a sufficiently high degree of probability—a fairly true reflection of the sampling population that is being studied.

Sampling theory is guided by two principles:

1 the avoidance of bias in the selection of a sample; and
2 the attainment of maximum precision for a given outlay of resources.

There are three categories of sampling design (Chapter 12):

1 random/probability sampling designs;
2 non-random/probability sampling designs; and
3 'mixed' sampling design.

There are several sampling strategies within the first two categories. You need to be acquainted with these sampling designs to select the one most appropriate for your study. You need to know the strengths and weaknesses of each and the situations in which they can or cannot be applied in order to select the most appropriate design. The type of sampling strategy you use also determines your ability to generalise from the sample to the total population and the type of statistical tests you can perform on the data.

Step V: writing a research proposal

Now, step by step, you have done all the preparatory work. Next put everything together in a way that provides adequate information, for your research supervisor and others, about your research study. This overall plan tells a reader about your research problem and how you are planning to investigate, and is called a *research proposal*. Broadly, a research proposal's main function is to detail the operational plan for obtaining answers to your research questions. In doing so it ensures—and reassures the readers of—the validity of the methodology to obtain answers accurately and objectively.

Universities and other institutions may have differing requirements regarding the style and content of a research proposal, but the majority of institutions would require most of what is set out here. Requirements may also vary within an institution, from discipline to discipline or from supervisor to supervisor. However, the guidelines set out in Chapter 13 provide a framework which will be acceptable to most.

A research proposal must tell you, your research supervisor and a reviewer the following information about your study:

- *what* you are proposing to do;
- *how* you plan to proceed;
- *why* you selected the proposed strategy.

Therefore it should contain the following information about your study (Chapter 13):

- a statement of the *objectives* of the study;
- a list of *hypotheses*, if you are testing any;
- the *study design* you are proposing to use;
- the *setting* for your study;
- the research *instrument(s)* you are planning to use;
- information on *sample size* and *sampling design*;
- information on *data-processing* procedures;
- an outline of the proposed *chapters* for the report;
- the study's *problems* and *limitations*; and
- the proposed *time-frame*.

Steps in conducting a study

Step VI: collecting data

Having formulated a research problem, developed a study design, constructed a research instrument and selected a sample, you then collect the data from which you will draw inferences and conclusions for your study.

Many methods could be used to gather the required information. As a part of the research design, you decided upon the procedure you wanted to adopt to collect your data. *At this stage you actually collect the data.* For example, depending upon your plans, you might commence interviews, mail out a questionnaire, conduct nominal/focused group discussions or make observations. Collecting data through any one of the methods may involve some ethical issues, which are discussed in Chapter 14.

Step VII: processing data

The way you analyse the information you collected largely depends upon two things:

1. type of information—descriptive, quantitative, qualitative or attitudinal;
2. the way you want to communicate your findings to your readers.

There are two broad categories of report: quantitative and qualitative. As mentioned earlier, the distinction is more academic than real as in most studies you need to combine quantitative and qualitative skills. Nevertheless, there are some solely qualitative and some solely quantitative studies. Chapter 15 describes different ways of analysing quantitative data and Chapter 16 details various methods of displaying analysed data.

In addition to the qualitative–quantitative distinction, it is equally important for data analysis that you consider whether the data is to be analysed manually or by a computer.

If your study is purely descriptive, you can write your dissertation/report on the basis of your field notes, manually analyse the contents of your notes (content analysis), or use a computer program such as NUD*DIST N6, NVIVO or Ethnograph for this purpose.

If you want quantitative analysis, it is also necessary to decide upon the type of analysis required (i.e. frequency distribution, cross-tabulations or other statistical procedures, such as regression analysis, factor analysis and analysis of variance) and how it should be presented. Also identify the variables to be subjected to these statistical procedures.

Step VIII: writing a research report

Writing the report is the last and, for many, the most difficult step of the research process. This report informs the world what you have done, what you have discovered and what conclusions you have drawn from your findings. If you are clear about the whole process, you will also be clear about the way you want to write your report. Your report should be written in an academic style and be divided into different chapters and/or sections based upon the main themes of your study. Chapter 17 suggests some of the ways of writing a research report.

SUMMARY

This chapter has provided an overview of the research process, which has been broken into eight steps, the details of which are covered in the remainder of this book. At each step the model provides a smorgasbord of methods, models, techniques and procedures so you can select the one most appropriate for your study. It is like a buffet party with eight tables, each with different dishes, but the dishes are made out of similar ingredients. You go to all eight tables and select the dish that you like most from each table. The main difference between the model and the example given is that in the model you select what is most appropriate for your study and not what you like the most, as in a buffet. For a beginner it is important to go through all the steps, although perhaps not in the same sequence. With experience you can take a number of short cuts.

The eight steps cover the total spectrum of a research endeavour, starting from problem formulation through to writing a research report. The steps are operational in nature, following a logical sequence, and detailing the various methods and procedures in a simple step-by-step manner.

STEP I

FORMULATING A RESEARCH PROBLEM

CHAPTER
three

Reviewing the literature

Place of literature review in research

One of the essential preliminary tasks when you undertake a research study is to go through the existing literature in order to acquaint yourself with the available body of knowledge in your area of interest. The literature review is an integral part of the entire research process and makes a valuable contribution to almost every operational step. It has value even before the first step; that is, when you are merely thinking about a research question that you may want to find answers to through your research journey. In the initial stages of research it helps you to establish the theoretical roots of your study, clarify your ideas and develop your methodology, but later on the literature review serves to enhance and consolidate your knowledge base and helps you to integrate your findings with the existing body of knowledge. Since an important responsibility in research is to compare your findings with those of others, it is here that the literature review plays an extremely important role. During the write-up of your report it helps you to integrate your findings with existing knowledge—that is, to either support or contradict earlier research. The higher the academic level of your research, the more important a thorough integration of your findings with exiting literature becomes.

Reviewing literature can be time-consuming, daunting and frustrating, but it is also rewarding. A literature review has a number of functions:

- It provides a theoretical background to your study.
- It reviews the means by which you establish the links between what you are proposing to examine and what has already been studied. In other words, it helps you to refine your research methodology.
- Through the literature review you are able to show how your findings have contributed to the existing body of knowledge in your profession.
- It enables you to contextualise your findings.

It also helps you to:
1 bring clarity and focus to your research problem;
2 improve your methodology;
3 broaden your knowledge base in your research area.
4 contextualise your findings.

Bring clarity and focus to your research problem

The literature review involves a paradox. On the one hand, you cannot effectively undertake a literature search without some idea of the problem you wish to investigate. On the other hand, the literature review can play an extremely important role in shaping your research problem because the process of reviewing the literature helps you to understand the subject area better and thus helps you to conceptualise your research problem clearly and precisely. It also helps you to understand the relationship between your research problem and the body of knowledge in the area.

Improve your methodology

Going through the literature acquaints you with the methodologies that have been used by others to find answers to research questions similar to the one you are investigating. A literature review tells you if others have used procedures and methods similar to the ones that you are proposing, which procedures and methods have worked well for them, and what problems they have faced with them. By becoming aware of any problems and pitfalls, you will be better positioned to select a methodology that is capable of providing valid answers to your research questions. This will increase your confidence in the methodology you plan to use and will equip you to defend its use.

Broaden your knowledge base in your research area

The most important function of the literature review is to ensure you read widely around the subject area in which you intend to conduct your research study. It is important that you know what other researchers have found in regard to the same or similar questions, what theories have been put forward and what gaps exist in the relevant body of knowledge. When you undertake a research project for a higher degree (that is, an MA or a PhD) you are expected to be an expert in your area of study. A thorough literature review helps to ensure that you fulfil this expectation. Another important reason for doing a literature review is that it helps you to understand how the findings of your study fit into the existing body of knowledge (Martin 1985: 30).

Contextualise your findings

Obtaining answers to your research questions is comparatively easy: the difficult part is examining how your findings fit into the existing body of knowledge. How do answers to your research questions compare with what others have found? What contribution have you been able to make to the existing body of knowledge? How are your findings different from those of others? For you to be able to answer these questions you need to go back to your literature review. It is important to place your findings in the context of what is already known in your field of inquiry.

Procedure for reviewing the literature

If you do not have a specific research problem, you should review the literature in your broad area of interest with the aim of gradually narrowing down to what you want to find out about. After that the literature review should be focused around your research problem. There is a danger in reviewing the literature without having a reasonably specific idea of what you want to study. It can condition your thinking about your study and the methodology you might use, resulting in a less innovative choice of research problem and methodology than otherwise would have been the case. Hence, you should try to conceptualise your research problem before undertaking your major literature review.

There are four steps involved in conducting a literature review:

1 search for existing literature in your area of study;
2 review the literature selected;
3 develop a theoretical framework;
4 develop a conceptual framework.

The skills required for these tasks are different. Developing theoretical and conceptual frameworks are more difficult than the other tasks.

Search for existing literature

To effectively search for literature in your field of inquiry, it is imperative that you have in mind at least some idea of the broad subject area and of the problem you wish to investigate, in order to set parameters for your search. Next compile a bibliography for this broad area. There are two sources that you can use to prepare a bibliography:

1 books;
2 journals.

The best way to search for a book is to look at your library catalogues. When librarians catalogue a book they also assign to it subject headings that usually are based on *Library of Congress Subject Headings*. If you are not sure, ask your librarian to help you to find the best subject heading for your area. This can save you a lot of time. Publications such as *Book Review Index* can help you to locate books of interest.

There are several sources designed to make your search for journals easier and these can save you enormous time. They are:

1 Indices of journals (e.g. *Humanities Index*);
2 Abstracts of articles (e.g. *ERIC*);
3 Citation indices (e.g. *Social Sciences Citation Index*).

All the above indexing, abstracting and citation services are available in print or on CD-ROM, or are stored on a mainframe computer accessible through the Internet, a world-wide electronic communication system.

In most libraries, information on books, journals, abstracts and so on is stored on computers and CD-ROMs. In each case the information is classified by subject, author and title. You may also have the keywords option (author/keyword; title/keyword; subject/keyword; expert/keyword; or just keywords). What system you use depends upon what is available in your library and what you are familiar with.

There are specially prepared electronic databases in a number of disciplines. These can also be helpful in preparing a bibliography. For example, most libraries carry the electronic databases shown in Table 3.1.

Table 3.1   Some commonly used electronic databases in public health, sociology, education and business studies

Electronic database	Description	Printed equivalent
ABI/INFORM	Abstracted Business Information contains references to business information worldwide. It covers subjects such as accounting, banking, data processing, economics, finance, health care, insurance, law, management, marketing, personnel, product development, public administration, real estate, taxation and telecommunications.	None
ERIC	ERIC is a database of educational material collected by the Education Resources Information Center of the US Department of Education. It covers subjects such as adult career or vocational education, counselling and personnel services, educational management, primary and early childhood education, handicapped and gifted children, higher education, information resources, language and linguistics, reading and communication, rural education, science, mathematics and environment education, social science education, teacher education, secondary education, evaluation and urban education.	*CIJE: Current Index to Journals in Education*
HEALTHROM	HEALTHROM provides references and some full-text publications on environment, health, HIV/AIDS and communicable diseases, Aboriginal health, clinical medicine, nutrition, alcohol and drug addiction.	None
MEDLINE	MEDLINE contains references to material in the biomedical sciences, including medicine, pharmacology, nursing, dentistry, allied health professions, public health, behavioural sciences, physiotherapy, occupational therapy, medical technology, hospital administration, and basic sciences such as anatomy and physiology.	*Index Medicus*
CINAHL	CINAHL (Cumulative Indices to Nursing and Allied Health Literature) provides access to virtually all English-language nursing journals and primary journals from 13 allied health disciplines including health education, medical records, occupational therapy, physical therapy and radiologic technology.	Cumulative indices to nursing and allied health literature

Select the database most appropriate to your area of study to see if there are any useful references. Of course, any computer database search is restricted to those journals and articles that are already on the database. You should also talk to your research supervisor and other available experts to find out about any additional relevant literature to include in your reading list.

Books

Books, though a central part of any bibliography, have their advantages as well as disadvantages. The main advantage is that the material published in books is usually important and of good quality, and the findings are 'integrated with other research to form a coherent body of knowledge' (Martin 1985: 33). The main disadvantage is that the material is not completely up to date, as it can take a few years between the completion of a work and its publication in the form of a book.

The best way to identify books is to use a computer catalogue. Use the *subject catalogue* or *keywords* option to search for books in your area of interest. Narrow the subject area searched by selecting the appropriate key-words. Look through these titles carefully and identify the books you think are likely to be of interest to you. If you think the titles seem appropriate to your topic, print them out if this facility is available (this will save you time) or note them down on a piece of paper. Be aware that sometimes a title does not provide enough information to decide if a book is going to be of use. To make this decision you may have to search for such books in the library and examine their contents.

When you have selected 10–15 books that you think are appropriate for your topic, examine the bibliography of each. It will save time to photocopy their bibliographies. Go through these bibliographies carefully to identify the books common to several of them. If a book has been referenced by a number of authors, you should include it in your reading list. Prepare a final list of books that you consider essential reading.

Having prepared your reading list, locate these books in your library or borrow them from other sources. Examine their contents to double-check that they really are relevant to your topic. If you find that a book is not relevant to your research, delete it from your reading list. If you find that something in a book's contents is relevant to your topic, make an annotated bibliography. An annotated bibliography contains a brief abstract of the aspects covered in a book and your own notes of its relevance. Be careful to keep track of your references. To do this you can prepare your own card index or use a computer program such as Endnotes or Pro-Cite.

Journals

In the same way, you need to go through the journals in your research area. Journals provide you with the most up-to-date information, even though there is often a gap of two to three years between the completion of a research project and its publication in a journal. You should select as many journals as you possibly can, though the number of journals available depends upon the field of study—certain fields have more journals than others. As with books, you need to prepare a list of the journals you want to examine for identifying literature relevant to your study. This can be done in a number of ways. You can:

- locate the hard copies of the journals that are appropriate to your study;
- look at citation or abstract indices to identify and/or read the abstracts of such articles;
- search electronic databases;
- use the Internet.

Whichever method you choose, first identify the journals that you want to look at in more detail for your review of the literature. The next step is to make preparations to go through them.

If you have been able to identify any useful journals and articles, prepare a list of those you want to examine, by journal. Select one of these journals and, starting with the latest issue, examine its contents page to see if there is an article of relevance to your research topic. If you feel that a particular article is of interest to you, read its abstract. If you think you are likely to use it, depending upon your financial resources, either photocopy it, or prepare a summary and record its reference for later use.

Review the literature selected

Now that you have identified several books and articles as useful, the next step is to start reading them critically to pull together themes and issues that are associated. If you do not have a theoretical framework of themes in mind to start with, use separate sheets of paper for each article or book. Once you develop a rough framework, slot the findings from the material so far reviewed into that framework, using a separate sheet of paper for each theme of that framework. As you read further, go on slotting the information where it logically belongs under the themes so far developed. You may need to add more themes as you go. In doing so, read critically with particular reference to the following aspects:

- Note whether the knowledge relevant to your theoretical framework has been confirmed beyond doubt.
- Note the theories put forward, the criticisms of these and their basis, the methodologies adopted (study design, sample size and its characteristics, measurement procedures, etc.) and the criticisms of them.
- Examine to what extent the findings can be generalised to other situations.
- Notice where there are significant differences of opinion among researchers and give your opinion about the validity of these differences.
- Ascertain the areas in which little or nothing is known—the gaps that exist in the body of knowledge.

Develop a theoretical framework

Examining the literature can be a never-ending task, but as you have limited time it is important to set parameters by reviewing the literature in relation to some main themes pertinent to your research topic. As you start reading the literature, you will soon discover that the problem you wish to investigate has its roots in a number of theories that have been developed from different perspectives. The information obtained from different books and journals now needs to be sorted under the main themes and theories, highlighting agreements and disagreements among the authors and identifying the unanswered questions or gaps. You will also realise that the literature deals with a number of aspects that have a direct or indirect bearing on your research topic. Use these aspects as a basis for developing your theoretical framework. Your review of the literature should sort out the information, as mentioned earlier, within this framework. Unless you review the literature in relation to this framework, you will not be able to develop a focus in your literature search: that is, your theoretical framework provides you with a guide as you read. This brings us to the paradox mentioned previously: until you go through the literature you cannot develop a theoretical framework and until you have developed a theoretical framework, you cannot effectively review the literature. The solution is to read some of the literature then attempt to develop a framework, even a loose one, within which you can organise the rest of the literature you read. As you read more about the area, you are likely to change the framework. However, without it, you will get bogged down in a great deal of unnecessary reading and note-taking that may not be relevant to your study.

Literature pertinent to your study may deal with two types of information:

1 universal;
2 more specific (i.e. local trends or a specific program).

In writing about such information you should start with the general information, gradually narrowing it down to the specific.

Look at the example in Figure 3.1.

Figure 3.1   Developing a theoretical framework—the relationship between mortality and fertility

If you want to study the relationship between mortality and fertility, you should review literature about:

- *fertility*—trends, theories, some of the indices and critiques of them, factors affecting fertility, methods of controlling fertility, factors affecting acceptance of contraceptives, and so on;
- *mortality*—factors affecting mortality, mortality indices and their sensitivity in measuring change in mortality levels of a population, trends in mortality, and so on; and, most importantly
- *the relationship between fertility and mortality*—theories that have been put forward to explain the relationship, implications of the relationship.

Out of this literature review you need to develop the theoretical framework for your study. Primarily this should revolve around theories that have been put forward about the relationship between mortality and fertility. You will discover that a number of theories has been proposed to explain this relationship. For example, it has been explained from economic, religious, medical and psychological perspectives. Within each perspective several theories have been put forward: 'insurance theory', 'fear of non-survival', 'replacement theory', 'price theory', 'utility theory', 'extra' or 'hoarding theory' and 'risk theory'.

Your literature review should be written under the following headings, with most of the review involving the examination of the relationships between fertility and mortality:

- fertility theories;
- the theory of demographic transition;
- trends in fertility (global, and then narrow it to national and local levels);
- methods of contraception (their acceptance and effectiveness);
- factors affecting mortality;
- trends in mortality (and their implications);
- measurement of mortality indices (their sensitivity);
- *relationships between fertility and mortality* (different theories such as 'insurance', 'fear of non-survival', 'replacement', 'price', 'utility', 'risk' and 'hoarding').

Develop a conceptual framework

The conceptual framework stems from the theoretical framework and concentrates, usually, on one section of that theoretical framework which becomes the basis of your study. The latter consists of the theories or issues in which your study is embedded, whereas the former describes the aspects you selected from the theoretical framework to become the basis of your inquiry. The conceptual framework is the basis of your research problem. For instance, in the example cited in Figure 3.1, the theoretical framework includes all the theories that have been put forward to explain the relationship between fertility and mortality. However, out of these, you may be planning to test only one, say, the fear of non-survival. Hence the conceptual framework grows out of the theoretical framework and relates to the specific research problem concerning the fear of non-survival theory.

Writing up the literature reviewed

Now, all that remains to be done is to write about the literature you have reviewed. As mentioned in the beginning of this chapter, the broad two functions of a literature review are (1) to provide a theoretical background to your study and (2) to enable you to contextualise your findings in relation to the existing body of knowledge in addition to refining your methodology. The content of your literature review reflects these two purposes. In order to fulfil the first purpose, you identify and describe various theories relevant to your field; and specify gaps in existing knowledge in the area, recent advances in the area of study, current trends and so on. In order to comply with the second function you integrate your results with specific and relevant findings from the existing literature by comparing the two for confirmation or contradiction.

While reading the literature for theoretical background of your study, you will realise that certain themes have emerged. List the main ones, converting them into subheadings. These subheadings should be precise, descriptive of the theme in question, and follow a logical progression. Now, under each subheading, record the main findings with respect to the theme in question, highlighting the reasons for and against an argument if they exist, and identifying gaps and issues. Some people write up the entire literature review in one section, entitled 'Review of the literature' or 'The literature review', without subheadings. The author strongly suggests that you write your literature review under subheadings. Figure 3.2 shows the subheadings used to describe the themes in a literature review for a study entitled *Intercountry adoption in Western Australia*, conducted by the author.

The second broad function of the literature review—contextualising the findings of your study—requires you to very systematically compare your findings with those made by others. Quote from these studies to show how your findings contradict, confirm or add to them. It places your findings in the context of what other have found out. This function is undertaken when writing about your findings, that is, after analysis of your data.

Figure 3.2   Sample of outline of a literature review

Intercountry adoption in Western Australia

(A profile of adoptive families)

The literature was reviewed under the following themes:

* Introduction (*introductory remarks about adoption*)
* History and philosophy of adoption
* Reasons for adoption
* Trends in adoption (*global and national*)
* Intercountry adoption
* History of intercountry adoption in Western Australia
* Trends in intercountry adoption in Western Australia
* The Adoption Act in Western Australia
* The adoption process in Western Australia
* Problems and issues in adoption
* Gaps in the literature (*in this case it was a lack of information about those parents who had adopted children from other countries that became the basis of the study*)

SUMMARY

Reviewing the literature is a continuous process. It begins before a research problem is finalised and continues until the report is finished. There is a paradox in literature review: you cannot undertake an effective literature review unless you have formulated a research problem, yet your literature search plays an extremely important role in helping you to formulate your research problem. The literature review brings clarity and focus to your research problem, improves your methodology and broadens your knowledge base.

Reviewing the literature involves a number of steps: searching for existing literature in your area of study; reviewing the selected literature; using it to develop a theoretical framework from which your study emerges and also using it to develop a conceptual framework which will become the basis of your investigation. The main sources for identifying literature are books and journals. There are several sources which can provide information about locating relevant journals.

CHAPTER
four

Formulating a research problem

The central aim of this chapter is to detail the process of problem formulation. However, the specific process that you are likely to adopt depends upon:

- your expertise in research methodology;
- your knowledge of the subject area;
- your understanding of the issues to be examined;
- the extent to which the focus of your study is predetermined.

If you are not very familiar with the research process and/or do not have a very specific idea about what is to be researched, you need to follow every step detailed in this chapter. However, more experienced researchers can take a number of short cuts. The process outlined here assumes that you have neither the required knowledge of the process of formulating a research problem nor a specific idea about what is to be researched.

The research problem

If you have a specific idea for the basis of your inquiry, you do not need to go through this chapter. However, you should make sure that your idea is researchable as not all problems lend themselves to research methodologies. Broadly speaking, any question that you want answered and any assumption or assertion that you want to challenge or investigate can become a research problem or a research topic for your study. However, it is important to remember that not all questions can be transformed into research problems and some may prove to be extremely difficult to study. According to Powers, Meenaghan & Twoomey (1985: 38), 'Potential research questions may occur to us on a regular basis, but the process of formulating them in a meaningful way is not at all an easy task'. As a newcomer it might seem easy to formulate a problem but it requires a considerable knowledge of both the subject area and research methodology. Once you examine a question more closely you will soon realise the complexity of formulating an idea into a problem which is researchable. 'First identifying and then specifying a research problem might seem like research tasks that ought to be easy and quickly accomplished. However, such is often not the case' (Yegidis & Weinback 1991: 35).

It is essential for the problem you formulate to be able to withstand scrutiny in terms of the procedures required to be undertaken. Hence you should spend considerable time in thinking it through.

The importance of formulating a research problem

The formulation of a research problem is the first and most important step of the research process. It is like the identification of a destination before undertaking a journey. As in the absence of a destination, it is impossible to identify the shortest—or indeed any—route, in the absence of a clear research problem, a clear and economical plan is impossible. A research problem is like the foundation of a building. The type and design of the building is dependent upon the foundation. If the foundation is well designed and strong you can expect the building to be also. The research problem serves as the foundation of a research study: if it is well formulated, you can expect a good study to follow. According to Kerlinger,

> If one wants to solve a problem, one must generally know what the problem is. It can be said that a large part of the problem lies in knowing what one is trying to do (1986: 17).

You must have a clear idea with regard to what it is that you want to find out **about** and not what you think you must find.

A research problem may take a number of forms, from the very simple to the very complex. The way you formulate a problem determines almost every step that follows: the type of study design that can be used; the type of sampling strategy that can be employed; the research instrument that can be used or developed; and the type of analysis that can be undertaken. The formulation of a problem is like the 'input' into a study, and the 'output'—the quality of the contents of the research report and the validity of the associations or causation established—is entirely dependent upon it. Hence the famous saying about computers—'garbage in, garbage out'—is equally applicable to a research problem.

In the beginning you may become more confused but this is normal and a sign of progression. *Remember: confusion is often but a first step towards clarity.* Take time over formulating your problem, for the clearer you are about your research problem/question, the easier it will be for you later on. *Remember, this is the most crucial step.*

Sources of research problems

This section is of particular relevance if you have not yet selected a research topic and do not know where to start. If you have already selected your topic or question, go to the next section.

Most research in the humanities revolves around four *P*s:

- People;
- Problems;
- Programs;
- Phenomena.

The emphasis on a particular '*P*' may vary from study to study but generally, in practice, most research studies are based upon at least a combination of two *P*s. You may select a group of individuals (a group or a community as such—'people'), either to examine the existence of certain issues or problems relating to their lives, to ascertain attitude of a group of people towards an issue ('problem'), to establish existence of a regularity ('phenomenon') or to evaluate the effectiveness of an intervention ('program'). Your focus may be the study of an issue, an association or a phenomenon *per se*; for example, the relationship between unemployment and street crime, smoking and cancer or fertility and mortality, which is done on the basis of information collected from individuals, groups, communities or organisations. The emphasis in these studies is on exploring, discovering or establishing associations or causation. Similarly, you can study different aspects of a program: its effectiveness, its structure, the need for it, consumers' satisfaction with it, and so on. In order to ascertain these you collect information from people. The 'people' provide you with the 'study population', whereas the other three *P*s furnish the 'subject areas'. Your study population—individuals, groups and communities—is the people from whom the information is collected. Your subject area is a 'problem', 'program' or 'phenomenon' about which the information is collected. A closer look at any academic discipline or occupational field will show that most research revolves around the four *P*s.

Every research study has two aspects:

1 the study population;
2) the subject area.

Table 4.1 shows aspects of a research problem.

Table 4.1   Aspects of a research problem

Aspects of a study	*About*	*Study of*	
Study population	People	Individuals, organisations, groups, communities	They provide you with the required information or you collect information from or about them
Subject area	Problem	Issues, situations, associations, needs, population composition, profiles, etc.	Information that you need to collect to find answers to your research questions
	Program	Contents, structure, outcomes, attributes, satisfaction, consumers, service providers, etc.	
	Phenomenon	Cause-and-effect relationships, the study of a phenomenon itself, etc.	

You can study a problem, a program or a phenomenon in any academic field or from any professional perspective. For example, you can measure the effectiveness of a program in the field of health, education, social work, industrial management, public health, nursing, health promotion or a welfare program, or you can look at a problem from a health, business or welfare perspective. Similarly you can gauge consumers' opinions about any aspect of a program in the above fields.

Examine your own academic discipline or professional field in the context of the four *P*s in order to identify anything that looks interesting. Consider some of the aspects identified under 'Study of' in Table 4.1 against problem, program or phenomenon for a possible research topic. For example, if you are a student in the health field there are an enormous number of issues, situations and associations within each subfield of health that you could examine. Issues relating to the spread of a disease, drug rehabilitation, an immunisation program, the effectiveness of a treatment, the extent of consumers' satisfaction or issues concerning a particular health program can all provide you with a range of research problems. Similarly, in education there are several issues: students' satisfaction with a teacher, attributes of a good teacher, the impact of the home environment on the educational achievement of students, and supervisory needs of postgraduate students in higher education. Any other academic or occupational field can similarly be dissected into subfields and examined for a potential research problem. Most fields lend themselves to the above categorisation even though specific problems and programs vary markedly from field to field.

Considerations in selecting a research problem

When selecting a research problem/topic there are a number of considerations to keep in mind. These help to ensure that your study will be manageable and that you will remain motivated. These considerations are interest, magnitude, measurement of concepts, level of expertise, relevance, availability of data and ethical issues.

- **Interest**—interest should be the most important consideration in selecting a research problem. A research endeavour is usually time-consuming, and involves hard work and possibly unforeseen problems. If you select a topic which does not greatly interest you, it could become extremely difficult to sustain the required motivation, and hence its completion as well as the amount of time taken could be affected.
- **Magnitude**—you should have sufficient knowledge about the research process to be able to visualise the work involved in completing the proposed study. Narrow the topic down to something manageable, specific and clear. It is extremely important to select a topic that you can manage within the time and resources at your disposal. Even if you are undertaking a descriptive study, you need to carefully consider its magnitude.
- **Measurement of concepts**—if you are using a concept in your study, make sure you are clear about its indicators and their measurement. For example, if you plan to measure the effectiveness of a health promotion program, you must be clear as to what determines effectiveness and how it will be measured. Do not use concepts in your research problem that you are not sure how to measure. This does not mean you cannot develop a measurement procedure as the study progresses. While most of the developmental work will be done during your study, it is imperative that you are reasonably clear about the measurement of these concepts at this stage.
- **Level of expertise**—make sure you have an adequate level of expertise for the task you are proposing. Allow for the fact that you will learn during the study and may receive help from your research supervisors and others, but remember you need to do most of the work yourself.

- **Relevance**—select a topic that is of relevance to you as a professional. Ensure that your study adds to the existing body of knowledge, bridges current gaps or is useful in policy formulation. This will help you to sustain interest in the study.
- **Availability of data**—if your topic entails collection of information from secondary sources (office records, client records, census or other already-published reports, etc.) before finalising your topic, make sure that these data are available and in the format you want.
- **Ethical issues**—another important consideration in formulating a research problem is the ethical issues involved. In the course of conducting a research study, the study population may be adversely affected by some of the questions (directly or indirectly); deprived of an intervention; expected to share sensitive and private information; or expected to be simply experimental 'guinea pigs'. How ethical issues can affect the study population and how ethical problems can be overcome should be thoroughly examined at the problem-formulation stage.

Steps in the formulation of a research problem

The formulation of a research problem is the most crucial part of the research journey on which the quality of the entire project depends. Yet the available books offer very little by way of specific guidance. This task is largely left either to the teachers of research methodology or to students like you to learn themselves. One of the strengths of this book is that it offers a beginner a very specific set of step-by-step guidelines in one place.

The process of formulating a research problem consists of a number of steps. Working through these steps presupposes a reasonable level of knowledge in the broad subject area within which the study is to be undertaken. A brief review of the relevant literature helps enormously in broadening this knowledge base. Without such knowledge it is difficult to clearly and adequately 'dissect' a subject area.

If you do not know what specific research topic, idea or issue you want to research (which is not uncommon among students) first go through the following two steps:

Steps 1   **Identify a broad field or subject area of *interest* to you.** Ask yourself, 'What is it that really interest me as a professional'? In the author's opinion, it is a good idea to think about the field in which you would like to work after graduation. This will help you to find an interesting topic, and one which may be of use to you in the future. For example, if you are a social work student, inclined to work in the area of youth welfare, refugees or domestic violence after graduation, you might take to research in one of these areas. Or if you are studying marketing you might be interested in researching consumer behaviour. Or, as a student of public health, intending to work with patients who have HIV/AIDS, you might like to conduct research on a subject area relating to HIV/AIDS. As far as the research journey goes, these are the broad research areas. It is imperative that you identify one of interest to you before undertaking your research journey.

Step 2   ***Dissect* the broad area into subareas**. At the onset, you will realise that all the broad areas mentioned above—youth welfare, refugees, domestic violence, consumer behaviour and HIV/AIDS—have many aspects. Take domestic violence for example. There are many aspects and issues in the area of domestic violence. Figure 4.1 shows some of its many aspects.

Figure 4.1   Dissecting the subject area of domestic violence into subareas

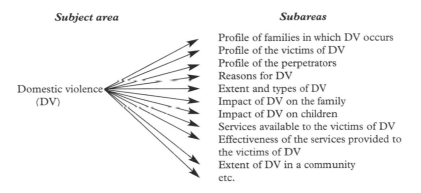

Similarly, you can select any subject area from other fields such as community health or consumer research and go through this dissection process. In preparing this list of subareas you should also consult others who have some knowledge of the area and the literature in your subject area. Once you have developed an exhaustive list of the subareas from various sources, you proceed to the next stage where you select what will become the basis of your inquiry.

Step 3   ***Select* what is of most interest to you.** It is neither advisable nor feasible to study all subareas. Out of this list, select issues or subareas about which you are passionate. This is because your interest should be the most important determinant for selection, even though there are other considerations which have been discussed in the previous section, 'Considerations in selecting a research problem'. One way to decide what interests you most is to start with the process of elimination. Go through your list and delete all those subareas in which you are not very interested. You will find that towards the end of this process, it will become very difficult for you to delete anything further. You need to continue until you are left with something that is *manageable* considering the time available to you, your level of expertise and other resources needed to undertake the study. Once you are confident that what you have selected you are passionate about and can manage, you are ready to go to the next step.

Step 4   **Raise research questions.** At this step you ask yourself, 'What is it that I want to find out about in this subarea'? Within your chosen subarea, first list whatever questions you want to find answers to. If you find yourself in a situation where you can think of many questions, too many to be manageable, again go through a process of elimination, as you did in Step 3.

Step 5   **Formulate objectives.** Formulate your main objectives and your subobjectives (see the following section on formulation of objectives). Your objectives grow out of your research questions. The main difference between objectives and research questions is the way in which they are written. Research questions are obviously that—questions. Objectives transform these questions into behavioural aims by using action-oriented words such as 'to find out', 'to determine', 'to ascertain' and 'to examine'. Some researchers prefer to reverse the process; that is, they start from objectives and formulate research questions from them. Some researchers are satisfied only with research questions, and do not formulate objectives at all. If you prefer to have only research questions or only objectives, this is fine but keep in mind the requirements of your institution for research proposals.

Step 6   **Assess your objectives.** Now examine your objectives to ascertain the feasibility of achieving them through your research endeavour. Consider them in the light of the time, resources (financial and human) and technical expertise at your disposal.

Step 7   **Double-check.** Go back and give final consideration to whether or not you are sufficiently interested in the study, and have adequate resources to undertake it. Ask yourself, 'Am I really enthusiastic about this study', and 'Do I really have enough resources to undertake it'? Answer these questions thoughtfully and realistically. If your answer to one of them is 'no', re-assess your objectives.

Figures 4.2 to 4.4 operationalise steps 1–7 with examples from different academic disciplines (health, social work/social sciences and community development).

So far we have focused on the basis of your study, the *research problem*. But every study in social sciences has a second element, *the study population*, from whom the required information to find answers to your research questions is obtained. As you narrow the research problem, similarly you need to decide very specifically who constitutes your study population, in order to select the appropriate respondents.

Figure 4.2   Steps in formulating a research problem—alcoholism

Example 1: Suppose you want to conduct a study in the area of alcoholism. In formulating your research problem take the following steps.

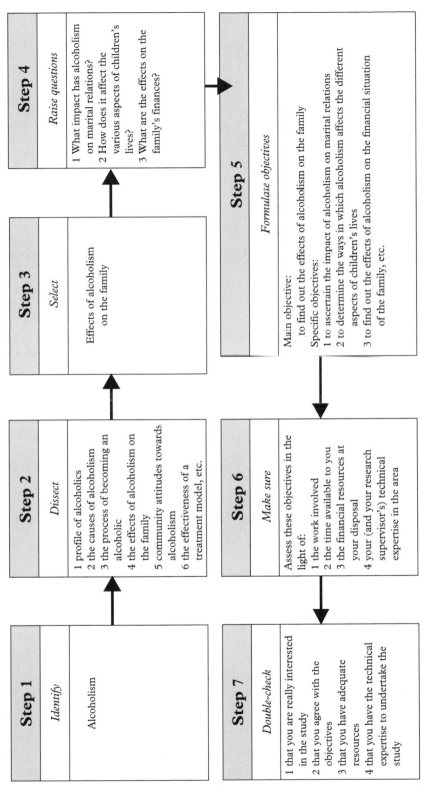

Figure 4.3   Formulating a research problem—the relationship between fertility and mortality

Example 2: Suppose you want to study the relationship between fertility and mortality. Follow these steps.

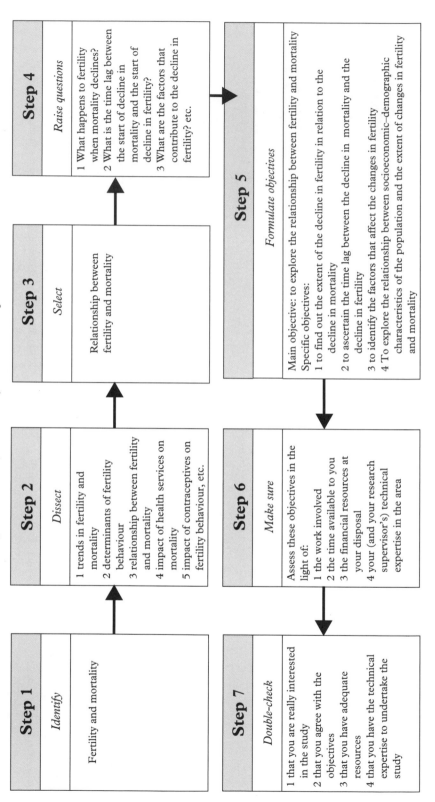

Step 1

Identify

Fertility and mortality

Step 2

Dissect

1 trends in fertility and mortality
2 determinants of fertility behaviour
3 relationship between fertility and mortality
4 impact of health services on mortality
5 impact of contraceptives on fertility behaviour, etc.

Step 3

Select

Relationship between fertility and mortality

Step 4

Raise questions

1 What happens to fertility when mortality declines?
2 What is the time lag between the start of decline in mortality and the start of decline in fertility?
3 What are the factors that contribute to the decline in fertility? etc.

Step 5

Formulate objectives

Main objective: to explore the relationship between fertility and mortality
Specific objectives:
1 to find out the extent of the decline in fertility in relation to the decline in mortality
2 to ascertain the time lag between the decline in mortality and the decline in fertility
3 to identify the factors that affect the changes in fertility
4 To explore the relationship between socioeconomic–demographic characteristics of the population and the extent of changes in fertility and mortality

Step 6

Make sure

Assess these objectives in the light of:
1 the work involved
2 the time available to you
3 the financial resources at your disposal
4 your (and your research supervisor's) technical expertise in the area

Step 7

Double-check

1 that you are really interested in the study
2 that you agree with the objectives
3 that you have adequate resources
4 that you have the technical expertise to undertake the study

Figure 4.4   Narrowing a research problem—health

Example 3: Suppose you want to conduct a study in the area of health. Follow these steps.

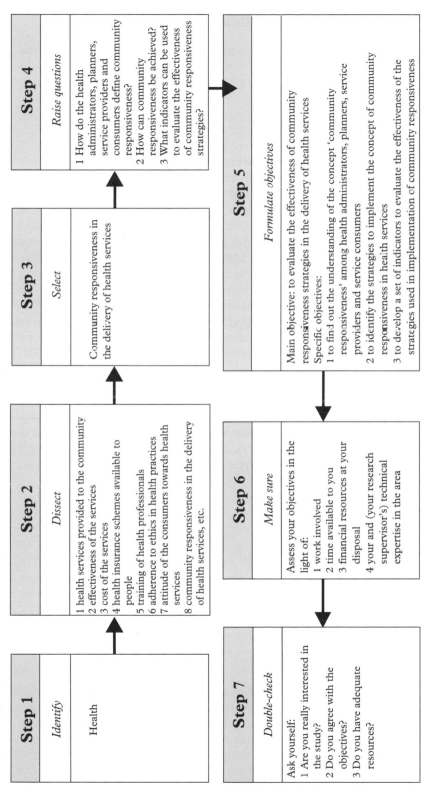

Step 1

Identify

Health

Step 2

Dissect

1 health services provided to the community
2 effectiveness of the services
3 cost of the services
4 health insurance schemes available to people
5 training of health professionals
6 adherence to ethics in health practices
7 attitude of the consumers towards health services
8 community responsiveness in the delivery of health services, etc.

Step 3

Select

Community responsiveness in the delivery of health services

Step 4

Raise questions

1 How do the health administrators, planners, service providers and consumers define community responsiveness?
2 How can community responsiveness be achieved?
3 What indicators can be used to evaluate the effectiveness of community responsiveness strategies?

Step 5

Formulate objectives

Main objective: to evaluate the effectiveness of community responsiveness strategies in the delivery of health services
Specific objectives:
1 to find out the understanding of the concept 'community responsiveness' among health administrators, planners, service providers and service consumers
2 to identify the strategies to implement the concept of community responsiveness in health services
3 to develop a set of indicators to evaluate the effectiveness of the strategies used in implementation of community responsiveness

Step 6

Make sure

Assess your objectives in the light of:
1 work involved
2 time available to you
3 financial resources at your disposal
4 your and (your research supervisor's) technical expertise in the area

Step 7

Double-check

Ask yourself:
1 Are you really interested in the study?
2 Do you agree with the objectives?
3 Do you have adequate resources?

The formulation of objectives

Objectives are the goals you set out to attain in your study. Since these objectives inform a reader of what you want to achieve through the study, it is extremely important to word them clearly and specifically.

Objectives should be listed under two headings:

- main objectives;
- subobjectives.

The main objective is an overall statement of the thrust of your study. It is also a statement of the main associations and relationships that you seek to discover or establish. The subobjectives are the specific aspects of the topic that you want to investigate within the main framework of your study.

Subobjectives should be numerically listed. They should be worded clearly and unambiguously. Make sure that each subobjective contains only one aspect of the study. Use action-oriented words or verbs when writing your objectives. The objectives should start with words such as 'to determine', 'to find out', 'to ascertain', 'to measure' and 'to explore'.

The way the main and subobjectives are worded determines how your research is classified (e.g. descriptive, correlational or experimental). In other words, the wording of your objectives determines the type of research design you need to adopt to achieve them. Hence, be careful about the way you word your objectives.

Irrespective of the type of research, the objectives should be expressed in such a way that the wording clearly, completely and specifically communicates to your readers your intention. There is no place for ambiguity, non-specificity or incompleteness, either in the wording of your objectives or in the ideas they communicate. Figure 4.5 displays the characteristics of the wording of objectives in relation to the type of research study.

Figure 4.5   Characteristics of objectives

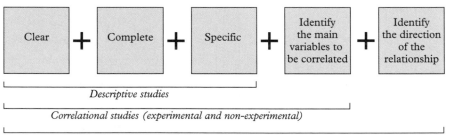

If your study is primarily descriptive, your main objective should clearly describe the major focus of your study, even mentioning the organisation and its location unless these are to be kept confidential (e.g. *to describe the types of treatment program provided by ... [name of the organisation] to alcoholics in ... [name of the place] ...* or *to find out the opinion of the community about the health services provided by ... [name of the health centre/department] in ... [name of the place] ...*). Identification of the organisation and its location is important as the services may be peculiar to the place and the organisation and may not represent the services provided by others to similar populations.

If your study is correlational in nature, in addition to the above three properties, the wording of the main objective should include the main variables being correlated (e.g. to ascertain the *impact of migration* on *family roles* or to compare the effectiveness of *different teaching methods* on the *comprehension of students*).

If the overall thrust of your study is to test a hypothesis, the wording of main objectives, in addition to the above, should indicate the direction of the relationship being tested (e.g. to ascertain if an *increase in youth unemployment* will *increase the incidence of street crime*, or to demonstrate that the provision of maternal and child health services to Aboriginal people in rural Australia will *reduce infant mortality*).

Establishing operational definitions

As mentioned earlier, in every study there are two components: the subject area and the study population (discussed in 'Sources of research problems' earlier in this chapter). The main aim of formulating a research problem is to clearly and precisely define the research problem. In defining the problem you may use certain words or items that are difficult to measure and/or the understanding of which may vary from respondent to respondent. In a research study it is important to develop, define or establish a set of rules, indicators or yardsticks in order to clearly establish the meaning of such words/items. On the other hand, it is sometimes also important to define clearly the study population from which you need to obtain the required information. The following example studies help to explain this. The main objectives are:

- to find out the number of *children* living below the *poverty line* in Australia;
- to ascertain the impact of immigration on *family roles* among *immigrants*;
- to measure the *effectiveness* of a retraining program designed to help *young people*.

Although these objectives clearly state the main thrust of the studies, they are not specific in terms of the main variables to be studied and the study populations. You cannot count the number of children living below the poverty line until you decide what constitutes the poverty line and how to determine it; you cannot find out the impact of immigration on family roles unless you identify which roles constitute family roles; and you cannot measure effectiveness until you define what effectiveness is. On the other hand, it is equally important to decide exactly what you mean by 'children', 'immigrants' or 'young'. Up to what age will you consider a person to be a child (i.e. 5, 10, 15 or 18)? Who would you consider young? A person 15 years of age, 20, 25 or 30? Who would you consider to be an immigrant? A person who immigrated 40, 20 or

5 years ago? In addition, are you going to consider immigrants from every country or only a few?

In many cases you need to develop operational definitions for the variable you are studying and for the population that becomes the source of the information for your study. Table 4.2 shows the concepts and the population groups to be operationalised for the above examples.

In a research study you need to define these clearly in order to avoid ambiguity and confusion. This is achieved through the process of developing operational/working definitions. You need to develop operational definitions for the major concepts you are using in your study and develop a framework for the study population enabling you to select appropriate respondents.

Table 4.2   Operationalisation of concepts and the study populations

Study	*Concept to be studied*		*Population to be studied*	
	Concepts	Issues	Study populations	Issues
1	Poverty line	What constitutes 'poverty line'?	Children	Who would you consider a child?
2	Family roles	What constitutes 'family roles'?	Immigrants	Who would you consider an immigrant?
3	Effectiveness	What constitutes 'effectiveness'?	The young	Who would you consider a young person?
You must	Operationalise the concepts: define in practical, observable and measurable terms 'poverty line', 'family roles' and 'effectiveness'		Operationalise the study population: define in identifiable terms 'children', 'immigrants' and 'young'.	

Operational definitions may differ from dictionary definitions as well as from day-to-day meanings. These meanings may not be helpful in either identifying your study population or the concepts you are studying. Though in daily life you often use words such as 'children', 'youth' and 'immigrant' loosely, you need to be more specific when using them in a research study. You should work through your own definition.

Operational definitions give an operational meaning to the study population and the concepts used. It is only through making your procedures explicit that you can validly describe, explain, verify and test. It is important to remember that there are no rules for deciding if an operational definition is valid. Your arguments must convince others about the appropriateness of your definitions.

SUMMARY

The formulation of a research problem is the most important step in the research process. It is the foundation, in terms of design, on which you build the whole study. Any defects in it will adversely affect the validity and reliability of your study.

There are no specific guidelines but the model suggested in this chapter could serve as a useful framework for the beginner. The seven-step model is operational in nature and follows a logical sequence that takes the beginner through the complexities of formulating a research problem in a simple and easy-to-understand manner.

It is important to articulate the objectives of your study clearly. Objectives should be specific and free from ambiguity, and each one should relate to only one aspect of the study. They should be under two headings: main objective and subobjectives. Use action-oriented words when writing your objectives.

CHAPTER
five

Identifying variables

If it exists, it can be measured (Babbie 1989: 105).

In the process of formulating a research problem there are two important considerations: the use of concepts and the construction of hypotheses. Concepts are highly subjective as their understanding varies from person to person and therefore, as such, may not be measurable. In a research study it is important that the concepts used should be operationalised in measurable terms so that the extent of variation in respondents' understanding is reduced if not eliminated. Techniques about how to operationalise concepts, and knowledge about variables, play an important role in reducing this variability. Their knowledge, therefore, is important in 'fine tuning' your research problem.

The definition of a variable

Whether we accept it or not, we all make value judgements constantly in our daily lives: 'This food is *excellent*'; 'I could not sleep *well* last night'; 'I do not *like* this'; and 'I think this is *wonderful*'. These are all judgements based upon our *own* preferences, indicators or assessment. Because these explain feelings or preferences, the basis on which they are made may vary markedly from person to person. There is no uniform yardstick with which to measure them. A particular food may be judged 'excellent' by one person but 'awful' by another, and something else could be wonderful to one person but ugly to another. When people express these feelings or preferences, they do so on the basis of certain criteria in their minds. If you take the time to question them you will discover that their judgement is based upon indicators that lead them to conclude and express that opinion.

Let us take the same issues at another level:

- 'This program is *effective*'.
- 'This program is *not effective*'.
- 'We are providing a *quality* service to our clients'.
- 'This is a *waste of time*'.
- 'In this institution women are *discriminated* against'.
- 'There is no *accountability* in this office'.
- 'This product is not doing *well*'.

These are not preferences *per se*; these are judgements that require a sound basis on which to proclaim. For example, if you want to find out if a program is effective, if a service is of quality or if there is discrimination, you need to be careful that such judgements have a rational and sound basis. This warrants the use of a measuring mechanism and it is in the process of measurement that knowledge about variables plays an important role.

An image, perception or concept that is capable of measurement—hence capable of taking on different values—is called a **variable**. In other words, a concept that can be measured is called a variable. According to Kerlinger,

'A variable is a property that takes on different values. Putting it redundantly, a variable is something that varies ... A variable is a symbol to which numerals or values are attached' (1986: 27). Black and Champion define a variable as 'rational units of analysis that can assume any one of a number of designated sets of values' (1976: 34). A concept that can be measured on any one of the four types of measurement scale, which have varying degrees of precision in measurement, is called a variable (measurement scales are discussed later in this chapter).

However, there are some who believe that scientific methods are incapable of measuring feelings, preferences, values and sentiments. In the author's opinion most of these things can be measured, though there are situations where such feelings or judgements are incapable of direct measurement (but can be measured indirectly). These feelings and judgements are based upon observable behaviours in real life, though the extent to which the behaviours reflect their judgements may vary from person to person. Cohen and Nagel express their opinion in the following words:

> There are, indeed, a great many writers who believe that scientific method is inherently inapplicable to such judgements as estimation or value, as 'This is beautiful', 'This is good' or 'This ought to be done' ... all judgements of the latter type express nothing but feelings, tastes or individual preferences, such judgements cannot be said to be true or false (except as descriptions of the personal feelings of the one who utters them) ... Almost all human discourse would become meaningless if we took the view that every moral or aesthetic judgement is no more true or false than any other (1966: 352).

The difference between a concept and a variable

Concepts are mental images or perceptions and therefore their meanings vary markedly from individual to individual, whereas variables are measurable, of course with varying degrees of accuracy. Measurability is the main difference between a concept and a variable. A concept cannot be measured whereas a variable can be subjected to measurement by crude/refined or subjective/objective units of measurement. Concepts are subjective impressions—their understanding may differ from person to person—which, if measured, would cause problems in comparing responses. According to Young,

> Each collaborator must have the same understanding of the concepts if the collaborative data are to be similarly classified and the findings pooled and tested, or reproduced. Classification and comparison demand uniform and precise definitions of categories expressed in concepts (1966: 18).

It is therefore important for the concepts to be converted into variables as they can be subjected to measurement even though the degree of precision with which they can be measured varies from scale to scale. Table 5.1 shows the difference between a concept and a variable.

Table 5.1   The difference between concepts and variables

Concept	*Variable*

• effectiveness
• satisfaction
• impact
• excellent
• high achiever
• self-esteem
• rich
• domestic violence
• extent and pattern of
  alcohol consumption
  etc.
	• gender (male/female)
	• attitude
	• age (*x* years, *y* months)
	• income ($ ___ per year)
	• weight (___ kg)
	• height (___ cm)
	• religion (Catholic, Protestant, Jew, Muslim)
	  etc.

—Subjective impression
 	
—No uniformity as to its understanding
  among different people
 	
—As such cannot be measured
	—Measurable though the degree of precision varies
	  from scale to scale and from variable to variable
	  (e.g., attitude—subjective, income—objective)

Concepts, indicators and variables

If you are using a concept in your study, you need to consider its operationalisation—that is, how it will be measured. In most cases, to operationalise a concept you first need to go through the process of identifying indicators—a set of criteria reflective of the concept—which can then be converted into variables. The choice of indicators for a concept might vary with the researcher but those selected must have a logical link with the concept. Some concepts, such as 'rich', can easily be converted into indicators and then variables. For example, to decide objectively if a person is 'rich', one first needs to decide upon the indicators of richness. Assume that we decide upon income and assets as the indicators. Income is also a variable since it can be measured in dollars; therefore, you do not need to convert this into a variable. Although the assets owned by an individual are indicators of his/her 'richness', they still belong to the category of concepts. You need to look further at the indicators of assets. For example, house, boat, car and investments are indicators of assets. Converting the value of each one into dollars will give the total value of the assets owned by a person. Next, fix a level, based upon available information on income distribution and an average level of assets owned by members of a community, which acts as the basis for classification. Then analyse the information on income and the total value of the assets to make a decision about whether the person should be classified as 'rich'. The operationalisation of other concepts, such as the 'effectiveness' or 'impact' of a program, may prove more difficult. Table 5.2 shows some examples that will help you to understand the process of converting concepts into variables.

Table 5.2   Converting concepts into variables

Concepts	Indicators	Variables	Decision level (working definitions)

Rich	1 Income
	2 Assets
		1 Income per year
		2 Total value of:
		    home(s); boat; car(s);
		    investments
			1 if > $100 000
			2 if > $250 000

High academic achievement	1 Average marks obtained in examinations 2 Average marks obtained in practical work 3 Aggregate marks 4 etc.	1 Percentage of marks 2 Percentage of marks 3 Percentage of marks	1 if > 75% 2 if > 75% 3 if > 80%

Effectiveness (of a health program)	1 Number of patients
	
	2 Changes in morbidity
	(a) Changes in the *extent* of morbidity
	(b) Changes in the *pattern* of morbidity
	
	3 Changes in mortality
	(a) Changes in the *Crude Death Rate* (CDR)
	(b) Changes in the *Age-Specific Death Rate* (ASDR)
	
	4 Changes in nutritional status
	(a) Changes in *weight*
	(b) Changes in *illness episodes*
	(c) Changes in *morbidity*
		1 number of patients serviced in a month/year
		
		2(a) Changes in morbidity rate (number of illness *or* episodes per 1000 pop.)
		
		(b) Changes in morbidity typology
		
		3 1 Changes in CDR
		  2 Changes in ASDR
		
		4 1 Changes in weight
		  2 Illness episodes in a year
		  3 Changes in morbidity type
			Whether the difference in before and after levels is statistically significant
			
			Point-prevalence increase or decrease in each variable as decided by the researcher or other experts

Figure 5.1 Types of variable

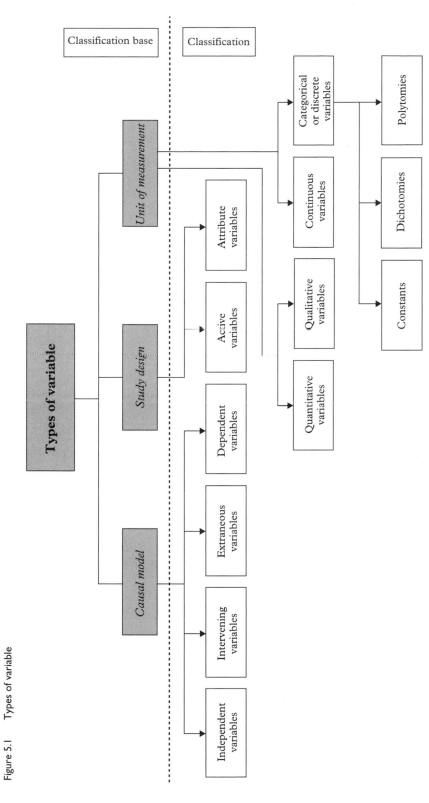

Note: Classification across a classification base is not mutually exclusive but classification within a classification base is. Within a study an independent variable can be an active variable, or a quantitative or a qualitative variable and it can also be a continuous or a categorical variable but it cannot be a dependent, an extraneous or an intervening variable.

Types of variable

A variable can be classified in a number of ways. The classification developed here results from looking at variables in three different ways (see Figure 5.1 on the previous page):

• the causal relationship;
• the design of the study;
• the unit of measurement.

From the viewpoint of causation

In studies that attempt to investigate a causal relationship or association, four sets of variables may operate (see Figure 5.2):

1 **change** variables, which are responsible for bringing about change in a phenomenon;
2 **outcome** variables, which are the effects of a change variable;
3 variables which **affect** the link between cause-and-effect variables;
4 **connecting** or **linking** variables, which in certain situations are necessary to complete the relationship between cause-and-effect variables.

Figure 5.2   Types of variable in a causal relationship

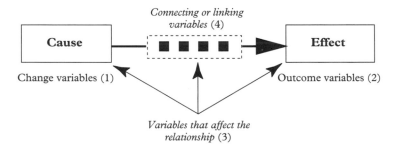

In research terminology, change variables are called *independent variables*, outcome/effect variables are called *dependent variables*, the unmeasured variables affecting the cause-and-effect relationship are called *extraneous variables* and the variables that link a cause-and-effect relationship are called *intervening variables*. Hence:

1 **Independent variable**—the cause supposed to be responsible for bringing about change(s) in a phenomenon or situation.
2 **Dependent variable** —the outcome of the change(s) brought about by introduction of an independent variable.
3 **Extraneous variable**—several other factors operating in a real-life situation may affect changes in the dependent variable. These factors, not measured in the study, may increase or decrease the magnitude or strength of the relationship between independent and dependent variables.

4   **Intervening variable**—sometimes called the confounding variable (Grinnell 1988: 203), links the independent and dependent variables. In certain situations the relationship between an independent and a dependent variable cannot be established without the intervention of another variable. The cause variable will have the assumed effect only in the presence of an intervening variable.

To explain these variables let us take some examples. Suppose you want to study the relationship between smoking and cancer. You assume that smoking is a cause of cancer. Studies have shown that there are many factors affecting this relationship, such as the number of cigarettes or the amount of tobacco smoked every day; the duration of smoking; the age of the smoker; dietary habits; and the amount of exercise undertaken by the individual. All of these factors may affect the extent to which smoking might cause cancer. These variables may either increase or decrease the magnitude of the relationship.

In the above example the extent of smoking is the independent variable, cancer is the dependent variable and all the variables that might affect this relationship, either positively or negatively, are extraneous variables. See Figure 5.3.

Figure 5.3   Independent, dependent and extraneous variables in a causal relationship

Smoking	Cancer
(Assumed cause)	(Assumed effect)
Independent variable	**Dependent variable**

Affect the relationship

• The age of the person
• The extent of his/her smoking
• The duration of smoking
• The extent of daily exercise
  etc.

Extraneous variables

Let us take another example. Suppose you want to study the effects of a marriage counselling service on marital problems among clients of an agency providing such a service. Figure 5.4 shows the sets of variables that may operate in studying the relationship between counselling and marriage problems.

Figure 5.4   Sets of variables in counselling and marriage problems

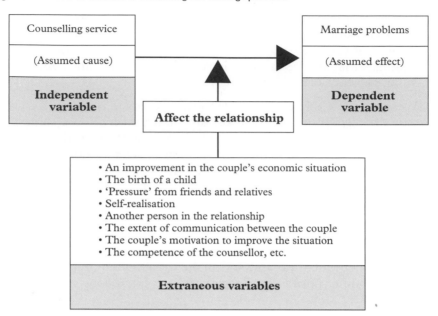

In studying the relationship between a counselling service and marriage problems, it is assumed that the counselling service will influence the extent of marital problems. Hence, in the study of the above relationship, the type of counselling service is the independent variable and the extent of marriage problems is the dependent variable. The magnitude or strength of this relationship can be affected, positively or negatively, by a number of other factors that are not the focus of the study. These extraneous variables might be the birth of a child; improvement in a couple's economic situation; the couple's motivation to change the situation; the involvement of another person; self-realisation; and pressure from relatives and friends. Extraneous variables that work both ways can increase or decrease the strength of the relationship.

The example in Figure 5.5 should help you to understand intervening variables. Suppose you want to study the relationship between fertility and mortality. Your aim is to explore what happens to fertility when mortality declines. The history of demographic transition has shown that a reduction in the fertility level follows a decline in the mortality level, though the time taken to attain the same level of reduction in fertility varies markedly from country to country. As such, there is no direct relationship between fertility and mortality. With the reduction in mortality, fertility will decline only if people attempt to limit their family size. History has shown that for a multiplicity of reasons (the discussion of which is beyond the scope of this book) people have used one method or another to control their fertility, resulting in lower fertility levels. It is thus the intervention of contraceptive methods that completes the relationship: the greater the use of contraceptives, the greater the decline in the fertility level. The extent of the use of contraceptives is also affected by a number of other factors, for example attitudes towards contraception, level of education, socioeconomic

Figure 5.5   Independent, dependent, extraneous and intervening variables

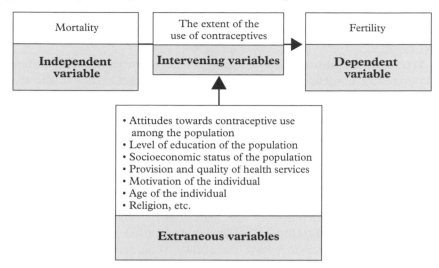

status and age, religion, and provision and quality of health services. These are classified as extraneous variables.

In the above example, decline in mortality is assumed to be the cause of a reduction in fertility, hence, the mortality level is the independent variable and fertility is the dependent variable. But this relationship will be completed only if another variable intervenes—that is, the use of contraceptives. A reduction in mortality (especially child mortality) increases family size, and an increase in family size creates a number of social, economic and psychological pressures on families, which in turn create attitudes favourable to a smaller family size. This change in attitudes is eventually operationalised in behaviour through the adoption of contraceptives. If people do not adopt methods of contraception, a change in mortality levels will not be reflected in fertility levels. The population explosion in developing countries is primarily due to lack of acceptance of contraceptives. The extent of the use of contraceptives determines the level of the decline in fertility. The extent of contraceptive adoption by a population is dependent upon a number of factors. In this causal model, the fertility level is the dependent variable, the extent of contraceptive use is the intervening variable, the mortality level is the independent variable, and the unmeasured variables such as attitudes, education, age, religion, the quality of services, and so on are all extraneous variables. Without the intervening variable the relationship between the independent and dependent variables will not be complete.

From the viewpoint of the study design

A study that examines association or causation may be a controlled/contrived experiment, a quasi-experiment or an *ex post facto* or non-experimental study. In controlled experiments the independent (cause) variable may be introduced or manipulated either by the researcher or by someone else who is providing the service. In these situations there are two sets of variables (see Figure 5.6):

- **Active variables**—those variables that can be manipulated, changed or controlled.
- **Attribute variables**—those variables that cannot be manipulated, changed or controlled, and that reflect the characteristics of the study population; For example, age, gender, education and income.

Suppose a study is designed to measure the relative effectiveness of three teaching models (Model A, Model B and Model C). The structure and contents of these models could vary and any model might be tested on any population group. The contents, structure and testability of a model on a population group may also vary from researcher to researcher. On the other hand, a researcher does not have any control over characteristics of the student population such as their age, gender or motivation to study. These characteristics of the study population are called attribute variables. However, a researcher does have the ability to control and/or change the teaching models. S/he can decide what constitutes a teaching model and on which group of the student population it should be tested (if randomisation is not used).

Figure 5.6   Active and attribute variables

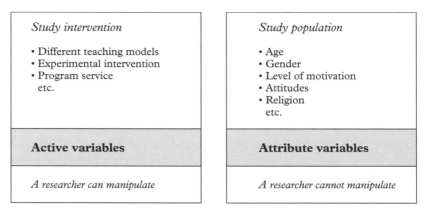

From the viewpoint of the unit of measurement

From the viewpoint of the unit of measurement, there are two ways of categorising variables:

- whether the unit of measurement is categorical (as in nominal and ordinal scales) or continuous in nature (as in interval and ratio scales);
- whether it is qualitative (as in nominal and ordinal scales) or quantitative in nature (as in interval and ratio scales).

The variables thus classified are called *categorical and continuous*, and *qualitative and quantitative*. On the whole there is very little difference between categorical and qualitative, and between continuous and quantitative, variables. The slight difference between them is explained below.

Categorical variables are measured on nominal or ordinal measurement scales, whereas for continuous variables the measurements are made either on an interval or a ratio scale. Categorical variables can be of three types:

1 constant;
2 dichotomous;
3 polytomous.

When a variable can have only one value or category, for example taxi, tree and water, it is known as a *constant variable*. When a variable can have only two categories as in yes/no, good/bad and rich/poor, it is known as a *dichotomous variable*. When a variable can be divided into more than two categories, for example: religion (Christian, Muslim, Hindu); political parties (Labor, Liberal, Democrat); and attitudes (strongly favourable, favourable, uncertain, unfavourable, strongly unfavourable), it is called a *polytomous variable*.

Continuous variables, on the other hand, have continuity in their measurement; for example, age, income and attitude score. They can take on any value on the scale on which they are measured. Age can be measured in years, months and days. Similarly, income can be measured in dollars and cents.

In many ways qualitative variables are similar to categorical variables as both use either nominal or ordinal measurement scales. However, there are some differences. For example, it is possible to develop categories on the basis of measurements made on a continuous scale, such as measuring the income of a population in dollars and cents and then developing categories such as 'low', 'middle' and 'high' income. The measurement of income in dollars and cents is classified as the measurement on a continuous variable, whereas its subjective measurement in categories such as 'low', 'middle' and 'high' groups is a qualitative variable.

Although this distinction exists, for most practical purposes there is no real difference between categorical and qualitative variables or between continuous and quantitative variables. Table 5.3 shows similarities and differences among the various types of variable.

For a beginner it is important to understand that the way a variable is measured determines the type of analysis that can be performed, the statistical procedures that can be applied to the data, the way the data can be interpreted and the findings that can be communicated. You may not realise in the beginning that the style of your report is entirely dependent upon the way the different variables have been measured—that is, the way a question has been asked and its response recorded. The way you measure the variables in your study determines whether a study is 'qualitative' or 'quantitative' in nature. It is therefore important to know about the measurement scales for variables.

Table 5.3   Categorical/continuous and quantitative/qualitative variables

Categorical			Continuous	Qualitative	Quantitative
Constant	*Dichotomous*	*Polytomous*			

- water	- yes/no	Attitudes
		  - strongly
		    favourable
		  - favourable
		  - uncertain
		  - strongly
		    unfavourable
		Political
		parties
		  - Labor
		  - Liberal
		  - Democrat
		Age*
		  - old
		  - young
		  - child
		Income ^
		  - high
		  - middle
		  - low
			Income ($)	Gender
				  - female
				  - male
				Educational
				level
				  - high
				  - average
				  - low
				Age*
				  - old
				  - young
				  - child
				Income
				  - high
				  - middle
				  - low
				Temperature+
				  - hot
				  - cold
					Educational
					level
					— no. of years
					completed
					
					Age:*
					
					—
					years/months
					
					Income ^
					—— $ per
					year
					
					Temperature:+
					—— C or F

- tree	- good/bad		Age (years)		
- taxi	- rich/poor		Weight (kg)		
	- day/night				
	- male/ female				
	- hot/cold*				

* Can be classified in qualitative categories, e.g. old, young, child; or quantitatively on a continuous scale, e.g. in years, months and days.
^ Can be measured quantitatively in dollars and cents as well as qualitatively in categories such as high, middle and low.
+ Similarly, temperature can be measured quantitatively in degrees on different scales (Celsius, Fahrenheit) or in qualitative categories such as hot and cold.

Types of measurement scale

> The frame into which we wish to make everything fit is one of our own construction; but we do not construct it at random, we construct it by measurement so to speak; and that is why we can fit the facts into it without altering their essential qualities (Poincaré 1952: xxv).

Measurement is central to any inquiry. The greater the refinement in the unit of measurement of a variable, the greater the confidence, other things being equal, one can place in the findings. One of the main differences between the physical and the social sciences is the units of measurement used and the degree of importance attached to them. In the physical sciences measurements have to be absolutely accurate and precise, whereas in the social sciences they may vary from the very subjective to the very quantifiable. Within the social sciences the emphasis on precision in measurement varies markedly from one discipline to another. An anthropologist normally uses very 'subjective' units of measurement, whereas an economist or an epidemiologist emphasises 'objective' measurement.

There are two main classification systems in the social sciences for measuring different types of variable. One was developed by S.S. Stevens (1946) and the other by Duncan (1984). According to Smith (1991: 72),

'Duncan (1984) has enumerated, in increasing order of interest to scientists, five types of measurement: nominal classification, ordinal scaling, cardinal scaling, ratio scaling, and probability scaling'. Duncan writes about Stevens's classification as follows:

> The theory of scale types proposed in 1946 by S S Stevens focused on nominal, ordinal, interval, and ratio scales of measurement. Some of his examples of these types—notably those concerning psychological test scores—are misleading (1984: viii).

However, Bailey considers that 'S S Stevens constructed a widely adopted classification of levels of measurement ...' (1978: 52). As this book is written for the beginner and as Stevens's classification is easier, it is used for discussion in this chapter. Stevens has classified the different types of measurement scale into four categories:

- nominal or classificatory scale;
- ordinal or ranking scale;
- interval scale;
- ratio.

Table 5.4 summarises the characteristics of the four scales.

The nominal or classificatory scale

A nominal scale enables the classification of individuals, objects or responses based on a common/shared property or characteristic. These people, objects or responses are divided into a number of subgroups in such a way that each member of the subgroup has a common characteristic. A variable measured on a nominal scale may have one, two or more subcategories depending upon the extent of variation. For example, 'water' and 'tree' have only one subgroup, whereas the variable 'gender' can be classified into two subcategories: male and female. Political parties in Australia can similarly be classified into four main subcategories: Labor, Liberal, Democrats and Greens. Those who identify themselves, either by membership or belief, as belonging to the Labor Party are classified as 'Labor', those identifying with the Liberals are classified as 'Liberal', and so on. The name chosen for a subcategory is notional, but for effective communication it is best to choose something that describes the characteristic of the subcategory.

Classification by means of a nominal scale ensures that individuals, objects or responses within the same subgroup have a common characteristic or property as the basis of classification. The sequence in which subgroups are listed makes no difference as there is no relationship among subgroups.

The ordinal or ranking scale

An ordinal scale has all the properties of a nominal scale plus one of its own. Besides categorising individuals, objects, responses or a property into subgroups on the basis of a common characteristic, it ranks the subgroups in a certain order. They are arranged either in ascending or descending order according to the extent a subcategory reflects the magnitude of variation in the variable. For example, income can be measured either quantitatively (in dollars and cents) or qualitatively, using subcategories: 'above average', 'average' and 'below average'. (These categories can also be developed on the basis of quantitative measures, for example below $10 000 = below average, $10 000–$25 000 = average and above $25 000 = above average.) The subcategory 'above average' indicates that people so grouped have more income than people in the 'average' category, and people in the 'average' category have more income than those in the 'below average' category. These subcategories of income are related to one another in terms of the magnitude of people's income, but the magnitude itself is not quantifiable, and hence the difference between 'above average' and 'average' or between 'average' and 'below average' subcategories cannot be ascertained. The same is true for other variables such as socioeconomic status and attitudes measured on an ordinal scale.

Therefore, an ordinal scale has all the properties/characteristics of a nominal scale, in addition to its own. Subcategories are arranged in the order of the magnitude of the property/characteristic. Also, the 'distance' between the subcategories is not equal as there is no quantitative unit of measurement.

The interval scale

An interval scale has all the characteristics of an ordinal scale; that is, individuals or responses belonging to a subcategory have a common characteristic and the subcategories are arranged in an ascending or descending order. In addition, an interval scale uses a unit of measurement that enables the individuals or responses to be placed at equally spaced intervals in relation to the spread of the variable. This scale has a starting and a terminating point that is divided into equally spaced units/intervals. The starting and terminating points and the number of units/intervals between them are arbitrary and vary from scale to scale.

Celsius and Fahrenheit scales are examples of the interval scale. In the Celsius system the starting point (considered as freezing point) is zero and the terminating point (considered as boiling point) is 100°C. The gap between freezing and boiling points is divided into 100 equally spaced intervals, known as degrees. In the Fahrenheit system the freezing point is 32°F and the boiling point is 212°F, and the gap between the two points is divided into 180 equally spaced intervals. Each degree or interval is a measurement of temperature—the higher the degree, the higher the temperature. As the starting and terminating points are arbitrary, they are not absolute; that is, you cannot say that 60°C is twice as hot as 30°C or 30°F is three times hotter than 10°F. This means that while no mathematical operation can be performed on the readings, it can be performed on the differences between readings. For example, if the difference in temperature between two objects, A and B, is 15°C and the difference in temperature between two other objects, C and D, is 45°C, you can say that the difference in temperature between C and D is three

Table 5.4   Characteristics and examples of the four measurement scales

Measurement scale	Examples	Characteristics of the scale

Nominal or classificatory	A Tree, house, taxi, etc.
	
	B Gender: male/female
	   Attitude: favourable
	   unfavourable
	
	C Political parties
	   - Labor
	   - Liberal
	   - Democrat
	   - Green
	   Psychiatric disorders
	   - Schizophrenic
	   - Paranoid
	   - Manic-depressive
	   etc.
	   Religions
	   - Christian
	   - Islam
	   - Hindu
	   etc
		Each subgroup has a characteristic/property which is common to all classified within that subgroup

Ordinal or ranking	Income
	   - above average
	   - average
	   - below average
	Socioeconomic status
	   - upper
	   - middle
	   - low
	Attitudes
	   - strongly favourable
	   - favourable
	   - uncertain
	   - unfavourable
	   - strongly unfavourable
	Attitudinal scale (Likert scale—these are numerical categories)
	   - 0–30
	   - 31–40
	   - 41–50
	   etc.
		It has the characteristics of a Nominal scale, e.g. individuals groups, characteristic classified under a subgroup have a common characteristic
		
		PLUS
		
		Subgroups have a relationship to one another. They are arranged in ascending or descending order.

Interval	Temperature:
	   - Celcius → 0°C
	   - Fahrenheit → 32°F
	Attitudinal scale (Thurstone scale):
	   - 10–20
	   - 21–30
	   - 31–40
	   - 41–50
	   etc.
		It has all the characteristics of an ordinal scale (which also includes a nominal scale).
		
		PLUS
		
		It has a unit of measurement with an arbitrary starting and terminating point.

Ratio	Height: cm Income $ Age: years/months Weight: kg Attitudinal score: Guttman scale	It has all the properties of an interval scale. PLUS It has a fixed starting point, e.g. a zero point.

times greater than that between A and B. An attitude towards an issue measured on the Thurstone scale is similar. However, the Likert scale does not measure the absolute intensity of the attitude but simply measures it in relation to another person.

The interval scale is relative; that is, it plots the position of individuals or responses in relation to one another with respect to the magnitude of the measurement variable. Hence, an interval scale has all the properties of an ordinal scale, plus it has a unit of measurement with an arbitrary starting and terminating point. Therefore, it is relative in nature. It helps to place individuals or responses in relation to each other with respect to the magnitude of the measuring variable. As it is a relative scale no mathematical operations can be performed on its readings.

The ratio scale

A ratio scale has all the properties of nominal, ordinal and interval scales plus its own property: the zero point of a ratio scale is fixed, which means it has a fixed starting point. Therefore, it is an absolute scale—the difference between the intervals is always measured from a zero point. This means the ratio scale can be used for mathematical operations. The measurement of income, age, height and weight are examples of this scale. A person who is 40 years of age is twice as old as a 20-year-old. A person earning $60 000 per year earns three times the salary of a person earning $20 000.

SUMMARY

Knowledge of the different types of variable and the way they are measured plays a crucial role in research. Variables are important in bringing clarity and specificity to the conceptualisation of a research problem, to the formulation of hypotheses, and to the development of a research instrument. They affect how the data can be analysed, what statistical tests can be applied to the data, what interpretations can be made, how the data can be presented and what conclusions can be drawn. The way you ask a question determines its categorisation on a measurement scale, which in turn affects how the data can be analysed, what statistical tests can be applied to the data, what interpretations can be made, how the data can be presented and what conclusions can be drawn. Also, the way a variable is measured at the data-collection stage to a great extent determines whether a study is considered to be predominantly 'qualitative' or 'quantitative' in nature. It is important for a beginner to understand the different ways in which a variable can be measured and the implications of this for the study. A variable can be classified from three perspectives that are not mutually exclusive: causal relationship, design of the study and unit of measurement.

There are four measurement scales used in the social sciences: nominal, ordinal, interval and ratio. Any concept that can be measured on these scales is called a variable. Measurement scales enable highly subjective responses, as well as responses that can be measured with extreme precision, to be categorised. The choice of measuring a variable on a measurement scale is dependent upon the purpose of your study and the way you want to communicate the findings to readers.

CHAPTER

six

Constructing hypotheses

> Almost every great step [in the history of science] has been made by the 'anticipation of nature', that is, by the invention of hypotheses which, though verifiable, often had very little foundation to start with. (T.H. Huxley cited in Cohen & Nagel 1966: 197).

The definition of a hypothesis

The second important consideration in the formulation of a research problem is the construction of hypotheses. Hypotheses bring clarity, specificity and focus to a research problem, but are not essential for a study. You can conduct a valid investigation without constructing a single formal hypothesis. On the other hand, within the context of a research study, you can construct as many hypotheses as you consider to be appropriate. Some believe that one must formulate a hypothesis to undertake an investigation; however, the author does not hold this opinion. Hypotheses primarily arise from a set of 'hunches' that are tested through a study and one can conduct a perfectly valid study without having these hunches or speculations. However, in epidemiological studies, to narrow the field of investigation, it is important to formulate hypotheses.

The importance of hypotheses lies in their ability to bring direction, specificity and focus to a research study. They tell a researcher what specific information to collect, and thereby provide greater focus.

Let us imagine you are at the races and you place a bet. You bet on a hunch that a particular horse will win. You will only know if your hunch was right after the race. Take another example. Suppose you have a hunch that there are more smokers than non-smokers in your class. To test your hunch, you ask either all or just some of the class if they are smokers. You can then conclude whether your hunch was right or wrong.

Now let us take a slightly different example. Suppose you work in the area of public health. Your clinical impression is that a higher rate of a particular condition prevails among people coming from a specific population subgroup. You want to find out the probable cause of this condition. There could be many causes. To explore every conceivable possibility would require an enormous amount of time and resources. Hence, to narrow the choice, based on your knowledge of the field, you could identify what you assume to be the most probable cause. You could then design a study to collect the information needed to verify your hunch. If on verification you were able to conclude that the assumed cause was the real cause of the condition, your assumption would have been right.

In these examples, you started with a superficial hunch or assumption. In one case (horse racing) you waited for the event to take place and in the other two instances you designed a study to assess the validity of your assumption, and only after careful investigation did you reach a conclusion about the validity of your assumptions.

Hypotheses are based upon similar logic. As a researcher you *do not know* about a phenomenon, a situation, the prevalence of a condition in a population or about the outcome of a program, but you *do have a hunch* to form the basis of certain *assumptions or guesses*. You test these by collecting information that will enable you to conclude if your hunch was right. The verification process can have one of the three outcomes. Your hunch may prove to be:

1 right;
2 partially right; or
3 wrong.

Without this process of verification, you cannot conclude anything about the validity of your assumption.

Hence, a hypothesis is a hunch, assumption, suspicion, assertion or an idea about a phenomenon, relationship or situation, the reality or truth of which you do not know. A researcher calls these assumptions, assertions, statements or hunches hypotheses and they become the basis of an inquiry. In most studies the hypothesis will be based upon either previous studies or on your own or someone else's observation.

There are many definitions of a hypothesis. According to Kerlinger, 'A hypothesis is a conjectural statement of the relationship between two or more variables' (1986: 17). *Webster's New International Dictionary of English Language* defines a hypothesis as:

> a proposition, condition, or principle which is assumed, perhaps without belief, in order to draw out its logical consequences and by this method to test its accord with facts which are known or may be determined.

Black and Champion define a hypothesis as, 'a tentative statement about something, the validity of which is usually unknown' (1976: 126). In another definition, Bailey defines a hypothesis as:

> a proposition that is stated in a testable form and that predicts a particular relationship between two (or more) variables. In other words, if we think that a relationship exists, we first state it as a hypothesis and then test the hypothesis in the field (1978: 35).

According to Grinnell and Stothers,

> A hypothesis is written in such a way that it can be proven or disproven by valid and reliable data—it is in order to obtain these data that we perform our study (Grinnell 1988: 200).

From the above definitions it is apparent that a hypothesis has certain characteristics:

1 It is a tentative proposition.
2 Its validity is unknown.
3 In most cases, it specifies a relationship between two or more variables.

The functions of a hypothesis

While some researchers believe that to conduct a study requires a hypothesis, having a hypothesis is not essential as already mentioned. However, a hypothesis is important in terms of bringing clarity to the research problem. See Figure 6.1.

Figure 6.1   The process of testing a hypothesis

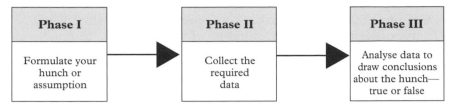

Specifically, a hypothesis serves the following functions.

- The formulation of a hypothesis provides a study with focus. It tells you what specific aspects of a research problem to investigate.
- A hypothesis tells you what data to collect and what not to collect, thereby providing focus to the study.
- As it provides a focus, the construction of a hypothesis enhances objectivity in a study.
- A hypothesis may enable you to add to the formulation of theory. It enables you to specifically conclude what is true or what is false.

The characteristics of a hypothesis

There are a number of considerations to keep in mind when constructing a hypothesis, as they are important for valid verification.

- **A hypothesis should be simple, specific and conceptually clear.** There is no place for ambiguity in the construction of a hypothesis, as ambiguity will make the verification of your hypothesis almost impossible. It should be 'unidimensional'—that is, it should test only one relationship or hunch at a time. To be able to develop a good hypothesis you must be familiar with the subject area (the literature review is of immense help). The more insight you have into a problem, the easier it is to construct a hypothesis. For example:

> The average age of the male students in this class is higher than that of the female students.

The above hypothesis is clear, specific and easy to test. It tells you what you are attempting to compare (average age of this class), which population groups are being compared (female and male students), and what you want to establish (higher average age of the male students).

Let us take another example.

> 'Suicide rates vary inversely with social cohesion' (Black & Champion 1976: 126).

This hypothesis is clear and specific, but a lot more difficult to test. There are three aspects of this hypothesis: 'suicide rates'; 'vary inversely', which stipulates the direction of the relationship; and 'social cohesion'. To find out the suicide rates and to establish whether the relationship is inverse or otherwise are comparatively easy, but to ascertain social cohesion is a lot more difficult. What determines social cohesion? How can it be measured? This problem makes it more difficult to test this hypothesis.

- **A hypothesis should be capable of verification.** Methods and techniques must be available for data collection and analysis. There is no point in formulating a hypothesis if it cannot be subjected to verification because there are no techniques to verify it. However, this does not necessarily mean that you should not formulate a hypothesis for which there are no methods of verification. You might, in the process of doing your research, develop new techniques to verify it.
- **A hypothesis should be related to the existing body of knowledge.** It is important that your hypothesis emerges from the existing body of knowledge, and that it adds to it, as this is an important function of research. This can only be achieved if the hypothesis has its roots in the existing body of knowledge.
- **A hypothesis should be operationalisable.** This means that it can be expressed in terms that can be measured. If it cannot be measured, it cannot be tested and, hence, no conclusions can be drawn.

Types of hypothesis

As explained, any assumption that you seek to validate through an inquiry is called a hypothesis. Hence, theoretically there should be only one type of hypothesis, that is, the research hypothesis—the basis of your investigation. However, because of the conventions in scientific inquiries and because of the wording used in the construction of a hypothesis, hypotheses can be classified into several types. Broadly, there are two categories of hypothesis:

1 research hypotheses;
2 alternate hypotheses.

The formulation of an **alternate hypothesis** is a convention in scientific circles. Its main function is to explicitly specify the relationship that will be considered as true in case the research hypothesis proves to be wrong. In a way, an alternate hypothesis is the opposite of the research hypothesis. Again, conventionally, a null hypothesis, or hypothesis of no difference, is formulated as an alternate hypothesis.

Let us take an example. Suppose you want to test the effect different combinations of maternal and child health services (MCH) and nutrition supplements (NS) have on the infant mortality rate. To test this a two-by-two factorial experimental design is adopted (see Figure 6.2).

There are several ways of formulating a hypothesis. For example:

1 There will be no difference in the level of infant mortality among the different treatment modalities.
2 The MCH and NS treatment group will register a greater decline in infant mortality than the MCH, the NS treatment or the control group.
3 Infant mortality in the MCH treatment group will reach a level of 30/1000 over five years.

Figure 6.2   Two-by-two factorial experiment to study the relationship between MCH, NS and infant mortality

		Maternal and child health services (MCH)	
		Yes	No
Nutrition supplements (NS)	Yes	MCH + NS	NS
	No	MCH	Control

4 Decline in the infant mortality rate will be three times greater in the MCH treatment group than in the NS one over five years.

Let us take another example. Suppose you want to study the smoking pattern in a community in relation to gender differentials. The following hypotheses could be constructed.

1 There is no significant difference in the proportion of male and female smokers in the study population.
2 A greater proportion of females than males are smokers in the study population.
3 A total of 60 per cent of females and 30 per cent of males in the study population are smokers.
4 There are twice as many female smokers as male smokers in the study population.

In both sets of examples, the way the first hypothesis has been formulated indicates that there is no difference either in the extent of the impact of different treatment modalities on the infant mortality rate or in the proportion of male and female smokers. When you construct a hypothesis stipulating that there is no difference between two situations, groups, outcomes, or the prevalence of a condition or phenomenon, this is called a **null hypothesis** and is usually written as Ho.

The second hypothesis in each example implies that there is a difference either in the extent of the impact of different treatment modalities on infant mortality or in the proportion of male and female smokers among the population, though the extent of the difference is not specified. A hypothesis in which a researcher stipulates that there will be a difference but does not specify its magnitude is called a **hypothesis of difference**.

A researcher may have enough knowledge about the smoking behaviour of the community or the treatment program and its likely outcomes to speculate almost the exact prevalence of the situation or the outcome of a treatment program in quantitative units. Examine the third hypothesis in both sets of examples: the level of infant mortality is 30/1000 and the proportion of female and male smokers is 60 and 30 per cent respectively. This type of hypothesis is known as a **hypothesis of point-prevalence**.

The fourth hypothesis in both sets of examples speculates a relationship between the impact of different combinations of MCH and NS programs on the dependent variable (infant mortality) or the relationship between the prevalence of a phenomenon (smoking) among different populations (male and female). This type of hypothesis stipulates the extent of the relationship in terms of the effect of different treatment groups on the dependent variable ('three times greater in the MCH treatment group than in the NS one over five years') or the prevalence of a phenomenon in different population groups ('twice as many female as male smokers'). This type of hypothesis is called a ***hypothesis of association***.

There may be some confusion about null and research hypotheses, as in Figure 6.3 the null hypothesis is also classified as hypothesis of no difference under 'research hypothesis'. Any type of hypothesis, including a null hypothesis, can become the basis of an inquiry. When a null hypothesis becomes the basis of an investigation, it becomes a research hypothesis.

Figure 6.3   Types of hypothesis

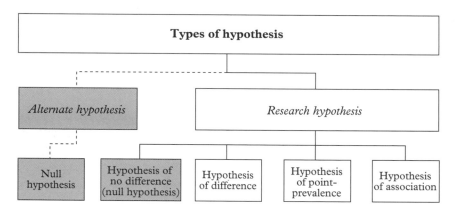

Errors in testing a hypothesis

As already mentioned, a hypothesis is an assumption thay may prove to be either correct or incorrect. It is possible to arrive at an incorrect conclusion about a hypothesis for a variety of reasons. Incorrect conclusions about the validity of a hypothesis may be drawn if:

- the study design selected is faulty;
- the sampling procedure adopted is faulty;
- the method of data collection is inaccurate;
- the analysis is wrong;
- the statistical procedures applied are inappropriate; or
- the conclusions drawn are incorrect.

Any, some or all of these aspects of the research process could be responsible for the inadvertent introduction of error in your study, making conclusions misleading. Hence, in the testing of a hypothesis there is always the possibility of errors attributable to the reasons identified above. Figure 6.4 shows the types of error that can result in the testing of a hypothesis.

Figure 6.4   Type I and Type II errors in testing a hypothesis

When a null hypothesis is actually:

	True	False
Accept	Correct decision	Type I error
Reject	Type II error	Correct decision

When your decision is to:

Hence in drawing conclusions about a hypothesis, two types of error can occur:

* *rejection* of a null hypothesis when it is true. This is known as a ***Type I error***.
* *acceptance* of a null hypothesis when it is false. This is known as a ***Type II error***.

SUMMARY

Hypotheses, though important, are not essential for a study. A perfectly valid study can be conducted without constructing a single hypothesis. Hypotheses are important for bringing clarity, specificity and focus to a research study.

A hypothesis is a speculative statement that is subjected to verification through a research study. In formulating a hypothesis it is important to ensure that it is simple, specific and conceptually clear; is able to be verified; is rooted in an existing body of knowledge; and able to be operationalised.

There are two broad types of hypothesis: a research hypothesis and an alternate hypothesis. A research hypothesis can be further classified, based upon the way it is formulated, as a null hypothesis, a hypothesis of difference, a hypothesis of point-prevalence and a hypothesis of association.

The testing of a hypothesis becomes meaningless if any one of the aspects of your study—design, sampling procedure, method of data collection, analysis of data, statistical procedures applied or conclusions drawn—is faulty or inappropriate. This can result in erroneous verification of a hypothesis: Type I where you reject a null hypothesis when it is true and should not have been rejected; and Type II where you accept a null hypothesis when it is false and should not have been accepted.

STEP II

CONCEPTUALISING A RESEARCH DESIGN

CHAPTER 7
The research design

CHAPTER 8
Selecting a study design

CHAPTER
seven

The research design

Having decided *what* you want to study *about*, the next question is: *how* are you going to conduct your study? What procedures will you adopt to obtain answers to research questions? How will you carry out the tasks needed to complete the different components of the research process? What should you do and what should you not do in the process of undertaking the study? These are some of the questions that need to be answered before you can proceed with the study. Basically, answers to these questions constitute the core of a research design.

The definition of a research design

> A research design is a plan, structure and strategy of investigation so conceived as to obtain answers to research questions or problems. The plan is the complete scheme or program of the research. It includes an outline of what the investigator will do from writing the hypotheses and their operational implications to the final analysis of data (Kerlinger 1986: 279).

> A traditional research design is a blueprint or detailed plan for how a research study is to be completed—operationalizing variables so they can be measured, selecting a sample of interest to study, collecting data to be used as a basis for testing hypotheses, and analysing the results (Thyer 1993: 94).

A research design is a procedural plan that is adopted by the researcher to answer questions validly, objectively, accurately and economically. According to Selltiz et al., 'A research design is the arrangement of conditions for collection and analysis of data in a manner that aims to combine relevance to the research purpose with economy in procedure' (1962: 50).

The functions of a research design

The above definitions suggest that a research design has two main functions. The first relates to the identification and/or development of procedures and logistical arrangements required to undertake a study, and the second emphasises the importance of quality in these procedures to ensure their validity, objectivity and accuracy. Hence, through a research design you:

- conceptualise an operational plan to undertake the various procedures and tasks required to complete your study;
- ensure that these procedures are adequate to obtain valid, objective and accurate answers to the research questions. Kerlinger calls this function the 'control of variance' (1986: 280).

Let us explain the second function first by taking a few examples. Suppose you want to find out the effectiveness of a marriage counselling service provided by an agency—that is, the extent to which the service has been able to resolve the marital problems of its clients. In studying such relationships you must understand that in real life there are many outside factors that can influence the outcome of your intervention. For example, during visits to your agency for counselling, your client may get a better job.

If some of the marital problems came about because of economic hardship, and, if the problem of money is now solved, it may be a factor in reducing the marital problems. On the other hand, if a client loses his/her job, the increase in the economic problems may either intensify or lessen the marital problems; that is, for some couples a perceived financial threat may increase marital problems, whereas for others, it may create more closeness between partners. In some situations, an improvement in a marriage may have very little to do with the counselling received, coming about almost entirely because of a change in economic circumstances. Other events such as the birth of a child to a couple or a couple's 'self-realisation', independently arriving at, may also affect the extent and nature of marital problems. Figure 7.1 lists other possible factors under the category of extraneous variables. This does not exhaust the list by any means.

Figure 7.1   Factors affecting the relationship between a counselling service and the extent of marital problems

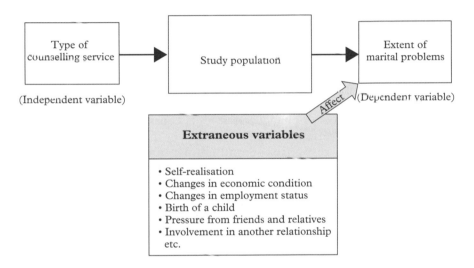

Continuing the example of marriage and counselling, there are sets of factors that can affect the relationship between counselling and marriage problems, and each is a defined category of variables:

1   Counselling *per se*;
2   All the factors other than counselling that affect the marital problems;
3   The outcome—that is, the change or otherwise in the extent of the marital problems;
4   Sometimes, the variation in response to questions about marital problems can be accounted for by the mood of respondents or ambiguity in questions. Some respondents may either overestimate or underestimate their marital problems because of the state of mind at that time. Or some respondents, in spite being exactly in the same situation, may respond to non-specific or ambiguous questions differently, according to how they interpret the question.

In the first category, any variable that is responsible for bringing about a change is called an ***independent variable***. In this example, the counselling is an independent variable. When you study a cause-and-effect relationship, usually you study the impact of only one independent variable. Occasionally you may study the impact of two independent variables, or (very rarely) more, but these study designs are more complex.

For this example *counselling* was the assumed cause of change in the *extent of marital problems*; hence, the extent of marital problems is the ***dependent variable***, as the change in the degree of marital problems was dependent upon counselling.

All other factors that affect the relationship between marital problems and counselling are called ***extraneous variables***. In the social sciences, extraneous variables operate in every study and cannot be eliminated. However, they can be controlled to some extent. (Some of the methods for controlling them are described later in this chapter.) However, it is possible to find out the impact attributable to extraneous variables. This is done with the introduction of a ***control group*** in the study design. The sole function of a control group is to quantify the impact of extraneous variables on the dependent variable(s).

Changes in the dependent variable because of the respondent's state of mood or ambiguity in the research instrument are called ***chance variables***, and the error thus introduced, ***chance*** or ***random error***. In most cases the net effect of chance variables is considered to be negligible as respondents who overreport tend to cancel out those who underreport. The same applies to responses to ambiguous questions in a research instrument.

Hence in any causal relationship, changes in the dependent variable may be attributed to three types of variable:

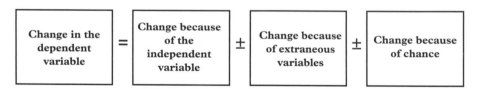

Let us take another example. Suppose you want to study the impact of different teaching models on the level of comprehension of students for which you adopt a comparative study design. In this study, the change in the level of comprehension, in addition to the teaching models, can be attributed to a number of other factors, some of which are shown in Figure 7.2.

Figure 7.2   The relationship between teaching models and comprehension

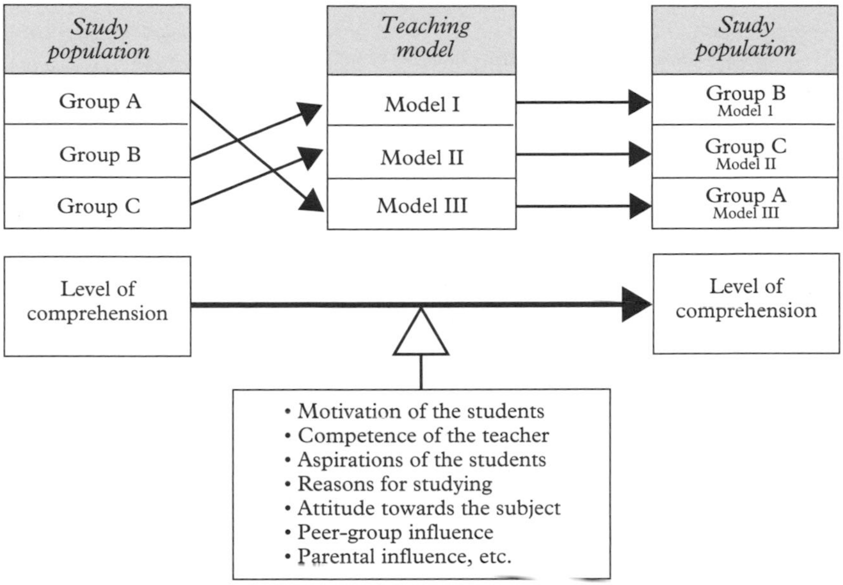

[Change in level of comprehension] =

>   [change attributable to the teaching model] ±
>   [change attributable to extraneous variables] ±
>   [change attributable to chance variables]

In fact, in any study that attempts to establish a causal relationship, you will discover that there are three sets of variables operating to bring about a change in the dependent variable. This can be expressed as an equation:

[change in the outcome variable] =

>   [change because of the chance variable] ±
>   [change because of extraneous variables] ±
>   [change because of chance or random variables]

or in other words:

[change in the dependent variable] =

>   [change attributable to the independent variable] ±
>   [change attributable to extraneous variables] ±
>   [change attributable to chance variables]

or in technical terms:

[total variance] =

>   [variance attributable to the independent variable] ±
>   [variance attributable to extraneous variables] ±
>   [random or chance variance]

It can also be expressed graphically (Figure 7.3).

Figure 7.3   The proportion attributable to the three components may vary markedly

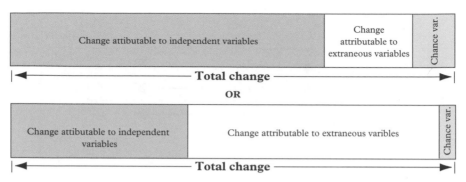

As the total change measures the combined effect of all three components it is difficult to isolate the impact of each of them (see Figure 7.3). Since your aim as a researcher is to determine the change that can be attributed to the independent variable, you need to design your study to ensure that the independent variable has the maximum opportunity to have its full effect on the dependent variable, while the effects that are attributed to extraneous and chance variables are minimised. This is what Kerlinger (1986: 286) calls the 'maxmincon' principle of variance.

One of the most important questions is: how do we minimise the effect attributable to extraneous and chance variables? The answer is that we cannot minimise it, but it can be quantified. The sole purpose of having a control group, as mentioned earlier, is to measure the change that is a result of extraneous variables. The effect of chance variables is often assumed to be none or negligible. As discussed, chance variation comes primarily from two sources: respondents and the research instrument. It is assumed that if some respondents affect the dependent variable positively, others will affect it negatively. For example, if some respondents are extremely positive in their attitude towards an issue, being very liberal or positively biased, there are bound to be others who are extremely negative (being very conservative or negatively biased). Hence, they tend to cancel out each other so the net effect is assumed to be zero. Therefore, in most studies chance variance is considered to be nil. However, if in a study population most individuals are either negatively or positively biased, a systematic error in the findings will be introduced. Similarly, if a research instrument is not reliable (that is, it is not measuring correctly what it is supposed to measure), a systematic bias may be introduced into the study.

In the physical sciences a researcher can control extraneous variables as experiments are usually done in a laboratory. By contrast, in the social sciences, the laboratory is society, over which the researcher lacks control. Since no researcher has control over extraneous variables their effect, as mentioned, is extremely difficult to minimise. The best option is to quantify their impact through the use of a control group, though the introduction of a control group creates the problem of ensuring that the extraneous variables have a similar effect on both control and experimental groups. In some situations their impact can be eliminated (this is possible only where one or two variables have a marked impact on the dependent variable). There are two methods used to ensure that extraneous variables have a similar effect on control and experimental groups and two methods for eliminating extraneous variables.

1 **Ensure that extraneous variables have a similar impact on control and experimental groups.** It is assumed that if two groups are comparable, the extent to which the extraneous variables will affect the dependent variable will be similar in both groups. The following two methods ensure that the control and experimental groups are comparable to one another:
   (a) **Randomisation**—ensures that the two groups are comparable with respect to the variable(s). It is assumed that if the groups are comparable, the extent to which extraneous variables are going to affect the dependent variable is the same in each group.
   (b) **Matching**—another way of ensuring that the two groups are comparable so that the effect of extraneous variables will be the same in both groups (discussed in Chapter 8).
2 **Eliminate extraneous variable(s).** Sometimes it is possible to eliminate the extraneous variable or to build it into the study design. This is usually done when there is strong evidence that the extraneous variable has a high correlation with the dependent variable, or when you want to isolate the impact of the extraneous variable separately. There are two methods used to achieve this:
   (a) **Build the affecting variable into the design of the study**—to explain this concept let us take an example. Suppose you want to study the impact of maternal health services on the infant mortality of a population. It can be assumed that the nutritional status of children also has a marked effect on infant mortality. To study the impact of maternal health services *per se*, you adopt a two-by-two factorial design as explained in Figure 7.4. In this way you can study the impact of the extraneous variables separately and interactively with the independent variable.

Figure 7.4   Building into the design

		Maternal health	
		Yes	No
Nutritional supplements	Yes	Maternal health + Nutritional supplements	Nutritional supplements
	No	Maternal health	Control

(b) **Eliminate the variable**—to understand this, let us take another example. Suppose you want to study the impact of a health education program on the attitudes towards, and beliefs about, the causation and treatment of a certain illness among non-Indigenous Australians and Indigenous Australians living in a particular community. As attitudes and beliefs vary markedly from culture to culture, studying non-Indigenous Australians and Indigenous Australians as one group will not provide an accurate picture. In such studies it is appropriate to eliminate the cultural variation in the study population by selecting and studying the populations separately or by constructing culture-specific cohorts at the time of analysis.

Let us now come back to the first function of a research design, which relates to the overall plan of the study. It details for you, your supervisor and other readers all the procedures you plan to use and the tasks you are going to perform to obtain answers to your research questions. One of the most important requirements of a research design is to specify everything clearly so a reader will understand what procedures to follow and how to follow them. A research design, therefore, should do the following:

- Name the study design *per se*—that is, 'cross-sectional', 'before-and-after', 'comparative', 'control experiment' or 'random control'.
- Provide detailed information about the following aspects of the study:
  - Who will constitute the study population?
  - How will the study population be identified?
  - Will a sample or the whole population be selected?
  - If a sample is selected, how will it be contacted?
  - How will consent be sought?
  - What method of data collection will be used and why?
  - In the case of a questionnaire, where will the responses be returned?
  - How should respondents contact you if they have queries?
  - In the case of interviews, where will they be conducted?
  - How will ethical issues be taken care of?

Chapter 8 describes some of the commonly used study designs. The rest of the topics that constitute a research design are covered in the subsequent chapters.

SUMMARY

In this chapter you have learnt about the functions of a research design: to detail the procedures for undertaking a study (e.g. study design, sampling, measurement); and to ensure that, if a study seeks to establish a causal relationship, the independent variable has the maximum opportunity to have its effect on the dependent variable while the effect of extraneous and chance variables is minimised.

A study without a control measures the total change (change attributable to independent variable ± extraneous variables ± chance variables) in a phenomenon or situation. The purpose of introducing a control group is to quantify the impact of extraneous and chance variables.

The study design is a part of the research design. It is the design of the study *per se*, whereas the research design also includes other details related to the carrying out of the study.

CHAPTER
eight

Selecting a study design

In this chapter we will discuss some of the most commonly used study designs. The various designs have been classified by examining them from three different perspectives:

1 the number of contacts with the study population;
2 the reference period of the study;
3 the nature of the investigation.

Every study design can be classified from each one of these perspectives. These perspectives are arbitrary bases of classification; hence, the terminology used to describe them is not universal. However, the names of the designs within each classification base are universally used. Note that the designs within each category are mutually exclusive; that is, if a particular study is cross-sectional in nature it cannot be at the same time a before-and-after or a longitudinal study, but it can be a non-experimental or experimental, as well as a retrospective or a prospective study. See Figure 8.1.

Another section has been added to the three sections listed above titled 'Others—some commonly used study designs'. This section includes some commonly used designs which are either based on certain philosophy or methology, and which have acquired their own names.

Study designs based on the number of contacts

Based on the number of contacts with the study population, designs can be classified into three groups:

- cross-sectional studies;
- before-and-after studies;
- longitudinal studies.

The cross-sectional study design

Cross-sectional studies, also known as one-shot or status studies, are the most commonly used design in the social sciences. This design is best suited to studies aimed at finding out the prevalence of a phenomenon, situation, problem, attitude or issue, by taking a cross-section of the population. They are useful in obtaining an overall 'picture' as it stands at the time of the study. They are 'designed to study some phenomenon by taking a cross-section of it at one time' (Babbie 1989: 89). Such studies are cross-sectional with regard to both the study population and the time of investigation.

A cross-sectional study is extremely simple in design. You decide what you want to find out, identify the study population, select a sample (if you need to) and contact your respondents to find out the required information. For example, a cross-sectional design would be the most appropriate for a study of the following topics:

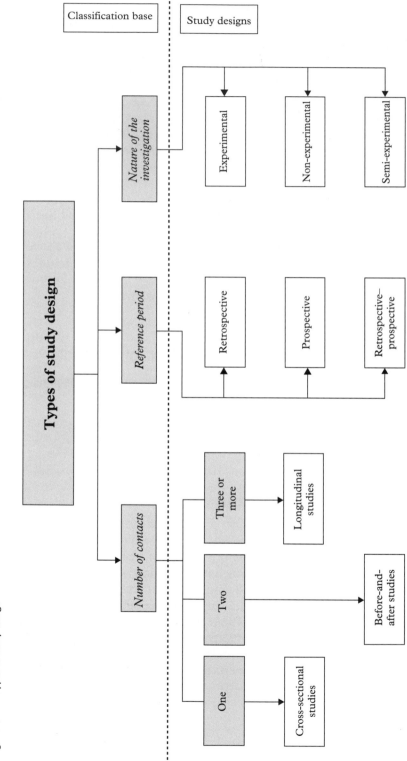

Figure 8.1   Types of study design

- The attitude of the study population towards uranium mining in Australia.
- The socioeconomic–demographic characteristics of immigrants in Western Australia.
- The incidence of HIV-positive cases in Australia.
- The reasons for homelessness among young people.
- The quality assurance of a service provided by an organisation.
- The impact of unemployment on street crime (this could also be a before-and-after study).
- The relationship between the home environment and the academic performance of a child at school.
- The attitude of the community towards equity issues.
- The extent of unemployment in a city.
- Consumer satisfaction with a product.
- The effectiveness of random breath testing in preventing road accidents (this could also be a before-and-after study).
- The health needs of a community.
- The attitudes of students towards the facilities available in their library.

As these studies involve only one contact with the study population, they are comparatively cheap to undertake and easy to analyse. However, their biggest disadvantage is that they cannot measure change. To measure change it is necessary to have at least two data collection points—that is, at least two cross-sectional studies, at two points in time, on the same population.

The before-and-after study design

The main advantage of the before-and-after design (also known as the pre-test/post-test design) is that it can measure change in a situation, phenomenon, issue, problem or attitude. It is the most appropriate design for measuring the impact or effectiveness of a program. A before-and-after design can be described as two sets of cross-sectional data collection points on the same population to find out the change in the phenomenon or variable(s) between two points in time. The change is measured by comparing the difference in the phenomenon or variable(s) before and after the intervention (see Figure 8.2).

Figure 8.2   Before-and-after (pre-test/post-test) study design

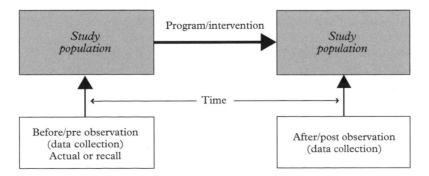

A before-and-after study is carried out by adopting the same process as a cross-sectional study except that it comprises two cross-sectional observations, the second being undertaken after a certain period. Depending upon how it is set up, a before-and-after study may be either an experiment or a non-experiment. It is one of the most commonly used designs in evaluation studies. The difference between the two sets of data collection points with respect to the dependent variable is considered to be the impact of the program. The following are examples of topics that can be studied using this design:

- The impact of administrative restructuring on the quality of the services provided by an organisation.
- The effectiveness of a marriage counselling service.
- The impact of sex education on sexual behaviour among schoolchildren.
- The effect of a drug awareness program on the knowledge about, and use of, drugs among young people.
- The impact of incentives on the productivity of employees in an organisation.
- The impact of increased funding on the quality of teaching in universities.
- The impact of maternal and child health services on the infant mortality rate.
- The effect of random breath testing on road accidents.
- The effect of an advertisement on the sale of a product.

Though a before-and-after design has advantages—the main one being its ability to measure change in a phenomenon or to assess the impact of an intervention—it can also have certain disadvantages. However, these do not occur, individually or collectively, in every study. The prevalence of a particular disadvantage or combination of disadvantages is dependent upon the nature of the investigation, the study population and the method of data collection. Some of the disadvantages are:

- Instead of collecting one set of data, two sets must be collected, which means two contacts with the study population. It is therefore more expensive and more difficult to implement. It requires a longer time to complete, particularly if you are using an experimental design, and hence need to wait until your intervention is completed.
- In some cases the time lapse between the two contacts may result in attrition in the study population. It is possible that some of those who participated in the pre-test may move out of the area or withdraw from the experiment for other reasons.
- One of the main limitations of this design is that, as it measures *total change*, you cannot ascertain whether independent or extraneous variables are responsible for producing change in the dependent variable. Also, is it not possible to quantify the contribution of independent and extraneous variables separately.
- If the study population is very young and if there is a significant time lapse between the before-and-after observations, changes in the study population may be because it is maturing. This is particularly true when

you are studying young children. The effect of this maturation, if it is significantly correlated with the dependent variable, is reflected at the 'after' observation and is known as the ***maturation effect***.

- Sometimes the instrument itself educates the respondents. This is known as the ***reactive effect*** of the instrument. For example, suppose you want to ascertain the impact of a program designed to create awareness of drugs in a population. To do this, you design a questionnaire listing various drugs and asking respondents to indicate whether they have heard of them. At the pre-test stage a respondent, while answering questions that include the names of the various drugs, is being made aware of them, and this will be reflected in his/her responses at the post-test stage. Thus, the research instrument itself has educated the study population and, hence, has affected the dependent variable. Another example of this effect is a study designed to measure the impact of a family planning education program on respondents' awareness of contraceptive methods. Most studies designed to measure the impact of a program on participants' awareness face the difficulty that a change in the level of awareness, to some extent, may be because of this reactive effect.

- Another disadvantage that may occur when you use a research instrument twice to gauge the attitude of a population towards an issue is a possible shift in attitude between the two points of data collection. Sometimes people who place themselves on the extreme positions of a measurement scale at the pre-test stage may, for a number of reasons, shift towards the mean at the post-test stage (see Figure 8.3). They might feel that they have been too negative or too positive at the pre-test stage. Therefore, the mere expression of an attitude in response to a questionnaire or interview has caused them to think about and alter their attitude at the time of the post-test. This type of effect is known as the ***regression effect***.

Figure 8.3   The regression effect

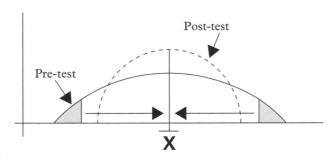

The longitudinal study design

The before-and-after study design is appropriate for measuring the extent of change in a phenomenon, situation, problem, attitude and so on, but is less helpful for studying the pattern of change. To determine the pattern of change in relation to time, a longitudinal design is used; for example, when you wish to study the proportion of people adopting a program in relation to time. Longitudinal studies are also useful when you need to collect factual information on a continuing basis. You may want to ascertain the trends in the demand for labour, immigration, changes in the incidence of a disease or in the mortality, morbidity and fertility patterns of a population.

In longitudinal studies the study population is visited a number of times at regular intervals, usually over a long period, to collect the required information (see Figure 8.4). These intervals are not fixed so their length may vary from study to study. Intervals might be as short as a week or longer than a year. Irrespective of the size of the interval, the information gathered each time is identical. Although the data collected is from the same study population, it may or may not be from the same respondents. A longitudinal study can be seen as a series of repetitive cross-sectional studies.

Figure 8.4   The longitudinal study design

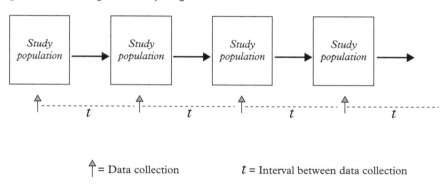

↑ = Data collection t = Interval between data collection

Longitudinal studies have the same disadvantages as before-and-after studies, in some instances to an even greater degree. In addition, longitudinal studies can suffer from the **conditioning effect**. This describes a situation where, if the same respondents are contacted frequently, they begin to know what is expected of them and may respond to questions without thought, or they may lose interest in the inquiry, with the same result.

The main advantage of a longitudinal study is that it allows the researcher to measure the pattern of change and obtain factual information, requiring collection on a regular or continuing basis, thus enhancing its accuracy.

Study designs based on the reference period

The *reference period* refers to the time-frame in which a study is exploring a phenomenon, situation, event or problem. Studies within this perspective are thus categorised as:

- retrospective;
- prospective;
- retrospective–prospective.

The retrospective study design

Retrospective studies investigate a phenomenon, situation, problem or issue that has happened in the past. They are usually conducted either on the basis of the data available for that period or on the basis of respondents' recall of the situation. For example, studies conducted on the following topics are classified as retrospective studies:

- The living conditions of Aboriginal and Torres Strait Islander peoples in Australia in the early twentieth century.
- The utilisation of land before World War II in Western Australia.
- A historical analysis of migratory movements in Eastern Europe between 1915 and 1945.
- The relationship between levels of unemployment and street crime.

The prospective study design

Prospective studies refer to the likely prevalence of a phenomenon, situation, problem, attitude or outcome in the future. Such studies attempt to establish the outcome of an event or what is likely to happen. Experiments are usually classified as prospective studies as the researcher must wait for an intervention to register its effect on the study population. The following are classified as prospective studies:

- To determine, under field conditions, the impact of maternal and child health services on the level of infant mortality.
- To establish the effects of a counselling service on the extent of marital problems.
- To determine the impact of random breath testing on the prevention of road accidents.
- To find out the effect of parental involvement on the level of academic achievement of their children.
- To measure the effects of a change in migration policy on the extent of immigration in Australia.

The retrospective–prospective study design

Retrospective–prospective studies focus on past trends in a phenomenon and study it into the future. A study is classified under this category when you measure the impact of an intervention without having a control group. In fact, most before-and-after studies, if carried out without having a control— where the baseline is constructed from the same population before introducing the intervention—will be classified as retrospective–prospective studies. In a retrospective–prospective study a part of the data is collected retrospectively from the existing records before the intervention is introduced and then the study population is followed to ascertain the impact of the intervention. Trend studies, which become the basis of projections, fall into this category. Some examples are:

- The effect of random breath testing on road accidents.
- The impact of incentives on the productivity of the employees of an organisation.
- The impact of maternal and child health services on the infant mortality rate.
- The effect of an advertisement on the sale of a product.

Study designs based on the nature of the investigation

On the basis of the nature of the investigation, studies can be classified as:

- experimental;
- non-experimental;
- quasi or semi-experimental.

To understand the differences, let us consider some examples. Suppose you want to test the following: the impact of a particular teaching method on the level of comprehension of students; the effectiveness of a program such as random breath testing on the level of road accidents; or the usefulness of a drug such as azidothymidine (AZT) in treating people who are HIV-positive. Imagine any similar situation in your own academic or professional field. In such situations there is assumed to be a *cause-and-effect* relationship. There are two ways of studying this relationship. The first involves the researcher (or someone else) introducing the intervention that is assumed to be the 'cause' of change, and waiting until it has produced—or has been given sufficient time to produce—the change. The second consists of the researcher observing a phenomenon and attempting to establish what caused it. In this instance the researcher starts from the effect(s) or outcome(s) and attempts to determine causation. If a relationship is studied in the first way, starting from the cause to establish the effects, it is classified as an ***experimental study***. If the second path is followed—that is, starting from the effects to trace the cause—it is classified as a ***non-experimental study*** (see Figure 8.5). In the former case the independent variable can be 'observed', introduced, controlled or manipulated by the researcher or someone else; whereas in the latter this cannot happen as the assumed cause has already occurred. Instead, the researcher retrospectively links the cause(s) to the outcome(s). A ***semi-experimental design*** has the properties of both experimental and non-experimental studies; part of the study may be non-experimental and the other part experimental.

An experimental study can be carried out in either a 'controlled' or a 'natural' environment. For an experiment in a controlled environment, the researcher (or someone else) introduces the intervention or stimulus to study its effects. The study population is in a 'controlled' situation such as a room. For an experiment in a 'natural' environment, the study population is exposed to an intervention in its own environment.

Experimental studies can be further classified on the basis of whether or not the study population is randomly assigned to different treatment groups. One of the biggest problems in comparable designs (those in which

Figure 8.5   Experimental and non-experimental studies

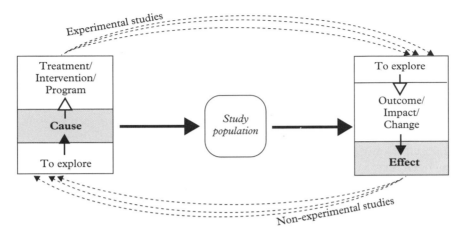

you compare two or more groups) is a lack of certainty that the different groups are in fact comparable in every respect except the treatment. The process of randomisation is designed to ensure that the groups are comparable. In a ***random design***, the study population, the experimental treatments or both are not predetermined but randomly assigned (see Figure 8.6). Random assignment in experiments means that any individual or unit of a study population group has an *equal* and *independent* chance of becoming a part of an experimental or control group or, in the case of multiple treatment modalities, any treatment has an equal and independent chance of being assigned to any of the population groups. It is important to note that the concept of randomisation can be applied to any of the experimental designs we discuss.

Figure 8.6   Randomisation in experiments

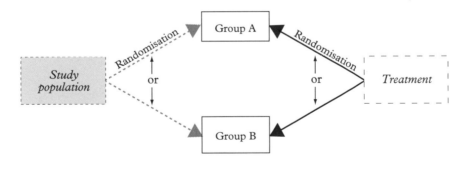

The experimental study designs

There are so many types of experimental design that not all of them can be considered within the scope of this book. This section, therefore, is confined to describing those most commonly used in the social sciences, the humanities, public health, marketing, education, epidemiology, social work and so on. These designs have been categorised as:

- the after-only design;
- the before-and-after design;
- the control-group design;
- the double-control design;
- the comparative design;
- the 'matched control' experimental design;
- the placebo design.

The after-only design

In an after-only design the researcher knows that a population is being, or has been, exposed to an intervention and wishes to study its impact on the population. In this design, information on baseline (pre-test or before observation) is usually 'constructed' on the basis of respondents' recall of the situation before the intervention, or from information available in existing records (Figure 8.7). The change in the dependent variable is measured by the difference between the 'before' (baseline) and 'after' observations. Technically, this is a very faulty design for measuring the impact of an intervention as there is no proper baseline data to compare the 'after' observation with. Therefore, one of the major problems of this design is that the two sets of data are not strictly comparable. Accordingly, some of the changes in the dependent variable may be attributable to the difference in the way the two sets of data were compiled. Another problem with this design is that it measures total change, including change attributable to extraneous variables; hence, it cannot identify the net effect of an intervention. However, this design is widely used in impact assessment studies, as in real-life many programs operate without the benefit of a planned evaluation at the program planning stage (though this is fast changing) in which case it is just not possible to follow strictly the sequence—collection of baseline information, implementation of the program and then program evaluation. An evaluator therefore has no choice but to adopt this design.

Figure 8.7   The after-only design

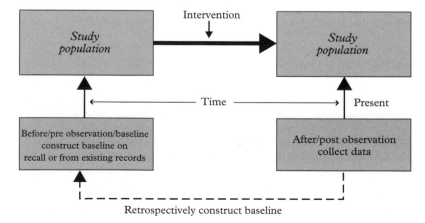

Retrospectively construct baseline

In practice, the adequacy of this design depends on having reasonably accurate data available about the prevalence of a phenomenon before the intervention is introduced. This might be the case for situations such as the impact of random breath testing on road accidents, the impact of a health program on the mortality of a population, the impact of an advertisement on the sale of a product, the impact of a decline in mortality on the fertility of a population, or the impact of a change in immigration policy on the extent of immigration. In these situations it is expected that accurate records are kept about the phenomenon under study and any change in trends is primarily because of the introduction of the intervention or change in the policy.

The before-and-after design

The before-and-after design overcomes the problem of retrospectively constructing the 'before' observation by establishing it before the intervention is introduced to the study population (see Figure 8.2). Then, when the program has been completely implemented or is assumed to have had its effect on the population, the 'after' observation is carried out to ascertain the impact attributable to the intervention (see Figure 8.8).

Figure 8.8   Measurement of change through a before-and-after design

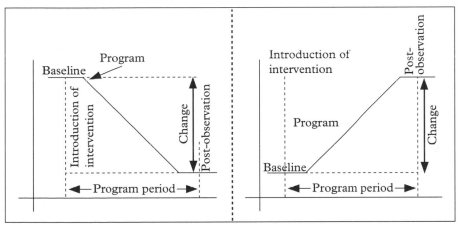

The before-and-after design takes care of only one problem of the after-only design—that is, the comparability of the before and after observations. It still does not enable one to conclude that any change—in whole or in part—can be attributed to the program intervention. To overcome this, a 'control' group is used. Before-and-after designs may also suffer from the problems identified earlier in this chapter in the discussion of before-and-after study designs. The impact of the intervention in before-and-after design is calculated as follows:

[Change in dependent variable] =

[status of the dependent variable at the 'after' observation] −
[status of the dependent variable at the 'before' observation]

The control-group design

In a study utilising the control-group design the researcher selects two population groups instead of one: a ***control group*** and an ***experimental group*** (Figure 8.9). These groups are expected to be comparable as far as possible in every respect except the intervention. The experimental group either receives or is exposed to the intervention, whereas the control group is not. First, the 'before' observations are made on both groups at the same time. The experimental group is then exposed to the intervention. When it is assumed that the intervention has had an impact, an 'after' observation is made on both groups. Any difference in the 'before' and 'after' observations between the groups regarding the dependent variable(s) is attributed to the intervention.

Figure 8.9   The control experimental design

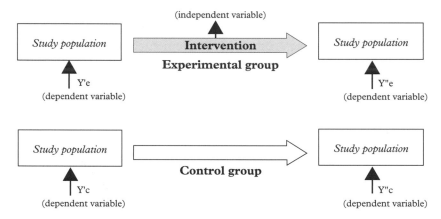

In the experimental group, total change in the dependent variable,

$(Ye) = (Y''e - Y'e)$, where
$Y''e$ = 'after' observation on the experimental group
$Y'e$ = 'before' observation on the experimental group

In other words:

$(Y''e - Y'e)$ = (Impact of program intervention) $\pm$ (Impact of extraneous variables) $\pm$ (Impact of chance variables)

In the control group, total change in the dependent variable,

$(Yc) = (Y''c - Y'c)$, where
$Y''c$ = post-test observation on the control group
$Y'c$ = pre-test observation on the control group

In other words:

$(Y''c - Y'c)$ = (Impact of extraneous variables) $\pm$ (Impact of chance variables)

The difference between control and experimental groups =

$(Y''e - Y'e) - (Y''c - Y'c)$, which is
{(Impact of program intervention) $\pm$ (Impact of extraneous variables in experimental groups) $\pm$ (Impact of chance variables in experimental groups)} − {(Impact of extraneous variables in control group) $\pm$ (Impact of chance variables in control group)}.

Using a simple arithmetic operation, this equals impact of the intervention.

Therefore, the impact of any intervention is equal to the difference in the 'before' and 'after' observations in the dependent variable between the experimental and control groups.

It is important to remember that the chief objective of the control group is to quantify the impact of extraneous variables. This helps you to ascertain the impact of the intervention only.

The double-control design

Although the control-group design helps the researcher to quantify the impact that can be attributed to extraneous variables, it does not separate out other effects that may be due to the research instrument (such as the reactive effect) or respondents (such as the maturation or regression effects, or placebo effect). When the researcher needs to identify and separate out these effects, a double-control design is required.

In a double-control study, the researcher has two control groups instead of one. To quantify, say, the reactive effect of an instrument, the researcher excludes one of the control groups from the 'before' observation (Figure 8.10).

Figure 8.10   Double-control designs

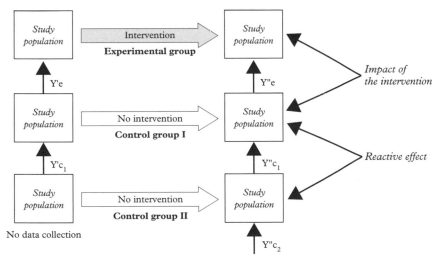

The different effects are calculated as follows:

$(Y''e - Y'e)$ = (Impact of program intervention) $\pm$ (Impact of extraneous variables) $\pm$ (Reactive effect) $\pm$ (Random effect)

$(Y''c_1 - Y'c_1)$ = (Impact of extraneous variables) $\pm$ (Reactive effect) $\pm$ (Random effect)

$(Y''c_2 - Y'c_1)$ = (Impact of extraneous variables) $\pm$ (Random effect).

(Note: $(Y''c_2 - Y'c_1)$ and not $(Y''c_2 - Y'c_2)$ as there is no 'before' observation for the second control group.)

$(Y''e - Y'e) - (Y''c_1 - Y'c_1) =$ Impact of program intervention

$(Y''c_1 - Y'c_1) - (Y'c_2 - Y'c_1) =$ Reactive effect

The net effect of the program intervention can be calculated in the same manner as for the control-group designs as explained earlier.

The comparative design

Sometimes a researcher seeks to compare the effectiveness of different treatment modalities. In such situations a comparative design is appropriate.

With a comparative design, as with most other designs, a study can be carried out either as an experiment or as a non-experiment. In the comparative experimental design, the study population is divided into the same number of groups as the number of treatments to be tested. For each group the baseline with respect to the dependent variable is established. The different treatment models are then introduced to the different groups. After a certain period, when it is assumed that the treatment models have had their effect, the 'after' observation is carried out to ascertain any change in the dependent variable. The degree of change in the dependent variable in the different population groups is then compared to establish the relative effectiveness of the various interventions.

In the non-experimental form of comparative design, groups already receiving different interventions are identified, and only the post-observation with respect to the dependent variable is conducted. The pre-test observation is constructed either by asking the study population in each group to recall the required information relating to the period before the introduction of the treatment or by extracting such information from existing records. Sometimes a pre-test observation is not constructed at all, on the assumption that if the groups are comparable the baseline must be identical. As each group is assumed to have the same baseline, the difference in the post-test observation is assumed to be because of the intervention.

To illustrate this, imagine you want to compare the effectiveness of three teaching models (A, B and C) on the level of comprehension of students in a class (Figure 8.11). To undertake the study, you divide the class into three groups (X, Y and Z), through randomisation, to ensure their comparability. Before exposing these groups to the teaching models, you first establish the baseline for each group's level of comprehension of the chosen subject. You then expose each group to a different teaching model to teach the chosen subject. Afterwards, you again measure the groups' levels of comprehension of the material. Suppose Xa is the average level of comprehension of group X before the material is taught, and Xa' is this group's average level of comprehension after the material is taught. The change in the level of comprehension, Xa' − Xa, is therefore attributed to model A. Similarly, changes in group Y and Z, Yb' − Yb and Zc' − Zc, are attributed to teaching models B and C respectively. The changes in the average level of comprehension for the three groups are then compared to establish which teaching model is the most effective. (Note that extraneous variables will affect the level of comprehension in all groups equally, as they have been formed randomly.)

It is also possible to set up this study as a non-experimental one, simply by exposing each group to the three teaching models, following up with an 'after' observation. The difference in the levels of comprehension is attributed to the difference in the teaching models as it is assumed that the three groups are comparable with respect to their original level of comprehension of the topic.

Figure 8.11   Comparative experimental design

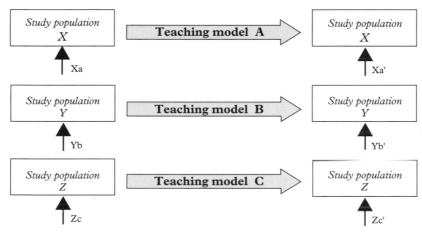

The matched-control experimental design

Comparative groups are usually formed on the basis of their overall comparability with respect to a relevant characteristic in the study population, such as socioeconomic status, the prevalence of a certain condition or the extent of a problem in the study population. In matched studies, comparability is determined on an individual-by-individual basis. Two individuals from the study population who are almost identical with respect to a selected characteristic and/or condition, such as age, gender or type of illness, are matched and then each is allocated to a different group (the matching is usually done on an easily identifiable characteristic). In the case of a matched-control experiment, once the two groups are formed, the researcher decides through randomisation or otherwise which group is to be considered control, and which, experimental.

The matched design can pose a number of problems:

* Matching increases in difficulty when carried out on more than one variable.
* Matching on variables that are hard to measure, such as attitude or opinion, is extremely difficult.
* Sometimes it is hard to know which variable to choose as a basis for matching. You may be able to base your decision upon previous findings or you may have to undertake a preliminary study to determine your choice of variable.

Matched groups are most commonly used in the testing of new drugs. Patients are matched on certain characteristics (type of illness, age or gender) to form pairs. The individuals forming each pair are then allocated to two different groups. On a random basis, one is provided with the treatment and the other is considered a control.

The 'placebo' design

A patient's belief that s/he is receiving treatment can play an important role in his/her recovery from an illness even if treatment is ineffective. This psychological effect is known as the **placebo effect**. A placebo design attempts to determine the extent of this effect. A placebo design involves two or three groups, depending on whether or not the researcher wants to have a control group (Figure 8.12). If the researcher decides to have a control group, the first group receives the treatment, the second receives the placebo treatment and the third—the control group—receives nothing. The decision as to which group will be the treatment, the placebo or the control group can also be made through randomisation.

Figure 8.12 The placebo design

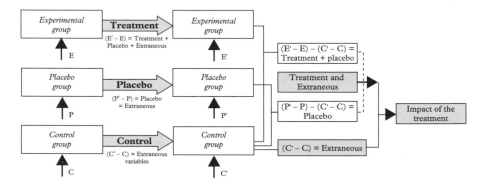

Others—some commonly used study designs

There are some commonly used research designs that may be classified in the typology described above; however, because of their uniqueness and prevalence they have acquired their own names. It is, therefore, important to mention them separately. These are described below.

Action research

As the name suggests, action research comprises two components: **action** and **research** (see Figure 8.13). Research is a means to action, either to improve your practice or to take action to deal with a problem or an issue. Since action research is guided by the desire to take action, strictly speaking it is not a design *per se*. Most action research is concerned with improving the quality of service. It is carried out to identify areas of concern, develop and test alternatives, and experiment with new approaches.

Action research seems to follow two traditions. The British tradition tends to view action research as a means of improvement and advancement of practice (Carr & Kemmins: 1986), whereas in the American tradition it is aimed at systematic collection of data that provides the basis for social change (Bogdan & Biklem: 1992).

Action research, in common with participatory research and collaborative inquiry, is based upon a philosophy of community development that seeks the involvement of community members. Involvement and participation of a community, in the total process from problem identification to implementation of solutions, are the two salient features of all three (action research, participatory research and collaborative inquiry). In all three, data are collected through a research process, and changes are achieved through action. This action is taken either by officials of an institution or the community itself in the case of action research, or by members of a community in the case of collaborate or participatory research.

There are two focuses of action research:

- An existing program or intervention is studied in order to identify possible areas of improvement in terms of enhanced efficacy and/or efficiency. The findings become the basis of bringing about changes.

- This is where a professional thinks that there is an unattended problem or unexplained issue in the community or among a client group. Through research, evidence is gathered to justify the introduction of a new service or intervention. Research techniques establish the prevalence of the problem or the importance of an issue so that appropriate action can be taken to deal with it.

Figure 8.13   Action research design

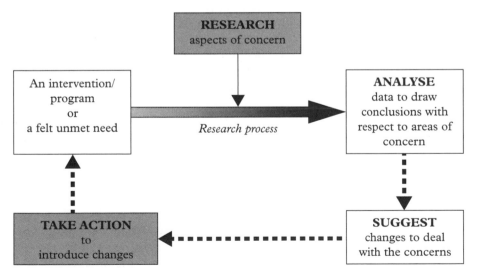

Feminist research

Like action research, feminist research is not a research design. It is characterised by its feminist theory philosophical base that underpins all inquiries. Feminist concerns and theory act as the guiding framework for this research. Feminist research differs from traditional research in three ways:

1 Its main focus is the experiences and viewpoints of women. It uses research methods aimed at exploring them.
2 It actively tries to remove or reduce the power imbalance between researcher and respondents.
3 The goal of feminist research is changing the social inequality between men and women. In fact, feminist research may be classified as action research in the area of gender inequality, using research techniques to create awareness of women's issues and concerns, and to foster action promoting equality between sexes.

The cross-over comparative experimental design

The denial of treatment to the control group is considered unethical by some professionals. In addition, the denial of treatment may be unacceptable to some individuals in the control group, which could result in them dropping out of the experiment and/or going elsewhere to receive treatment. The former increases 'experimental mortality' and the latter may contaminate the study. The cross-over experimental design makes it possible to measure the impact of a treatment without denying treatment to any group, though this design has its own problems.

In the cross-over design, also called the ABAB design (Grinnell 1993: 104) two groups are formed, the intervention is introduced to one of them and, after a certain period, the impact of this intervention is measured. Then the interventions are 'crossed over'; that is, the experimental group becomes the control and vice versa (Figure 8.14). However, in this design, population groups do not constitute experimental or control groups but only segments upon which experimental and control observations are conducted.

One of the main disadvantages of this design is discontinuity in treatment. The main question is: what impact would intervention have produced had it not been provided in segments?

The replicated cross-sectional design

In practice one usually examines programs already in existence and ones in which clients are at different stages of an intervention. Evaluating the effectiveness of such programs within a conventional experimental design is impossible because a baseline cannot be established as the intervention has already been introduced. In this situation, the usual method of selecting a group of people who were recently recruited to the program and following them through till the intervention has been completed may take a long time.

Figure 8.14   The cross-over experimental design

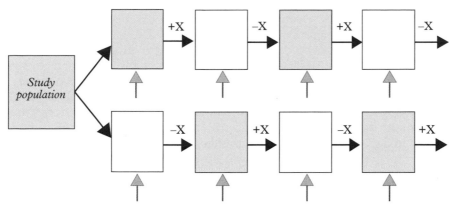

+X = treatment provided (experimental segment)
−X = no treatment (control segment)

In such situations, it is possible to choose clients who are at different phases of the program to form the basis of your study (Figure 8.15).

This design is based upon the assumption that participants at different stages of a program are similar in terms of their socioeconomic–demographic characteristics and the problem for which they are seeking intervention.

Figure 8.15   The replicated cross-sectional design

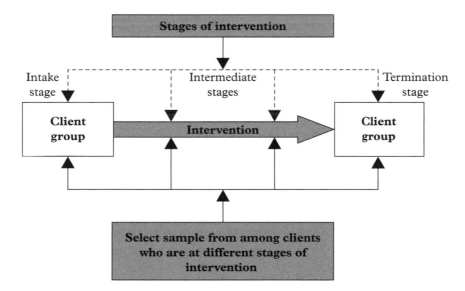

Trend studies

If you want to map change over a period, a trend study is the most appropriate method of investigation. Trend analysis enables you to find out what has happened in the past, what is happening now and what is likely to happen in the future in a population group. Trend studies are also useful in forecasting trends by extrapolating from present and past trends.

This design involves selecting a number of data observation points in the past, together with a picture of the present or immediate past with respect to the phenomenon under study and then making certain assumptions as to future trends. On the basis of the classification system developed in this chapter, this design can be classified under retrospective–prospective studies.

Trends regarding the phenomenon under study can be correlated with other characteristics of the study population. For example, you may want to examine the changes in political preference of a study population in relation to age, gender, income or ethnicity.

Cohort studies

Cohort studies are based upon the existence of a common characteristic such as year of birth, graduation or marriage, within a subgroup of a population. Suppose you want to study the employment pattern of a batch of accountants who graduated from a university in 1975, or study the fertility behaviour of women who were married in 1930. To study the accountants' career paths you would contact all the accountants who graduated from the university in 1975 to find out their employment histories. Similarly, you would investigate the fertility history of those women who married in 1930. Both of these studies could be carried out either as cross-sectional or longitudinal designs. In the case of a longitudinal design, it is not important for the required information to be collected from the same respondents; however, it is important that the respondents belong to the cohort. (In the above examples they must have graduated in 1975 or married in 1930.)

Panel studies

Trend, cohort and panel studies are similar except that panel studies are longitudinal and prospective in nature and collect information from the same respondents. In trend and cohort studies the information can be collected in a cross-sectional manner and the observation points can be retrospectively constructed, whereas in a panel study the observations are made over a period of time and are prospective in nature. Suppose you want to study the changes in the pattern of expenditure on household items in a community. To do this, you would select a few families to find out the amount they spend every fortnight on household items. You would keep collecting the same information from the same families over a period of time to ascertain the changes in the expenditure pattern. Such a study is called a panel study. Similarly, a panel study design could be used to study the morbidity pattern in a community.

Blind studies

The concept of a blind study can be used with comparable and placebo experimental designs and is applied to studies measuring the effectiveness of a drug. In a blind study, the study population does not know whether it is getting real or fake treatment. The main objective of designing a blind study is to isolate the placebo effect: the psychological effect on the recovery process of a patient's knowledge that s/he is receiving the treatment.

Double-blind studies

The concept of a double-blind study is very similar to that of a blind study except that it also tries to eliminate the researcher's bias: the researcher does not know the identity of experimental and placebo groups. In a double-blind study neither the researcher nor the study participants know who is receiving real and who is receiving fake treatment.

Case studies

The case study method is an approach to studying a social phenomenon through a thorough analysis of an individual case. The case may be a person, group, episode, process, community, society or any other unit of social life. All data relevant to the case are gathered and organised in terms of the case. It provides an opportunity for the intensive analysis of many specific details often overlooked by other methods. This approach rests on the assumption that the case being studied is typical of cases of a certain type so that, through intensive analysis, generalisations may be made that will be applicable to other cases of the same type.

SUMMARY

In this chapter the various study designs have been examined, along with their advantages and disadvantages, from three perspectives. The terminology used to describe these perspectives is that of the author but the names of the study designs are universally used. The different designs across each category are mutually exclusive but not so within a category.

The three perspectives are the number of contacts, the reference period and the nature of the investigation. The first comprises cross-sectional studies, before-and-after studies and longitudinal studies. The second categorises the studies as retrospective, prospective and retrospective–prospective. The third perspective classifies studies as experimental, non-experimental and semi-experimental studies.

Some commonly used designs that may be classified in the above typology have also been discussed in a separate section called 'Others' because they have acquired their own names as a result of their uniqueness and prevalence among certain professional groups.

STEP III

CONSTRUCTING AN INSTRUMENT FOR DATA COLLECTION

CHAPTER 9
Selecting a method of data collection

CHAPTER 10
Collecting data using attitudinal scales

CHAPTER 11
Establishing the validity and reliability of a research instrument

CHAPTER
nine

Selecting a method
of data collection

Methods of data collection

There are two major approaches to gathering information about a situation, person, problem or phenomenon. Sometimes, information required is already available and need only be extracted. However, there are times when the information must be collected. Based upon these broad approaches to information gathering, data are categorised as:

- secondary data;
- primary data.

Information gathered using the first approach is said to be collected from **secondary sources**, whereas the sources used in the second approach are called **primary sources**. Examples of secondary sources include the use of census data to obtain information on the age–sex structure of a population; the use of hospital records to find out the morbidity and mortality patterns of a community; the use of an organisation's records to ascertain its activities; and the collection of data from sources such as articles, journals, magazines, books and periodicals to obtain historical and other types of information. On the other hand, finding out first-hand the attitudes of a community towards health services, ascertaining the health needs of a community, evaluating a social program, determining the job satisfaction of the employees of an organisation, and ascertaining the quality of services provided by a worker are examples of information collected from primary sources. In summary, primary sources provide first-hand information and secondary sources provide second-hand data. Figure 9.1 shows the various methods of data collection.

Figure 9.1   Methods of data collection

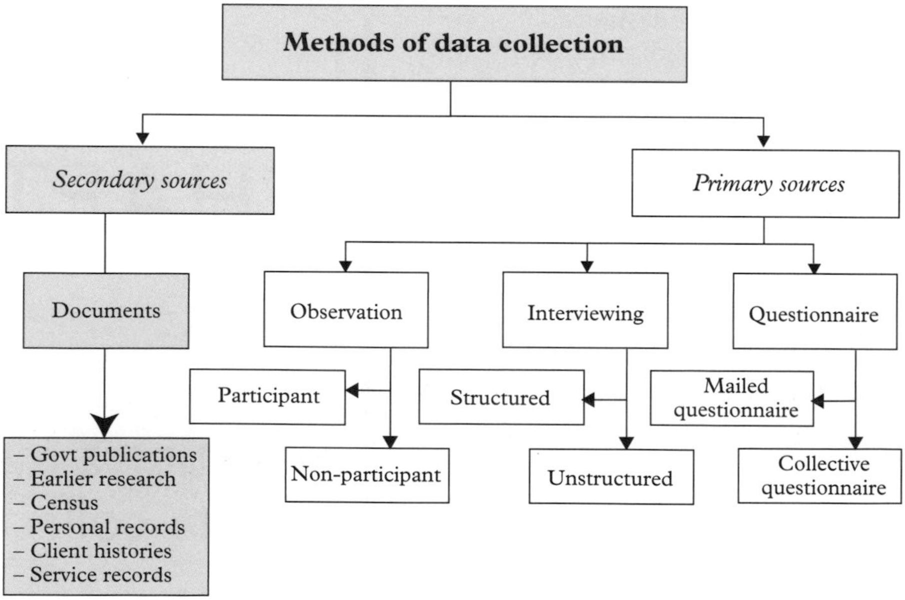

None of the methods of data collection provides 100 per cent accurate and reliable information. The quality of the data gathered is dependent upon a number of other factors, which we will identify as we discuss each method. Your skill as a researcher lies in your ability to take care of the factors that could affect the quality of your data. One of the main differences between experienced and amateur researchers lies in their understanding of, and ability to control, these factors. It is therefore important for a beginner to be aware of them.

Collecting data using primary sources

Several methods can be used to collect primary data. The choice of a method depends upon the purpose of the study, the resources available and the skills of the researcher. There are times when the method most appropriate to achieve the objectives of a study cannot be used because of constraints such as a lack of resources and/or required skills. In such situations you should be aware of the problems these limitations impose on the quality of the data.

In selecting a method of data collection, the socioeconomic–demographic characteristics of the study population play an important role: you should know as much as possible about characteristics such as educational level, age structure, socioeconomic status and ethnic background. If possible, it is helpful to know the study population's interest in, and attitude towards, participation in the study. Some populations, for a number of reasons, may not feel either at ease with a particular method of data collection (such as being interviewed) or comfortable to express opinions in a questionnaire. Furthermore, people with little education may respond differently to certain methods of data collection compared to people with more education.

Another important determinant of the quality of your data is the way the purpose and relevance of the study is explained to potential respondents. Whatever method of data collection is used, make sure that respondents clearly understand the purpose and relevance of the study. This is particularly important when you use a questionnaire to collect data because in an interview situation you can answer a respondent's questions but in a questionnaire you will not have this opportunity.

In the following sections each method of data collection is discussed from the point of view of its applicability and suitability to a situation, and the problems and limitations associated with it.

Observation

Observation is one way to collect primary data. Observation is a purposeful, systematic and selective way of watching and listening to an interaction or phenomenon as it takes place. There are many situations in which observation is the most appropriate method of data collection; for example, when you want to learn about the interaction in a group, study the dietary patterns of a population, ascertain the functions performed by a worker, or study the behaviour or personality traits of an individual. It is also appropriate in situations where full and/or accurate information cannot be elicited by questioning, because respondents either are not co-operative or are unaware of the answers because it is difficult for them to detach themselves from the interaction. In summary, when you are more interested in the behaviour than in the perceptions of individuals, or when subjects are so involved in the interaction that they are unable to provide objective information about it, observation is the best approach to collect the required information.

Types of observation

There are two types of observation:

- participant observation;
- non-participant observation.

Participant observation is when you, as a researcher, participate in the activities of the group being observed in the same manner as its members, with or without their knowing that they are being observed. For example, you might want to examine the reactions of the general population towards people in wheelchairs. You can study their reactions by sitting in a wheelchair yourself. Or you might want to study the life of prisoners and pretend to be a prisoner in order to do this.

Non-participant observation, on the other hand, is when you, as a researcher, do not get involved in the activities of the group but remains a passive observer, watching and listening to its activities and drawing conclusions from this. For example, you might want to study the functions carried out by nurses in a hospital. As an observer, you could watch, follow, and record the activities as they are performed. After making a number of observations, conclusions could be drawn about the functions nurses carry out in the hospital. Any occupational group in any setting can be observed in the same manner.

Problems with using observation as a method of data collection

The use of observation as a method of data collection may suffer from a number of problems, which is not to suggest that all or any of these necessarily prevails in every situation. But as a beginner you should be aware of these problems.

- When individuals or groups become aware that they are being observed, they may change their behaviour. Depending upon the situation, this change could be positive or negative—it may increase or decrease, for example, their productivity—and may occur for a number of reasons. When a change in the behaviour of persons or groups is attributed to their being observed it is known as the *Hawthorne Effect*. The use of observation in such a situation may introduces distortion: what is observed may not represent their normal behaviour.
- There is always the possibility of observer bias. If an observer is biased, s/he can easily introduce bias and there is no easy way to verify the observations and the inferences drawn from them.

- The interpretations drawn from observations may vary from observer to observer.
- There is the possibility of incomplete observation and/or recording, which varies with the method of recording. An observer may watch keenly but at the expense of detailed recording. The opposite problem may occur when the observer takes detailed notes but in doing so misses some of the interaction.

Situations in which observations can be made

Observations can be made under two conditions:

- natural;
- controlled.

Observing a group in its natural operation rather than intervening in its activities is classified as observation under natural conditions. Introducing a stimulus to the group for it to react to and observing the reaction is called controlled observation.

The recording of observation

There are many ways of recording observation. The selection of a method of recording depends upon the purpose of the observation. Keep in mind that each method has its advantages and disadvantages.

- **Narrative**—in this form of recording the researcher records a description of the interaction in his/her own words. Usually, s/he makes brief notes while observing the interaction and soon after the observation makes detailed notes in narrative form. In addition, some researchers may interpret the interaction and draw conclusions from it. The biggest advantage of narrative recording is that it provides a deeper insight into the interaction. However, a disadvantage is that an observer may be biased in his/her observation and, therefore, the interpretations and conclusions drawn from the observation may also be biased. Also, if a researcher's attention is on observing, s/he might forget to record an important piece of interaction and, obviously, in the process of recording, part of the interaction may be missed. Hence, there is always the possibility of incomplete recording and/or observation. In addition, with different observers the comparability of narrative recording can be a problem.
- **Scales**—at times some observers may prefer to develop a scale in order to rate various aspects of the interaction or phenomenon. The recording is done on a scale developed by the observer/researcher. A scale may be one-, two- or three-directional, depending upon the purpose of the observation. For example, in the scale in Figure 9.2—designed to record the nature of the interaction within a group—there are three directions: positive, negative, and neutral.

One of the problems with using a scale to record observations is that it does not provide in-depth information about the interaction. In addition, it may suffer from any of the following problems:

Figure 9.2   A three-directional rating scale

A study of the nature of interaction in a group

Aspects of interaction		Positive				Neutral			Negative		
Participation	5	4	3	2	1	0	1	2	3	4	5
Rapport	5	4	3	2	1	0	1	2	3	4	5
Confidence	5	4	3	2	1	0	1	2	3	4	5
Aggressiveness	5	4	3	2	1	0	1	2	3	4	5
Withdrawnness	5	4	3	2	1	0	1	2	3	4	5
Friendliness	5	4	3	2	1	0	1	2	3	4	5
Aloofness	5	4	3	2	1	0	1	2	3	4	5

- Unless the observer is extremely confident of his/her ability to assess an interaction, s/he may tend to avoid the extreme positions on the scale, using mostly the central part. The error this tendency creates is called the ***error of central tendency***.
- Some observers may prefer certain sections of the scale in the same way that some teachers are strict markers and others are not. When observers have a tendency to use a particular part of the scale in recording an interaction, this phenomenon is known as the ***elevation effect***.
- Another type of error that may be introduced is when the way an observer rates an individual on one aspect of the interaction influences the way s/he rates that individual on another aspect of the interaction. Again something similar to this can happen in teaching when a teacher's assessment of the performance of a student in one subject may influence his/her rating of that student's performance in another. This type of effect is known as the ***halo effect***.

• **Categorical recording**—sometimes an observer may decide to record her/his observation using categories. The type and number of categories depend upon the type of interaction and the observer's choice about how to classify the observation. For example: passive/active (two categories); introvert/extrovert (two categories); always/sometimes/never (three categories); strongly agree/agree/uncertain/disagree/strongly disagree (five categories). The use of categories to record an observation may suffer from the same problems as those associated with scales.

• **Recording on mechanical devices**—observation can also be recorded on a videotape and then analysed. The advantage of taping the inter-action is that the observer can see it a number of times before drawing any conclusions, and can invite other professionals to view the tape in order to arrive at more objective conclusions. However, one of the disadvantages is that some people may feel uncomfortable or may behave differently before a camera. Therefore the interaction may not be a true reflection of the situation.

The choice of a particular method for recording your observation is dependent upon the purpose of the observation, the complexity of the interaction and the type of population being observed. It is important to consider these factors before deciding upon the method for recording your observation.

The interview

Interviewing is a commonly used method of collecting information from people. In many walks of life we collect information through different forms of interaction with others. Any person-to-person interaction between two or more individuals with a specific purpose in mind is called an interview. On the one hand, interviewing can be very flexible, when the interviewer has the freedom to formulate questions as they come to mind around the issue being investigated; and on the other hand, it can be inflexible, when the investigator has to keep strictly to the questions decided beforehand. Interviews are classified according to the degree of flexibility as in Figure 9.3.

Figure 9.3   Types of interview

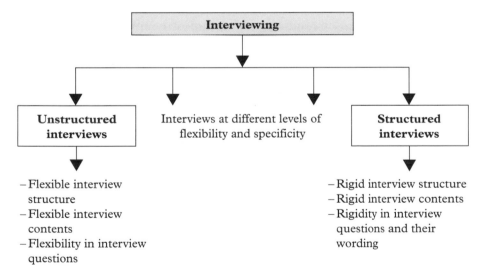

Unstructured Interviews

The strength of *unstructured interviews* is the almost complete freedom they provide in terms of content and structure. You are free to order these in whatever sequence you wish. You also have complete freedom in terms of the wording you use and the way you explain questions to your respondents. You may formulate questions and raise issues on the spur of the moment, depending upon what occurs to you in the context of the discussion.

There are several types of unstructured interviewing; for example: in-depth interviewing, focus group interviewing, narratives and oral histories.

In-depth interviews

The theoretical roots of in-depth interviewing are in what is known as the interpretive tradition. According to Taylor and Bogdan, in-depth interviewing is, 'repeated face-to-face encounters between the researcher and informants directed towards understanding informants' perspectives on their lives, experiences, or situations as expressed in their own words' (1984: 77). This definition underlines two essential characteristics of in-depth interviewing: (1) it involves face-to-face, repeated interaction between the researcher and his/her informant(s); and (2) it seeks to understand the latter's perspectives. Because of repeated contacts and hence extended length of time spent with an informant, it is assumed that the rapport between researcher and informant will be enhanced, and that the corresponding understanding and confidence between the two will lead to in-depth and accurate information.

Focus group interviews

The only difference between a focus group interview and an in-depth interview is that the former is undertaken with a group and the latter with an individual. In a focus group interview, you explore the perceptions, experiences and understandings of a group of people who have some experience in common with regard to a situation or event. For example, you may explore with relevant groups such issues as domestic violence, physical disability or refugees.

In focus group interviews, broad discussion topics are developed beforehand, either by the researcher or by the group. These provide a broad frame for discussions which follow. The specific discussion points emerge as a part of the discussion. Members of a focus group express their opinions while discussing these issues.

You, as a researcher, need to ensure that whatever is expressed or discussed is recorded accurately. Use the method of recording that suits you the best. You may audiotape discussions, employ someone else to record them or record them yourself immediately after each session. If you are taking your own notes during discussions, you need to be careful not to lose something of importance because of your involvement in discussions. You can and should take your write-up on discussions back to your focus group for correctness, verification and confirmation.

Narratives

The narrative technique of gathering information has even less structure than the focus group. Narratives have almost no predetermined contents except that the researcher seeks to hear the personal experience of a person with an incident or happening in his/her life. Essentially, the person tells his/her story about an incident or situation and you, as the researcher, listen passively. And, occasionally, you encourage the individual by using techniques of active listening; that is, you say words such as 'uh huh', 'mmmm', 'yeah', 'right' and nod as appropriate. Basically, you let the person talk freely and without interrupting.

Narratives are a very powerful method of data collection for situations which are sensitive in nature. For example, you may want to find out about the impact of child sexual abuse on people who have gone through such an experience. You, as a researcher, ask these people to narrate their experiences and how they have been affected. Narratives may have a therapeutic impact; that is, sometimes simply telling his/her story may help a person to feel more at ease with the event. Some therapists specialise in narrative therapy. But here, we are concerned with narratives as a method of data collection.

As with focus group interviews, you need to choose the recording system that suits you the best. Having completed narrative sessions you need to write your detail notes and give them back to the respondent to check for accuracy.

Oral histories

Oral histories, like narratives, involve the use of both passive and active listening. Oral histories, however, are more commonly used for learning about a historical event or episode that took place in the past or for gaining information about a cultural, custom or story that has been passed from generation to generation. Narratives are more about a person's personal experiences whereas, historical, social or cultural events are the subjects of oral histories.

Suppose you want to find out about the life after World War II in some regional town of Western Australia or about the living conditions of Aboriginal and Torres Strait Islander people in the 1930s. You would talk to persons who were alive during that period and ask them about life at that time.

Data collection through unstructured interviewing is extremely useful in situations where either in-depth information is needed or little is known about the area. The flexibility allowed to the interviewer in what s/he asks of a respondent is an asset as it can elicit extremely rich information. As it provides in-depth information, many researchers use this technique for constructing a structured research instrument. On the other hand, since an unstructured interview does not list specific questions to be asked of respondents, the comparability of questions asked and responses obtained may become a problem. As the researcher gains experience during the interviews, the questions asked of respondents change; hence, the type of information obtained from those who are interviewed at the beginning may be markedly different from that obtained from those interviewed towards the end. Also, this freedom can introduce investigator bias into the study. Using an interview guide as a means of data collection requires much more skill on the part of the researcher than does using a structured interview.

Structured interviews

In a *structured interview* the researcher asks a predetermined set of questions, using the same wording and order of questions as specified in the interview schedule. An *interview schedule* is a written list of questions, open-ended or closed-ended, prepared for use by an interviewer in a person-to-person interaction (this may be face-to-face, by telephone or by other electronic media). Note that an interview schedule is a research tool/instrument for collecting data, whereas interviewing is a method of data collection.

One of the main advantages of the structured interview is that it provides uniform information, which assures the comparability of data. Structured interviewing requires fewer interviewing skills than does unstructured interviewing.

The questionnaire

A questionnaire is a written list of questions, the answers to which are recorded by respondents. In a questionnaire respondents read the questions, interpret what is expected and then write down the answers. The only difference between an interview schedule and a questionnaire is that in the former it is the interviewer who asks the questions (and if necessary, explains them) and records the respondent's replies on an interview schedule, and in the latter replies are recorded by the respondents themselves. This distinction is important in accounting for the respective strengths and weaknesses of the two methods.

In the case of a questionnaire, as there is no one to explain the meaning of questions to respondents, it is important that questions are clear and easy to understand. Also, the layout of a questionnaire should be such that it is easy to read and pleasant to the eye, and the sequence of questions should be easy to follow. A questionnaire should be developed in an interactive style. This means respondents should feel as if someone is talking to them. In a questionnaire, a sensitive question or a question respondents may feel hesitant about answering should be prefaced by an interactive statement explaining the relevance of the question. It is a good idea to use a different font for these statements to distinguish them from the actual questions. Examples in Figures 9.4 and 9.5 taken from two surveys recently carried out by the author with the help of two students explain some of the above points.

Choosing between an interview schedule and a questionnaire

The choice between a questionnaire and an interview schedule is important and should be considered thoroughly as the strengths and weaknesses of the two methods can affect the validity of the findings. The nature of the investigation and the socioeconomic–demographic characteristics of the study population are central in this choice. The selection between an interview schedule and a questionnaire should be based upon the following criteria.

- **The nature of the investigation**—if the study is about issues that respondents may feel reluctant to discuss with an investigator, a questionnaire may be the better choice as it ensures anonymity. This may be the case with studies on drug use, sexuality, indulgence in criminal activities and personal finances. However, there are situations where better information about sensitive issues can be obtained by interviewing respondents. It depends on the type of study population and the skills of the interviewer.
- **The geographical distribution of the study population**—if potential respondents are scattered over a wide geographical area, you have no choice but to use a questionnaire, as interviewing in these circumstances would be extremely expensive.
- **The type of study population**—if the study population is illiterate, very young or very old, or handicapped, there may be no option but to interview respondents.

Figure 9.4   Example 1: Where to go? A study of occupational mobility among immigrants

Where to go?

A study of occupational mobility among immigrants

The questionnaire opened with the following interactive statement:

Personal circumstances, and educational and occupational background, to a great extent determine the occupational mobility of an individual. This is especially true for immigrants. We would therefore like to ask you some questions about you and your family background. Knowledge of these factors is also important for assessing the representativeness of those who participated in the study and to understand the extent, nature and reasons of occupational mobility in relation to your background. We would appreciate your answering these questions as the information you provide will be very useful to us. We would like to emphasise that your responses are extremely valuable to us and we would greatly appreciate your answering all questions. However, if you feel that you do not want to answer a particular question, we will gladly accept your decision. We can assure you that your responses will be completely anonymous and will not be used for any other purpose.

Before asking questions about family background, the following interactive statement was inserted in the questionnaire:

Now, we would like to ask some questions about your family. Your family circumstances can affect your choice of an occupation after immigration. Again, we assure you of the complete anonymity of your responses.

Before ascertaining respondents' experiences with respect to recognition of their qualifications in Australia, the following interactive statement prepared them to be at ease with the area of inquiry:

Recognition of educational and professional qualifications, in addition to

(Continued on next page)

other factors, plays a major role in determining an individual's occupational mobility in a new country. In this section we would like to ask your opinion about the process of getting your qualifications recognised. We would also like to know how satisfied or dissatisfied you are with the outcome. If you are dissatisfied, we would like to know your reasons as this information may help decision makers to improve the process. Again, we assure you that your answers will be completely confidential. However, if you still feel that you do not want to answer a particular question, please feel free to omit it.

Figure 9.5   Example 2: Occupational redeployment—a study of occupational redeployment among state government employees

Occupational redeployment

A study of occupational redeployment among state government employees

The following interactive statement was inserted in the questionnaire before questions asking about the socioeconomic–demographic background of respondents:

In order to gain an understanding of the situation of employees who have experienced occupational redeployment in state government departments during the last three years, we would like to ask some questions about your background. Your answers will help us to determine the types of occupation where redeployment has occurred and the backgrounds of the employees who have been affected by it. Please do not feel obliged to answer a question if you do not wish to, though we assure you that any information you provide will be treated with strict confidentiality.

Questions about occupational history were prefaced by the following statement:

We would like to ask some questions about your work history. The answers to these questions will enable us to compare the type of work you have been doing since entering the workforce with the job you have been assigned after redeployment. This will help us to establish the nature and extent of change in your job before and after redeployment. Again, there is no obligation to answer a question if you do not want to. However, answers to these questions are extremely important to us. We assure you of the anonymity of the information you provide.

Before asking questions about the impact of redeployment, the following interactive statement was incorporated into the questionnaire:

The following questions ask you to express your opinion about different aspects of your job after *and* before *redeployment. Your answers will help us to gauge the impact of redeployment on different aspects of your work and family situation. We would appreciate your honest opinions. Be assured that your responses will be completely anonymous.*

Different ways of administering a questionnaire

A questionnaire can be administered in different ways.

- **The mailed questionnaire**—the most common approach to collecting information is to send the questionnaire to prospective respondents by mail. Obviously this approach presupposes that you have access to their addresses. Usually it is a good idea to send a prepaid, self-addressed envelope with the questionnaire as this might increase the response rate. A mailed questionnaire *must* be accompanied by a covering letter (see below for details). One of the major problems with this method is the low response rate. In the case of an extremely low response rate, the findings have very limited applicability to the population studied.

- **Collective administration**—one of the best ways of administering a questionnaire is to obtain a captive audience such as students in a classroom, people attending a function, participants in a program or people assembled in one place. This ensures a very high response rate as you will find few people refuse to participate in your study. Also, as you have personal contact with the study population, you can explain the purpose, relevance and importance of the study and can clarify any questions that respondents may have. The author's advice is that if you have a captive audience for your study, don't miss the opportunity—it is the quickest way of collecting data, ensures a very high response rate and you save money on postage.

- **Administration in a public place**—sometimes you can administer a questionnaire in a public place such as a shopping centre, health centre, hospital, school or pub. Of course this depends upon the type of study population you are looking for and where it is likely to be found. Usually the purpose of the study is explained to potential respondents as they approach and their participation in the study is requested. Apart from being slightly more time-consuming, this method has all the advantages of administering a questionnaire collectively.

The contents of the covering letter

It is essential that you write a covering letter with your mailed questionnaire. It should very briefly:

- introduce you and the institution you are representing;
- describe in two or three sentences the main objectives of the study;
- explain the relevance of the study;
- convey any general instructions;
- indicate that participation in the study is voluntary—if recipients do not want to respond to the questionnaire, they have the right not to;
- assure respondents of the anonymity of the information provided by them;
- provide a contact number in case they have any questions;
- give a return address for the questionnaire and a deadline for its return;
- thank them for their participation in the study.

Advantages of a questionnaire

A questionnaire has several advantages.

- **It is less expensive**. As you do not interview respondents, you save time, and human and financial resources. The use of a questionnaire, therefore, is comparatively convenient and inexpensive. Particularly, when it is administered collectively to a study population, it is an extremely inexpensive method of data collection.
- **It offers greater anonymity**. As there is no face-to-face interaction between respondents and interviewer, this method provides greater anonymity. In some situations when sensitive questions are asked it helps to increase the likelihood of obtaining accurate information.

Disadvantages of a questionnaire

Although a questionnaire has several disadvantages, it is important to note that not all data collection using this method has these disadvantages. The prevalence of a disadvantage depends on a number of factors, but you need to be aware of them to understand their possible bearing on the quality of the data. These are:

- **Application is limited**. One main disadvantage is that its application is limited to a study population that can read and write. It cannot be used on a population that is illiterate, very young, very old, or handicapped.
- **Response rate is low**. Questionnaires are notorious for their low response rates; that is, people fail to return them. If you plan to use a questionnaire, keep in mind that because not everyone will return their questionnaire, your sample size will in effect be reduced. The response rate depends upon a number of factors: the interest of the sample in the topic of the study; the layout and length of the questionnaire; the quality of the letter explaining the purpose and relevance of the study; and the methodology used to deliver the questionnaire. You should consider yourself lucky to obtain a 50 per cent response rate and sometimes it may be as low as 20 per cent. However, as mentioned, the response rate is not a problem when a questionnaire is administered in a collective situation.
- **There is a self-selecting bias**. Not everyone who receives a questionnaire returns it, so there is a self-selecting bias. Those who return their questionnaire may have attitudes, attributes or motivations that are different from those who do not. Hence, if the response rate is very low, the findings may not be representative of the total study population.
- **Opportunity to clarify issues is lacking**. If, for any reason, respondents do not understand some questions, there is no opportunity for them to have the meaning clarified. If different respondents interpret questions differently, this will affect the quality of the information provided.
- **Spontaneous responses are not allowed for**. Mailed questionnaires are inappropriate when spontaneous responses are required, as a questionnaire gives them time to reflect before answering.

- **The response to a question may be influenced by the response to other questions**. As respondents can read all the questions before answering (which usually happens), the way they answer a particular question may be affected by their knowledge of other questions.
- **It is possible to consult others**. With mailed questionnaires respondents may consult other people before responding. In situations where an investigator wants to find out only the study population's opinions, this method may be inappropriate, though requesting respondents to express their own opinion may help.
- **A response cannot be supplemented with other information**. An interview can sometimes be supplemented with information from other methods of data collection such as observation. However, a questionnaire lacks this advantage.

Advantages of the interview

- **The interview is more appropriate for complex situations**. It is the most appropriate approach for studying complex and sensitive areas as the interviewer has the opportunity to prepare a respondent before asking sensitive questions and to explain complex ones to respondents in person.
- **It is useful for collecting in-depth information**. In an interview situation it is possible for an investigator to obtain in-depth information by probing. Hence, in situations where in-depth information is required, interviewing is the preferred method of data collection.
- **Information can be supplemented**. An interviewer is able to supplement information obtained from responses with those gained from observation of non-verbal reactions.
- **Questions can be explained**. It is less likely that a question will be misunderstood as the interviewer can either repeat a question or put it in a form that is understood by the respondent.
- **Interviewing has a wider application**. An interview can be used with almost any type of population: children, handicapped, illiterate or the very old.

Disadvantages of the interview

- **Interviewing is time-consuming and expensive**. This is especially so when potential respondents are scattered over a wide geographical area. However, if you have a situation such as an office, a hospital or an agency where potential respondents come to obtain a service, interviewing them in that setting may be less expensive and less time-consuming.
- **The quality of data depends upon the quality of the interaction**. In an interview the quality of interaction between an interviewer and interviewee is likely to affect the quality of the information obtained. Also, because the interaction in each interview is unique, the quality of the responses obtained from different interviews may vary significantly.

- **The quality of data depends upon the quality of the interviewer**. In an interview situation the quality of the data generated is affected by the experience, skills and commitment of the interviewer.
- **The quality of data may vary when many interviewers are used**. Use of multiple interviewers may magnify the problems identified in the two previous points.
- **The researcher may introduce his/her bias**. Researcher bias in the framing of questions and the interpretation of responses is always possible.
- **The interviewer may be biased**. If the interviews are conducted by a person or persons, paid or voluntary, other than the researcher, it is also possible that they may exhibit bias in the way they interpret responses, select response categories or choose words to summarise respondents' expressed opinions.

Forms of question

The form and wording of questions is extremely important in a research instrument as they have an effect on the type and quality of information obtained. The questions should therefore be appropriate, relevant and free from any of the problems discussed in the section titled 'Considerations in formulating questions'. This present section discusses open-ended and closed-ended questions, which are both commonly used in the social sciences.

In an interview schedule or a questionnaire, questions may be formulated as:

- open-ended; or
- closed-ended.

In an ***open-ended question*** the possible responses are *not* given. In the case of a questionnaire, the respondent writes down the answers in his/her words, whereas in the case of an interview schedule the investigator records the answers either verbatim or in a summary describing a respondent's answer. In a ***closed-ended question*** the possible answers are set out in the questionnaire or schedule and the respondent or the investigator ticks the category that best describes the respondent's answer. It is usually wise to provide a category 'Other/please explain' to accommodate any response listed. The questions in Figure 9.6 are classified as closed-ended questions. The same questions could be asked as open-ended questions, as shown in Figure 9.7.

When deciding whether to use open-ended or closed-ended questions to obtain information about a variable, visualise how you plan to use the information generated. This is important because the way you frame your questions determines the unit of measurement by which the responses can be classified. In turn the unit of measurement dictates what statistical procedures can be applied to the data and the way the information can be analysed and displayed.

Let us take, as an example, the question about the variable: 'income'. In closed-ended questions income can be qualitatively recorded in categories

Figure 9.6   Examples of closed-ended questions

A. Please indicate your age by placing a tick in the appropriate category.

Under 15 ☐
15–19 years ☐
20–24 years ☐

B. How would you describe your current marital status?

Married ☐
Single ☐
De facto ☐
Divorced ☐
Separated ☐

C. What is your average annual income?

Under 10 000 ☐
10 000–19 999 ☐
20 000–29 999 ☐
30 000–39 999 ☐
40 000+ ☐

OR

C(a) How would you categorise your average annual income?

Above average ☐
Average ☐
Below average ☐

D. What, in your opinion, are the qualities of a good administrator?

Able to make decisions ☐
Fast decision maker ☐
Able to listen ☐
Impartial ☐
Skilled in interpersonal communication ☐
Other, please specify

_____

_____

such as 'above average/average/below average', or quantitatively in categories such as 'under $10 000/$10 000–$19 999/…'. Your choice of qualitative and quantitative categories affects the unit of measurement for income, which in turn will affect the application of statistical procedures. For example, you

Figure 9.7   Examples of open-ended questions

> A. What is your current age? _____years
>
> B. How would you describe your current marital status? _____
>
> C. What is your average annual income? _____$
>
> D. What, in your opinion, are the qualities of a good administrator?
>
>   1 _____
>
>   2 _____
>
>   3 _____
>
>   4 _____
>
>   5 _____

cannot calculate the average income of a person from the responses to question C(a) in Figure 9.6; nor can you calculate the median or modal category of income. But from the responses to question C, you can accurately calculate modal category of income. However, the average and the median income cannot be accurately calculated (such calculations are usually made under certain assumptions). From the responses to question C in Figure 9.7, where the income for a respondent is recorded in exact dollars, the different descriptors of income can be calculated very accurately. In addition, information on income can be displayed in any form. You can calculate average, median or mode. The same is true for any other information obtained in response to open-ended and closed-ended questions.

In closed-ended questions, having developed categories, you cannot change them; hence, you should be very certain about your categories when developing them. If you ask an open-ended question, you can develop any catogories at the time of analysis.

Both open-ended and closed-ended questions have their advantages and disadvantages in different situations. To some extent, their advantages and disadvantages depend upon whether they are being used in an interview or in a questionnaire and on whether they are being used to seek information about facts or opinions. As a rule, closed-ended questions are extremely useful for eliciting factual information and open-ended questions for seeking opinions, attitudes and perceptions. The choice of open-ended or closed-ended questions should be made according to the purpose for which a piece of information is to be used, the type of study population from which information is going to be obtained, the method proposed for communicating the findings and the readership.

Advantages and disadvantages of open-ended questions

Open-ended questions have a number of advantages and disadvantages.

- Open-ended questions provide in-depth information if used in an interview by an experienced interviewer. In a questionnaire, open-ended questions can provide a wealth of information provided respondents feel comfortable about expressing their opinions and are fluent in the language used. On the other hand, analysis of open-ended questions is more difficult. The researcher usually needs to go through another process—**content analysis**—in order to classify the data.

- In a questionnaire, open-ended questions provide respondents with the opportunity to express themselves freely, resulting in a greater variety of information. Thus respondents are not 'conditioned' by having to select answers from a list. The disadvantage of free choice is that, in a questionnaire, some respondents may not be able to express themselves, and so information can be lost.

- As open-ended questions allow respondents to express themselves freely, they virtually eliminate the possibility of investigator bias (investigator bias is introduced through the response pattern presented to respondents). On the other hand, there is a greater chance of interviewer bias in open-ended questions.

Advantages and disadvantages of closed-ended questions

Closed-ended questions, like open-ended questions, have many advantages and disadvantages.

- One of the main disadvantages of closed-ended questions is that the information obtained through them lacks depth and variety.

- There is a greater possibility of investigator bias because the researcher may list only the response patterns that s/he is interested in or those that come to mind. Even if the category of 'other' is offered, most people will usually select from the given responses, and so the findings may still reflect the researcher's bias.

- In a questionnaire, the given response pattern for a question could condition the thinking of respondents, and so the answers provided may not truly reflect respondents' opinions. Rather, they may reflect the extent of agreement or disagreement with the researcher's opinion or analysis of a situation.

- The ease of answering a ready-made list of responses may create a tendency among some respondents and interviewers to tick a category or categories without thinking through the issue.

- Closed-ended questions, as they provide 'ready made' categories within which respondents reply to the questions asked by the researcher, help to ensure that the information needed by the researcher is obtained.

- Because the possible responses are already categorised, they are easy to analyse.

Considerations in formulating questions

The wording and tone of your questions are important because the information and its quality largely depend upon these factors. It is therefore important to be careful about the way you formulate questions. The following are some considerations to keep in mind when formulating questions:

- **Always use simple and everyday language**. Your respondents may not be highly educated, and even if they are they still may not know some of the 'simple' technical jargon that you are used to. Particularly in a questionnaire, take extra care to use words that your respondents will understand as you will have no opportunity to explain questions to them. A pre-test should show you what is and what is not understood by your respondents. For example:

'Is anyone in your family a *dipsomaniac*?' (Bailey 1978: 100)

In this question many respondents, even some who are well educated, will not understand 'dipsomaniac' and, hence, they either do not answer or answer the question without understanding.

- **Do not use ambiguous questions**. An ambiguous question is one that contains more than one meaning and that can be interpreted differently by different respondents. This will result in different answers, making it difficult, if not impossible, to draw any valid conclusions from the information. The following questions highlight the problem:

'Is your work made difficult because you are expecting a baby?' (Moser & Kalton 1989: 323)   Yes ☐ No ☐

In the survey all women were asked this question. Those women who were not pregnant ticked 'no', meaning no they were not pregnant, and those who were pregnant and who ticked 'no' meant pregnancy had not made their work difficult. The question has other ambiguities as well: it does not specify the type of work and the stage of pregnancy.

'Are you satisfied with your canteen?' (Moser & Kalton 1989: 319)

This question is also ambiguous as it does not ask respondents to indicate the aspects of the canteen with which they may be satisfied or dissatisfied. Is it with the service, the prices, the physical facilities, the attitude of the staff or the quality of the meals? Respondents may have any one of these aspects in mind when they answer the question.

- **Do not ask double-barrelled questions**. A double-barrelled question is a question within a question. The main problem with this type of question is that one does not know which particular question a respondent has answered. Some respondents may answer both 'questions' and others may answer only one of them.

'How often and how much time do you spend on each visit?'

This question was asked in a survey in Western Australia to ascertain the need for child-minding services in one of the hospitals. The question has two parts: how often do you visit and how much time is spent on each visit? In this type of question some respondents may answer the first part, whereas others may answer the second and some may answer both parts. Incidentally, this question is also ambiguous in that it does not specify 'how often' in terms of a period of time. Is it in a week, a fortnight, a month or a year?

> 'Does your department have a special recruitment policy for racial minorities and women?' (Bailey 1978: 97)

This question is double-barrelled in that it asks respondents to indicate whether their office has a special recruitment policy for two population groups: racial minorities and women. A 'yes' response does not necessarily mean that the office has a special recruitment policy for both groups.

• **Do not ask leading questions**. A leading question is one which, by its contents, structure or wording, leads a respondent to answer in a certain direction. Such questions are judgemental and lead respondents to answer either positively or negatively.

> 'Unemployment is increasing, isn't it?'
>
> 'Smoking is bad, isn't it?'

The first problem is that these are not questions but statements. Because the statements suggest that 'unemployment is increasing' and 'smoking is bad', respondents may feel that to disagree with them is to be in the wrong, especially if they feel that the researcher is an authority and that if s/he is saying that 'unemployment is increasing' or 'smoking is bad', it must be so. The feeling that there is a 'right' answer can 'force' people to respond in a way that is contrary to their true position.

• **Do not ask questions that are based on presumptions**. In such questions the researcher assumes that respondents fit into a particular category and seeks information based upon that assumption.

> 'How many cigarettes do you smoke in a day? (Moser & Kalton 1989: 325)
>
> 'What contraceptives do you use?'

Both these questions were asked without ascertaining whether or not respondents were smokers or sexually active. In situations like this it is important to first ascertain whether or not a respondent fits into the category about which you are inquiring.

The construction of a research instrument

The construction of a research instrument or tool is the most important aspect of a research project because anything you say by way of findings or conclusions is based upon the type of information you collect, and the data you collect is entirely dependent upon the questions that you ask of your respondents. The famous saying about computers—'garbage in garbage out'—is also applicable to data collection. The research tool provides the input into a study and therefore the quality and validity of the output, the findings, are solely dependent upon it.

In spite of its immense importance, to the author's knowledge, no specific guidelines for beginners on how to construct a research tool exist. Students are left to learn for themselves under the guidance of their research supervisor. The guidelines suggested below outline a broad approach, especially for beginners. The underlying principle is to ensure the validity of your instrument by making sure that *your questions relate to the objectives of your study*. Therefore, clearly defined objectives play an extremely important role as each question in the instrument must stem from the objectives, research questions and/or hypotheses of the study. It is suggested that a beginner should adopt the following procedure.

Step I:　If you have not already done so, clearly define and individually list all the specific objectives, research questions or hypotheses, if any, to be tested.

Step II:　For each objective, research question or hypothesis, list all the associated questions that you want to answer through your study.

Step III: Take each research question identified in step II and list the information required to answer it.

Step IV: Formulate question(s) to obtain this information.

In the above process you may find that the same piece of information is required for a number of questions. In such a situation the question should be asked once only. To understand this process see Table 9.1 for which we have already developed a set of objectives in Figure 4.4 on p. 49.

Asking personal and sensitive questions

In the social sciences, sometimes one needs to ask questions that are of a personal nature. Some respondents may find this offensive. It is important to be aware of this as it may affect the quality of information or even result in an interview being terminated or failure to return questionnaires. Researchers have used a number of approaches to deal with this problem. Which approach is best is a difficult question to answer. According to Bradburn and Sudman,

'... no data collection method is superior to other methods for all types of threatening questions. If one accepts the results at face value, each of the data gathering methods is best under certain conditions' (1979: 12–13).

In terms of the best technique for asking sensitive or threatening questions, there appears to be two opposite opinions, referring to the manner in which the question is asked:

• a direct manner;
• an indirect manner.

The advantage with the first approach is that one can be sure that an affirmative answer is accurate. Those who advocate the second approach believe that direct questioning is likely to offend respondents and hence they are unlikely to answer even the non-sensitive questions. Some ways of asking personal questions in an indirect manner are as follows:

Table 9.1   Guidelines for constructing a research instrument: a study to evaluate community responsiveness in a health program

Objectives/research questions/ hypotheses Step I	Main and associated research questions Step II	Information required Step III	Questions Step IV
1 To find out the understanding of the concept 'community responsiveness' among health administrators, planners, service providers and consumers of health services	What is community responsiveness? What does it mean when people use the term 'community responsiveness'? What are the differences in the perception of community responsiveness among health administrators, planners, service providers and consumers of health services?	1 Perception of community responsiveness	Q1.1 When you use the term 'community responsiveness', what do you mean by it? Q1.2 What comes to your mind when you use the term 'community responsiveness' in the delivery of health services? Q1.3 What, in your opinion, are the characteristics of 'community responsiveness'? Q1.4 What, in your opinion, is the difference between 'community development and community responsiveness'?
2 To identify the strategies needed to foster community responsiveness in the delivery of health services		2 Occupational status, i.e. health administrator, planner, service provider or consumer	Q2.1 What would you categorise your job as? Health administrator/planner Service provider Health consumer
3 To develop a set of indicators to evaluate the effectiveness of strategies to foster community responsiveness		3 Age, gender, education	Q3.1 How old are you? ____ Q3.2 Are you ____ female ____ male? Q3.3 What is the highest level of educational achievement you have attained? ____

- by showing drawings or cartoons;
- by asking a respondent to complete a sentence;
- by asking a respondent to sort cards containing statements;
- by using random devices.

To describe these methods is beyond the scope of this book.

The order of questions

The order of questions in a questionnaire or in an interview schedule is important as it affects the quality of information, and the interest and even willingness of a respondent to participate in a study. Again, there are two categories of opinion as to the best way to order questions. The first is that questions should be asked in a random order and the second is that they should follow a logical progression based upon the objectives of the study. The author believes that the latter procedure is better as it gradually leads respondents into the themes of the study, starting with simple themes and progressing to complex ones. This approach sustains the interest of respondents and gradually stimulates them to answer the questions. However, the random approach is useful in situations where a researcher wants respondents to express their agreement or disagreement with different aspects of an issue. In this case a logical listing of statements or questions may 'condition' a respondent to the opinions expressed by the researcher through the statements.

Prerequisites for data collection

Before you start obtaining information from potential respondents it is imperative that you make sure of their:

- **motivation to share the required information**—it is essential for respondents to be willing to share information with you. You should make every effort to motivate them by explaining clearly and in simple terms the objectives and relevance of the study, either at the time of the interview or through the questionnaire.
- **clear understanding of the questions**—respondents must understand what is expected of them in the questions. If respondents do not understand a question clearly, the response given may either be wrong or irrelevant, or make no sense.
- **possession of the required information**—the third prerequisite is that respondents must have the information sought. This is of particular importance when you are seeking factual or technical information. If respondents do not have the required information, they cannot provide it. In the case of opinions this does not necessarily apply as all of us have opinions.

Collecting data using secondary sources

So far we have discussed the primary sources of data collection where the required data was collected either by you or by someone else for the specific purpose you have in mind. There are occasions when your data has already been collected by someone else and you need only to extract the required information for the purpose of your study. This section lists some of the many secondary sources that can be grouped into the following categories:

- **Government or semi-government publications**—there are many government and semi-government organisations that collect data on a regular basis in a variety of areas and publish it for use by members of the public and interest groups. Some common examples are the census, vital statistics registration, labour force surveys, health reports, economic forecasts and demographic information.
- **Earlier research**—for some topics, an enormous number of research studies that have already been done by others can provide you with the required information.
- **Personal records**—some people write historical and personal records that may provide the information you need.
- **Mass media**—reports published in newspapers, magazines and so on may be another good source of data.

Problems with using data from secondary sources

When using data from secondary sources you need to be careful as there may be certain problems with the availability, format and quality of data. The extent of these problems varies from source to source. While using such data some issues you should keep in mind are:

- **Validity and reliability**—the validity of information may vary markedly from source to source. For example, information obtained from a census is likely to be more valid and reliable than that obtained from most personal diaries.
- **Personal bias**—the use of information from personal diaries, newspapers and magazines may have the problem of personal bias as these writers are likely to exhibit less rigorousness and objectivity than one would expect in research reports.
- **Availability of data**—it is common for beginning researchers to assume that the required data will be available, but you cannot and should not make this assumption. Therefore, it is important to make sure that the required data are available before you proceed further with your study.
- **Format**—before deciding to use data from secondary sources it is equally important to ascertain that the data are available in the required format. For example, you might need to analyse age in the categories 23–33, 34–48 and so on, but in your source, age may be categorised differently, for example 21–24, 25–29 and so on.

SUMMARY

In this chapter you have learnt about the various methods of data collection. The methods used to collect information about a situation, phenomenon, issue or group of people can be classified as:

- primary sources;
- secondary sources.

Interviewing, observation and the use of questionnaires are the three main methods classified under primary sources. All other sources, where the information required is already available, such as government publications, reports and previous research, are called secondary sources.

The choice of a particular method of collecting data depends upon the purpose of collecting information, the type of information being collected, the resources available to you, your skills in the use of a particular method of data collection and the socioeconomic–demographic characteristics of your study population. Each method has its own advantages and disadvantages and each is appropriate for certain situations. The choice of a particular method for collecting data is important in itself for ensuring the quality of the information. No method of data collection will guarantee 100 per cent accurate information. The quality of your information is dependent upon several methodological, situational and respondent-related factors and your ability as a researcher lies in either controlling or minimising the effect of these factors in the process of data collection.

The use of open-ended and closed-ended questions is appropriate for different situations. Both of them have strengths and weaknesses. You should be aware of these so that you can use them appropriately.

The construction of a research instrument is the most important aspect of any research endeavour as it determines the nature and quality of the information. This is the input of your study and the output is entirely dependent upon it. A research instrument must be developed in the light of the objectives of your study. The method suggested in this chapter ensures that questions in an instrument have a direct link to your objectives. The wording of questions can have several problems and you should keep them in mind while formulating your questions.

CHAPTER
ten

Collecting data using attitudinal scales

Functions of attitudinal scales

If you want to find out the attitude of respondents towards an issue, you can ask either a closed-ended or an open-ended question. For example, let us say that you want to ascertain the attitude of students in a class towards their lecturer. To achieve this, further suppose that you have asked them to respond to the following question: '*What is your attitude towards your lecturer?*' If your question is open-ended, it invites each respondent to describe the attitude that s/he holds towards the lecturer. If you have framed a closed-ended question, with categories such as '*extremely positive*', '*positive*', '*uncertain*', '*negative*' and '*extremely negative*', this guides the respondents to select a category that best describes his/her attitude. This type of questioning, whether framed descriptively or in a categorical form, elicits an overall attitude towards the lecturer. While ascertaining the overall attitude may be sufficient in some situations, in many others, where the purpose of attitudinal questioning is to develop strategies for improvement of a service or intervention, or to formulate policy, eliciting attitudes on various aspects of the issue under study is required.

But as you know, every issue, including that of the attitude of students towards their lecturers, has many aspects. For example, the attitude of the members of a community towards the provision of a particular service comprised of their attitude towards the need for the service; its manner of delivery; its location; the physical facilities provided to users; the behaviour of the staff; the competence of the staff; the effectiveness and efficiency of the service; and so on. Similarly, other examples—such as the attitude of employees towards the management of their organisation; the attitude of employees towards occupational redeployment and redundancy; the attitude of nurses towards death and dying; the attitude of consumers towards a particular product; the attitude of students towards a lecturer; or the attitude of staff towards the strategic plan for their organisation—can be broken down in the same manner.

Respondents usually have different attitudes towards different aspects. Only when you ascertain the attitude of respondents to an issue by formulating a question for each aspect, using either open-ended or closed-ended questions, do you find out their attitude towards each aspect. The main limitation of this method is that it is difficult to draw any conclusion about the overall attitude of a respondent from the responses. For example, suppose you want to find out the attitude of students towards a lecturer. There are different aspects of teaching: the contents of lectures; the organisation of material; the lecturer's ability to communicate material; the presentation and style; knowledge of the subject; responsiveness; punctuality; and so on. Students may rate the lecturer differently on different aspects. That is, the lecturer might be considered extremely competent and knowledgeable in his/her subject but may not be considered a good communicator by a majority of students. Further, students may differ markedly in their opinion regarding any one aspect of a lecturer's teaching. Some might consider the lecturer to be a good communicator and others might not. The main problem is: how do we find out the 'overall' attitude of the students towards the lecturer? In other words, how do we combine the responses to different aspects of any issue to come up with one indicator that is reflective of an overall attitude? Attitudinal scales play an important role in overcoming this problem.

Attitudinal scales measure the intensity of respondents' attitudes towards the various aspects of a situation or issue and provide techniques to combine the attitudes towards different aspects into one overall indicator. This reduces the risk of an expression of opinion by respondents being influenced by their opinion on only one or two aspects of that situation or issue.

Difficulties in developing an attitudinal scale

In developing an attitudinal scale there are three problems:

1 Which aspects of a situation or issue should be included when seeking to measure an attitude? For instance, in the example cited above, what aspects of teaching should be included in a scale to find out the attitude of students towards their lecturer?
2 What procedure should be adopted for combining the different aspects to obtain an overall picture?
3 How can one ensure that a scale really is measuring what it is supposed to measure?

The first problem is extremely important as it largely determines the third problem: the extent to which the statements on different aspects are reflective of the main issue largely determines the validity of the scale. You can solve the third problem by ensuring that your statements on the various aspects have a logical link with the main issue under study—the greater the link, the higher the validity. The different types of attitudinal scale (Likert, Thurstone and Guttman) provide an answer to the second problem. They guide you as to the procedure for combining the attitudes towards various aspects of an issue, though the degree of difficulty in following the procedure for these scales varies from scale to scale. For example, the Guttman scale is much more difficult to construct than the Likert scale.

Types of attitudinal scale

There are three major types of attitudinal scale:

1 the summated rating scale, also known as the Likert scale;
2 the equal-appearing interval scale or differential scale, also known as the Thurstone scale;
3 the cumulative scale, also known as the Guttman scale.

The summated rating or Likert scale

The summated rating scale, more commonly known as the Likert scale, is the easiest to construct. This scale is based upon the assumption that each statement/item on the scale has equal 'attitudinal value', 'importance' or 'weight' in terms of reflecting an attitude towards the issue in question. This assumption is also the main limitation of this scale as statements on a scale seldom have equal attitudinal value. For instance, in the examples in Figures 10.1 and 10.2, 'knowledge of subject' is not as important in terms of the degree to which it reflects the attitude of the students towards the lecturer as 'has published a great deal' or 'some students like, some do not', but, on the Likert scale, each is treated as having the same 'weight'. A student may not bother much about whether a lecturer has published a great deal, but may be more concerned about 'knowledge of the subject', 'communicates well' and 'knows how to teach'.

Figure 10.1   An example of a categorical scale

The lecturer:	Strongly agree	Agree	Uncertain	Disagree	Strongly disagree
1 Knows the subject well	☐	☐	☐	☐	☐
2 Is unenthusiastic about teaching	☐	☐	☐	☐	☐
3 Shows concern for students	☐	☐	☐	☐	☐
4 Makes unreasonable demands	☐	☐	☐	☐	☐
5 Has *poor* communication skills	☐	☐	☐	☐	☐
6 Knows how to teach	☐	☐	☐	☐	☐
7 Can explain difficult concepts in simple terms	☐	☐	☐	☐	☐
8 Is hard to approach	☐	☐	☐	☐	☐
9 Is liked by some students and not by others	☐	☐	☐	☐	☐
10 Is difficult to get along with	☐	☐	☐	☐	☐

Figure 10.2   An example of a seven-point numerical scale

The lecturer:

1 Knows the subject well	7	6	5	4	3	2	1
2 Is enthusiastic about teaching	7	6	5	4	3	2	1
3 Shows no concern for students	7	6	5	4	3	2	1
4 Demands too much	7	6	5	4	3	2	1
5 Communicates well	7	6	5	4	3	2	1
6 Knows how to teach	7	6	5	4	3	2	1
7 Can explain difficult concepts in simple terms	7	6	5	4	3	2	1
8 Is seldom available to the students	7	6	5	4	3	2	1
9 Is liked by some students and not by others	7	6	5	4	3	2	1
10 Has published a great deal	7	6	5	4	3	2	1

It is important to remember that the Likert scale does not measure attitude *per se*. It does help to place different respondents in relation to each other in terms of the intensity of their attitude towards an issue: it shows the strength of one respondent's view in relation to that of another.

Considerations in constructing a Likert scale

In developing a Likert scale, there are a number of things to consider. First, decide whether the attitude to be measured is to be classified into one-, two- or three-directional categories (that is, whether you want to determine positive, negative and neutral positions in the study population) with respect to their attitude towards the issue under study. Next, consider whether you want to use categories or a numerical scale. This should depend upon whether you think that your study population can express itself better on a numerical scale or in categories. The decision about the number of points or the number of categories on a categorical scale depends upon how finely you want to measure the intensity of the attitude in question and on the capacity of the population to make fine distinctions. Figure 10.1 shows a five-point categorical scale that is three-directional and Figure 10.2 illustrates a seven-point numerical scale that is one-directional. Sometimes you can also develop statements reflecting opinion about an issue in varying degrees (Figure 10.3). In this instance a respondent is asked to select the statement which best describes the opinion.

Figure 10.3   An example of a scale with statements reflecting varying degrees of an attitude

1: The lecturer

(a) knows the subject _extremely well_
(b) knows the subject _well_
(c) has an _average_ knowledge of the subject
(d) _does not know_ the subject
(e) has an _extremely poor knowledge_ of the subject

The procedure for constructing a Likert scale

Figure 10.4 shows the procedure used in constructing a Likert scale.

Figure 10.4   The procedure for constructing a Likert scale

Procedure

Step 1   Assemble or construct statements that are reflective of the attitudes towards the main issue in question. Statements should be worded to reflect both positive and negative attitudes towards the issue; that is, they should be for, as well as against, the issue. (If your scale is one-directional, you need only positive statements.) Make sure that all the statements have a logical link with the main issue. You also need to decide whether you want respondents to answer in categories or on a numerical scale.

Step 2   Administer the statements to a small group of people.

(Continued on next page)

Step 3   Analyse the responses by assigning a weighting—a numerical value—to the responses. Numerical values are assigned differently to positive and negative statements. For a positive statement the response indicating the most favourable attitude is to be given the highest score. For example, on a five-category or five-point scale, 5 is assigned to the response that indicates the most favourable attitude and 1 to the response which indicates the least favourable attitude. By contrast, a person who agrees strongly with a negative statement indicates that s/he does not have a favourable attitude; hence, the scoring is reversed, i.e. 1 is assigned to the response where a respondent strongly agrees with a negative statement and 5 to the response where s/he strongly disagrees with it.

Step 4   Calculate each respondent's attitudinal score by adding numerical values assigned in step 3 to the responses s/he gave to each statement.

Step 5   Compare all respondents' scores for each item to identify non-discriminative items. Non-discriminative statements do not help you to distinguish respondents with respect to attitude as almost everyone responds to them in the same way. (Refer to a book specifically written for measuring attitudes.)

Step 6   Eliminate non-discriminative items.

Step 7   Construct a questionnaire/interview schedule comprising the selected statements/items.

Calculating attitudinal scores

Suppose you have developed a questionnaire/interview schedule to measure the attitudes of a class of students towards their lecturer. Also, assume you have decided to use a categorical scale using five categories (a smaller or larger number could also have been used).

In Figure 10.5, statement no. 1 is a positive statement; hence, if a respondent ticks 'strongly agree', s/he is assumed to have a more positive attitude on this item than a person who ticks 'agree'. The person who ticks 'agree' has a more positive attitude than a person who ticks 'uncertain', and so on. Therefore, a person who ticks 'strongly agree' has the most positive attitude compared with all of the others with different responses. Hence, the person is given the highest score, 5, as there are only five response categories. If there were four categories you could assign a score of 4. As a matter of fact, any score can be assigned as long as the intensity of the response pattern is reflected in the score and the highest score is assigned to the response with the highest intensity.

Figure 10.5   Scoring positive and negative statements

The lecturer:	SA	A	U	D	SD
1 Knows the subject well (+)	5	4	3	2	1
2 Is unenthusiastic about teaching (−)	1	2	3	4	5
3 Shows concern for students (+)	5	4	3	2	1
4 Makes unreasonable demands (−)	1	2	3	4	5
5 Has poor communication skill) (−)					
6 Knows how to teach (+)					
7 Can explain difficult concepts in simple terms (+)					
8 Is hard to approach (−)					
9 Is liked by some students and not by others (+/−)					
10 Is difficult to get along with (−)					

SA = strongly agree, A = agree, U = uncertain, D = disagree, SD = strongly disagree

Statement no. 2 is a negative statement. In this case a person who ticks 'strongly disagree' has the most positive attitude on this item; hence, the highest score is assigned, 5. On the other hand, a respondent who ticks 'strongly agree' has the least positive attitude on the item and therefore is assigned the lowest score, 1. The same scoring system is followed for the other statements.

Note statement no. 9. There will always be some people who like a lecturer and some who do not; hence this type of statement is neutral. There is no point in including it as most respondents are likely to answer in the same way.

To illustrate how to calculate an individual's attitudinal score, let us take the example of two respondents who have ticked the different statements marked in our example by # and @ (see Figure 10.6).

Figure 10.6   Calculating an attitudinal score

The lecturer:	SA	A	U	D	SD
1 Knows the subject well (+)	@				#
2 Is unenthusiastic about teaching (−)		#			@
3 Shows concern for students (+)			@		#
4 Makes unreasonable demands (−)		#			@
5 Communicates poorly (−)		#			@
6 Knows how to teach (+)			@	#	
7 Can explain difficult concepts in simple terms (+) @	#				
8 Is hard to approach (−)			@#		
9 Is liked by some students and not by others (+/−)				@#	
10 Is difficult to get along with (−)			#		@

SA = strongly agree, A = agree, U = uncertain, D = disagree, SD = strongly disagree

Let us work out their attitudinal score.

Statement no.	1	2	3	4	5	6	7	8	9	10

Respondent @ =   5 + 5 + 3 + 5 + 5 + 4 + 5 + 3 + 2 + 5 = 42
Respondent # =   1 + 2 + 1 + 2 + 2 + 2 + 4 + 3 + 2 + 3 = 20

The analysis shows that, overall, respondent @ has a 'more' positive attitude towards the lecturer than respondent #. You cannot say that the attitude of respondent @ is twice (42/20 = 2.10) as positive as that of respondent #. The attitudinal score only places respondents in a position relative to one another. Remember that the Likert scale does not measure the attitude *per se* but helps you to rate a group of individuals in descending or ascending order with respect to their attitudes towards the issues in question.

The equal-appearing interval or Thurstone scale

To overcome this problem with the Likert scale, the Thurstone scale calculates a 'weight' or 'attitudinal value' for each statement. The weight (equivalent to the median value) for each statement is calculated on the basis of rating assigned by a group of judges. Each statement with which respondents express agreement (or to which they respond in the affirmative) is given an attitudinal score equivalent to the 'attitudinal value' of the statement. The procedure for constructing the Thurstone scale is as follows:

Figure 10.7   The procedure for constructing the Thurstone scale

Step 1	Assemble or construct statements reflective of attitudes towards the issue in question.
Step 2	Select a panel of judges who are experts in the field of attitudes being explored.
Step 3	Send the statements to these judges with a request to rate each statement's importance in reflecting an attitude towards the issue being studied. Ask them to rate each statement on an 11-point scale.
Step 4	On the basis of the judges' ratings, calculate the median value of their ratings for each item.
Step 5	If the judges' ratings of any item are scattered over the scale, this indicates that, even among the experts, there is no agreement as to the degree to which that statement reflects an attitude towards the issue in question. Discard such statements.
Step 6	From the remaining statements select items that best reflect attitudes towards various aspects of the issue.
Step 7	Construct a questionnaire/interview schedule comprising the selected items.

The main advantage of this scale is that, as the importance of each statement is determined by judges, it reflects the absolute rather than relative attitudes of respondents. The scale is thus able to indicate the intensity of people's attitudes and any change in this intensity should the study be replicated. On the other hand, the scale is difficult to construct, and a major criticism is that judges and respondents may assess the importance of a particular statement differently and, therefore, the respondents' attitudes might not be reflected.

The cumulative or Guttman scale

The Guttman scale is one of the most difficult scales to construct and therefore is rarely used. This scale does not have much relevance for beginners in research and so is not discussed in this book. For information about this scale, consult books specifically dealing with attitudinal scales.

The relationship between attitudinal and measurement scales

Different attitudinal scales use different measurement scales. It is important to know which attitudinal scale belongs to which measurement scale as this will help you in the interpretation of respondents' scores. Table 10.1 shows attitudinal scales in relation to measurement scales.

Table 10.1 The relationship between attitudinal and measurement scales

Attitudinal scales	*Measurement scales*
Likert scale	Ordinal scale
Thurstone scale	Interval scale
Guttman scale	Ratio scale

SUMMARY

Attitudinal scales measure attitudes towards an issue. Their strength lies in their ability to combine attitudes towards different aspects of an issue and to provide an indicator that is reflective of an overall attitude. There are problems in developing an attitudinal scale. Which aspects should be included when measuring attitudes towards an issue? How should the responses given by a respondent to ascertain the overall attitude be combined? How does one ensure the scale developed really measures attitude towards the issue in question?

There are three types of scale that measure attitude: the Likert, Thurstone and Guttman scales. The Likert scale is the most common because it is easy to construct. The main assumption of the scale is that each statement is 'equally important'. The 'importance' of each item for the Thurstone scale is determined by a panel of judges. Arranging statements in a perfect cumulative order is the main problem in developing the Guttman scale.

CHAPTER
eleven

Establishing the validity and reliability of a research instrument

In the last two chapters we discussed various methods of data collection. The questions asked of your respondents are the basis of your findings and conclusions. These questions constitute the 'input' for your conclusions (the 'output'). This input passes through a series of steps—the selection of a sample, the collection of information, the processing of data, the application of statistical procedures and the writing of a report—and the manner in which all of these are done can affect the accuracy and quality of your conclusions. Hence, it is important for you to attempt to establish the quality of your results, for as a researcher you can also be asked by others to establish the validity of the procedures you adopted for finding answers to your research questions. As inaccuracies can be introduced into a study at any stage, the concept of validity can be applied to the research process as a whole or to any of its steps. We can talk about the validity of the study design used, the sampling strategy adopted, the conclusions drawn, the statistical procedures applied or the measurement procedures used. Broadly, there are two perspectives on validity:

1 Is the research investigation providing answers to the research questions for which it was undertaken?
2 If so, is it providing these answers using appropriate methods and procedures?

In this chapter we will discuss the concept of validity as applied to measurement procedures or the research tools used to collect the required information from your respondents.

The concept of validity

To examine the concept of validity, let us take a very simple example. Suppose you have designed a study to ascertain the health needs of a community. In doing so, you have developed an interview schedule. Further suppose that most of the questions in the interview schedule relate to the attitude of the study population towards the health services being provided to them. Note that your aim was to *find out about health needs* but the interview schedule is finding out what *attitudes respondents have to the health services*; thus, the instrument is not measuring what it was designed to measure. The author has come across many similar examples among students and less skilled researchers.

In terms of measurement procedures, therefore, validity is the ability of an instrument to measure what it is designed to measure. 'Validity is defined as the degree to which the researcher has measured what he has set out to measure' (Smith 1991: 106). According to Kerlinger, 'The commonest definition of validity is epitomised by the question: Are we measuring what we think we are measuring?' (1973: 457). Babbie writes, 'validity refers to the extent to which an empirical measure adequately reflects the real meaning of the concept under consideration' (1990: 133). These definitions raise some questions:

• Who decides that an instrument is measuring what it is supposed to measure?

- How can it be established that an instrument is measuring what it is supposed to measure?

Obviously the answer to the first question is the person who has designed the study and experts in the field. The second question is extremely important. On what basis do you (as a researcher) or an expert make this judgement? In the social sciences there appear to be two approaches to establishing the validity of a research instrument: logic and statistical evidence. Establishing validity through logic implies justification of each question in relation to the objectives of the study, whereas the statistical procedures provide hard evidence by way of calculating the coefficient of correlations between the questions and the outcome variables.

Establishing a logical link between the questions and the objectives is both simple and difficult. It is simple in the sense that you may find it easy to see a link for yourself, and difficult because your justification may lack the backing of experts and the statistical evidence to convince others. Establishing a logical link between questions and objectives is easier when the questions relate to tangible matters. For example, if you want to find out about age, income, height or weight, it is relatively easy to establish the validity of the questions, but to establish whether a set of questions is measuring, say, the effectiveness of a program, the attitudes of a group of people towards an issue, or the extent of satisfaction of a group of consumers with the service provided by an organisation is more difficult. When a less tangible concept is involved, such as effectiveness, attitude or satisfaction, you need to ask several questions in order to cover different aspects of the concept and demonstrate that the questions asked are actually measuring it. Validity in such situations becomes more difficult to establish.

It is important to remember that the concept of validity is pertinent only to a particular instrument and it is an ideal state that you as a researcher aim to achieve.

Types of validity

There are three types of validity:

1 Face and content validity;
2 Concurrent and predictive validity;
3 Construct validity.

Face and content validity

The judgement that an instrument is measuring what it is supposed to is primarily based upon the logical link between the questions and the objectives of the study. Hence, one of the main advantages of this type of validity is that it is easy to apply. Each question or item on the scale must have a logical link with an objective. Establishment of this link is called *face validity*. It is equally important that the items and questions cover the full range of the issue or attitude being measured. Assessment of the items of an instrument in this respect is called ***content validity***. In addition, the coverage of the issue or attitude should be balanced; that is, each aspect should have similar and adequate representation in the questions or items. Content validity is also judged on the basis of the extent to which statements or questions represent the issue they are supposed to measure, as judged by you as a researcher and experts in the field. Although it is easy to present logical arguments to establish validity, there are certain problems:

1 The judgement is based upon subjective logic; hence, no definite conclusions can be drawn. Different people may have different opinions about the face and content validity of an instrument.
2 The extent to which questions reflect the objectives of a study may differ. If the researcher substitutes one question for another, the magnitude of the link may be altered. Hence, the validity or its extent may vary with the questions selected for an instrument.

Concurrent and predictive validity

'In situations where a scale is developed as an indicator of some observable criterion, the scale's validity can be investigated by seeing how good an indicator it is' (Moser & Kalton 1989: 356). Suppose you develop an instrument to determine the suitability of applicants for a profession. The instrument's validity might be determined by comparing it with another assessment, for example by a psychologist, or with a future observation of how well these applicants have done in the job. If both assessments are similar, the instrument used to make the assessment is assumed to have higher validity. These types of comparisons establish two types of validity: ***predictive*** and ***concurrent***. Predictive validity is judged by the degree to which an instrument can forecast an outcome. Concurrent validity is judged by how well an instrument compares with a second assessment concurrently done. 'It is usually possible to express predictive validity in terms of the correlation coefficient between the predicted status and the criterion. Such a coefficient is called a validity coefficient' (Burns 1994: 220).

Construct validity

Construct validity is a more sophisticated technique for establishing the validity of an instrument. It is based upon statistical procedures. It is determined by ascertaining the contribution of each construct to the total variance observed in a phenomenon.

Suppose you are interested in carrying out a study to find the degree of job satisfaction among employees of an organisation. You consider status, the nature of the job and remuneration as the three most important factors indicative of job satisfaction, and construct questions to ascertain the degree to which people consider each important for job satisfaction. After the pre-test or data analysis you use statistical procedures to establish the contribution of each construct (status, the nature of the job and remuneration) to the total variance (job satisfaction). The contribution of these factors to the total variance is an indication of the degree of validity of the instrument. The greater the variance attributable to the constructs, the higher the validity of the instrument.

One of the main disadvantages of construct validity is that you need to know about the required statistical procedures.

The concept of reliability

We use the word 'reliability' very often in our lives. When we say that a person is reliable, what do we mean? We infer that s/he is dependable, consistent, predictable, stable and honest.

The concept of reliability in relation to a research instrument has a similar meaning: if a research tool is consistent and stable, and, hence, predictable and accurate, it is said to be reliable. The greater the degree of consistency and stability in an instrument, the greater is its reliability. Therefore, 'a scale or test is reliable to the extent that repeat measurements made by it under constant conditions will give the same result' (Moser & Kalton 1989: 353).

The concept of reliability can be looked at from two sides:

1 How reliable is an instrument?
2 How unreliable is it?

The first question focuses on the ability of an instrument to produce consistent measurements. When you collect the same set of information more than once, using the same instrument and get the same or similar results under the same or similar conditions, an instrument is considered to be reliable. The second question focuses on the degree of inconsistency in the measurements made by an instrument—that is, the extent of difference in the measurements when you collect the same set of information more than once, using the same instrument under the same or similar conditions. Hence, the degree of inconsistency in the different measurements is an indication of the extent of its inaccuracy. This 'error' is a reflection of an instrument's unreliability. Therefore, reliability is the degree of accuracy or precision in the measurements made by a research instrument. The lower the degree of 'error' in an instrument, the higher is the reliability.

Let us take an example. Suppose you develop a questionnaire to ascertain the prevalence of domestic violence in a community. You administer this questionnaire and find that domestic violence is prevalent in, say, 5 per cent of households. If you follow this with another survey using the same questionnaire on the same population under the same conditions, and discover that the prevalence of domestic violence is, say, 15 per cent, the questionnaire has not given a comparable result, which may mean it is unreliable. The less the difference between the two sets of results, the higher the reliability of the instrument.

Factors affecting the reliability of a research instrument

In the social sciences it is impossible to have a research tool which is 100 per cent accurate, not only because a research instrument cannot be so but also because it is impossible to control the factors affecting reliability. Some of these factors are:

- **The wording of questions**—a slight ambiguity in the wording of questions or statements can affect the reliability of a research instrument as respondents may interpret the questions differently at different times, resulting in different responses.
- **The physical setting**—in the case of an instrument being used in an interview, any change in the physical setting at the time of the repeat interview may affect the responses given by a respondent, which may affect reliability.
- **The respondent's mood**—a change in a respondent's mood when responding to questions or writing answers in a questionnaire can change and may affect the reliability of that instrument.
- **The nature of interaction**—in an interview situation, the interaction between the interviewer and the interviewee can affect responses significantly. During the repeat interview the responses given may be different due to a change in interaction, which could affect reliability.
- **The regression effect of an instrument**—when a research instrument is used to measure attitudes towards an issue, some respondents, after having expressed their opinion, may feel that they have been either too negative or too positive towards the issue. The second time they may express their opinion differently, thereby affecting reliability.

Methods of determining the reliability of an instrument

There are a number of ways of determining the reliability of an instrument. The various procedures can be classified into two groups:

1 external consistency procedures;
2 internal consistency procedures.

External consistency procedures

External consistency procedures compare findings from two independent processes of data collection with each other as a means of verifying the reliability of the measure. The two methods are as follows.

- **Test/re-test**—this is a commonly used method for establishing the reliability of a research tool. In the test/re-test (repeatability test) an instrument is administered once, and then again, under the same or similar conditions. The ratio between the test and re-test scores (or any other finding, for example the prevalence of domestic violence, a disease or incidence of an illness) is an indication of the reliability of the instrument—the greater the value of the ratio, the higher the reliability of the instrument. As an equation:

$$(\text{Test score}) / (\text{Re-test}) = 1$$
or
$$(\text{Test score}) - (\text{Re-test}) = 0$$

A ratio of 1 shows 100 per cent reliability (no difference between test and re-test) and any deviation from it indicates less reliability—the less the value of this ratio, the less the reliability of the instrument. Expressed in another way, zero difference between the test and re-test scores is an indication of 100 per cent reliability. The greater the difference between the test scores/findings, the greater the unreliability of the instrument.

The main advantage of the test/re-test procedure is that it permits the instrument to be compared with itself, thus avoiding the sort of problems that could arise with the use of another instrument.

The main disadvantage is that a respondent may recall the responses that s/he gave in the first round, which in turn may affect the reliability of the instrument. Where an instrument is reactive in nature (when an instrument educates the respondent with respect to what the researcher is trying to find out) this method will not provide an accurate assessment of its reliability. One of the ways of overcoming this problem is to increase the time span between the two tests, but this may affect reliability for other reasons, such as the maturation of respondents and the impossibility of achieving conditions similar to those under which the questionnaire was first administered.

- **Parallel forms of the same test**—in this procedure you construct two instruments that are intended to measure the same phenomenon. The two instruments are then administered to two similar populations. The results obtained from one test are compared with those obtained from the other. If they are similar, it is assumed that the instruments are reliable.

  The main advantage of this procedure is that it does not suffer from the problem of recall found in the test/re-test procedure. Also, a time lapse between the two tests is not required. A disadvantage is that you need to construct two instruments instead of one. Moreover, it is extremely difficult to construct two instruments that are comparable in their measurement of a phenomenon. It is equally difficult to achieve comparability in the two population groups and in the two conditions under which the tests are administered.

Internal consistency procedures

The idea behind internal consistency procedures is that items measuring the same phenomenon should produce similar results. The following method is commonly used for measuring the reliability of an instrument.

- **The split-half technique**—this technique is designed to correlate half of the items with the other half and is appropriate for instruments that are designed to measure attitudes towards an issue or phenomenon. The questions or statements are divided in half in such a way that any two questions or statements intended to measure the same aspect fall into different halves. The scores obtained by administering the two halves are correlated. Reliability is calculated by using the product moment correlation between scores obtained from the two halves. Because the product moment correlation is calculated on the basis of only half the instrument, it needs to be corrected to assess reliability for the whole. This is known as *stepped-up reliability*. The stepped-up reliability for the whole instrument is calculated by a formula called the Spearman-Brown formula.

SUMMARY

The concept of validity refers to quality and can be applied to any aspect of the research process. With respect to measurement procedures it relates to whether a research instrument is measuring what it set out to measure. There are two approaches used to establish the validity of an instrument: the establishment of a logical link between the objectives of a study and the questions used in an instrument, and the use of statistical analysis to demonstrate this link. There are three types of validity: face and content, concurrent and predictive, and construct validity.

The reliability of an instrument refers to its ability to produce consistent measurements each time. When we administer an instrument under the same or similar conditions to the same population and obtain similar results, we say that the instrument is 'reliable'—the more similar the results, the greater the reliability. You can look at reliability from two sides: reliability (the extent of accuracy) and unreliability (the extent of inaccuracy). Ambiguity in the wording of questions, a change in the physical setting for data collection, a respondent's mood when providing information, the nature of the interaction between interviewer and interviewee, and the regressive effect of an instrument are factors that can affect the reliability of a research instrument.

There are external and internal consistency procedures for determining reliability. Test/re-test and parallel forms of the same test are the two procedures that determine the external reliability of a research instrument, whereas the split-half technique is classified under internal consistency procedures.

STEP IV

SELECTING
A SAMPLE

CHAPTER 12
Sampling

CHAPTER
twelve

Sampling

The concept of sampling

Let us take a very simple example to explain the concept of sampling. Suppose you want to estimate the average age of the students in your class. There are two ways of doing this. The first method is to contact all students in the class, find out their ages, add them up and then divide this by the number of students (the definition of an average). The second method is to select a few students from the class, ask them their ages, add them up and then divide by the number of students you have asked. From this you can make an **estimate** of the average age of the class. Take another example: suppose you want to find out the average income of families living in a city. You could follow the procedures described above, but imagine the amount of effort and resources required to go to each family in the city to find out their income! You could follow the second method by selecting a few families to become the basis of your inquiry and then, from what you have found out from the few families, make an *estimate* of the average income of families in the city. A further example would be the outcome of an election: the result is decided after voting on election day, but predictions about the outcome are usually made on the basis of opinion polls. These polls are based upon a very small group of people who are questioned about their voting preferences. On the basis of these results, a *prediction* is made about the outcome.

Sampling, therefore, is the process of selecting a few (a sample) from a bigger group (the sampling population) to become the basis for estimating or predicting the prevalence of an unknown piece of information, situation or outcome regarding the bigger group. A sample is a subgroup of the population you are interested in. See Figure 12.1.

Figure 12.1   The concept of sampling

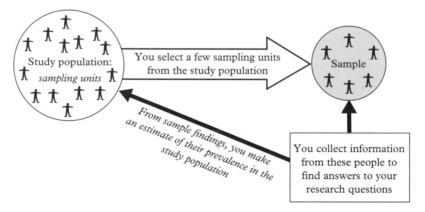

This process of selecting a sample from the total population has advantages and disadvantages. The advantages are that it saves time as well as financial and human resources. However, the disadvantage is that you *do not find out the information* about the population's characteristics of interest to you but *only estimate* or *predict* them. Hence, the possibility of an error in your estimation exists.

Sampling is thus a trade-off between certain gains and losses. While on the one hand you save time and resources, on the other hand you may compromise the level of accuracy in your findings. Through sampling you only make an estimate about the actual situation prevalent in the total population from which the sample is drawn. If you ascertain a piece of information from the total sampling population, and if your method of inquiry is correct, your findings should be reasonably accurate. However, if you select a sample and use this as the basis from which to estimate the situation in the total population, an error is possible. Tolerance of this possibility of error is an important consideration in selecting a sample.

The concept of sampling in qualitative research

In qualitative research the issue of sampling has little significance as the main aim of most qualitative inquiries is either to explore or describe the diversity in a situation, phenomenon or issue. Qualitative research does not make an attempt to either quantify or determine the extent of this diversity. You can select even one individual as your sample and describe whatever the aim of your inquiry is. A study based upon the information obtained from one individual, or undertaken to describe one event or situation is perfectly valid. In qualitative research, to explore the diversity, you need to reach what is known as *saturation point* in terms of your findings; for example, you go on interviewing or collecting information as long as you keep discovering new information. When you find that you are not obtaining any new data or the new information is negligible, you are assumed to have reached saturation point. Some researchers prefer to select a sample using non-probability designs and to collect data till they have reached saturation point. Keep in mind that saturation point is a subjective judgement which you, as a researcher, decide.

Sampling terminology

Let us, again, consider the examples used above. Our main aims are to find out the average age of the class, the average income of the families living in the city, and the likely election outcome for a particular state or country. Let us assume that we adopt the second method—that is, we select a few students, families or electorates to achieve these aims. In this process there are a number of aspects:

- The class, families living the city or electorates from which you select a few students, families, electors to question in order to find answers to your research questions are called the *population* or *study population*, and are usually denoted by the letter (N).
- The small group of students, families or electors from whom you collect the required information to estimate the average age of the class, average income or the election outcome is called the *sample*.
- The number of students, families or electors from whom you obtain the required information is called the *sample size* and is usually denoted by the letter (n).

- The way you select students, families or electors is called the ***sampling design*** or ***strategy***.
- Each student, family or elector that becomes the basis for selecting your sample is called the ***sampling unit*** or ***sampling element***.
- A list identifying each student, family or elector in the study population is called the ***sampling frame***. If all elements in a sampling population cannot be individually identified, you cannot have a sampling frame for that study population.
- Your findings based on the information obtained from your respondents (sample) are called ***sample statistics.*** Examples of this information are the average age of students (calculated from the information obtained from those students who responded to your question on age); the average income of a family (calculated from the relevant information obtained from those families who participated in your study); and the expected outcome (predicted on the basis of the information obtained from those who expressed their intention in voting). Your sample statistics become the basis of estimating the prevalence of the above characteristics in the study population.
- Your main aim is to find answers to your research questions in the study population, not in the sample you collected information from. In the examples we have been talking about, our aims are to find out the average age of students in a *class*, the average income of *families living in a city* and the expected *outcome of the election* respectively. From sample statistics we make an estimate of the answers to our research questions in the study population. The estimates arrived at from sample statistics are called ***population parameters*** or the ***population mean***.
- As mentioned earlier, in qualitative research, when you reach a stage where no new information is coming from your respondents, this is called ***saturation point***.

Principles of sampling

The theory of sampling is guided by three principles. To effectively explain these, we will take an extremely simple example. Suppose there are four individuals: A, B, C and D. A is 18 years of age, B is 20, C is 23 and D is 25. As you know their ages, you can *find out* (calculate) their average age by simply adding 18 + 20 + 23 + 25 = 86 and dividing by 4. This gives the average age of A, B, C and D as 21.5 years.

Now let us suppose that you want to select a sample of two individuals to make an ***estimate*** of the average age of the four individuals. If you adopt the theory of probability, we can have six possible combinations of two: A and B; A and C; A and D; B and C; B and D; and C and D. Let us take each of these pairs to calculate the average age of the sample:

1 A + B = 18 + 20 = 38/2 = 19.0 years;
2 A + C = 18 + 23 = 41/2 = 20.5 years;
3 A + D = 18 + 25 = 43/2 = 21.5 years;
4 B + C = 20 + 23 = 43/2 = 21.5 years;

5 B + D = 20 + 25 = 45/2 = 22.5 years;
6 C + D = 23 + 25 = 48/2 = 24.0 years.

Notice that in most cases the average age calculated on the basis of these samples of two (sample statistics) is different. Now compare these sample statistics with the average of all four individuals—the population mean (population parameter) of 21.5 years. Out of a total of six possible sample combinations, only in the case of two is there no difference between the sample statistics and the population mean. Where there is a difference, this is attributed to the sample and is known as ***sampling error***. Again, the size of the sampling error varies markedly. Let us consider the difference in the sample statistics and the population mean for each of the six samples (Table 12.1).

Table 12.1 The difference between sample statistics and the population mean

Sample	Sample average (Sample statistics) (1)	Population mean (Population parameter) (2)	Difference between (1) and (2)
1	19.0	21.5	−2.5
2	20.5	21.5	−1.5
3	21.5	21.5	0.0
4	21.5	21.5	0.0
5	22.5	21.5	+1.0
6	24.0	21.5	+2.5

This analysis suggests a very important principle of sampling:

Principle one—*In a majority of cases of sampling there will be a difference between the sample statistics and the true population mean, which is attributable to the selection of the units in the sample.*

To understand the second principle, let us continue with the above example, but instead of a sample of two individuals take a sample of three. There are four possible combinations of three that can be drawn.

1 A + B + C = 18 + 20 + 23 = 61/3 = 20.33 years;
2 A + B + D = 18 + 20 + 25 = 63/3 = 21.00 years;
3 A + C + D = 18 + 23 + 25 = 66/3 = 22.00 years;
4 B + C + D = 20 + 23 + 25 = 68/3 = 22.67 years.

Now, let us compare the difference between the sample statistics and the population mean (Table 12.2).

Table 12.2 The difference between a sample and a population average

Sample	Sample average (1)	Population average (2)	Difference between (1) and (2)
1	20.33	21.5	−1.17
2	21.00	21.5	−0.5
3	22.00	21.5	+0.5
4	22.67	21.5	+1.17

Compare the difference between the differences calculated in Table 12.1 and Table 12.2. In Table 12.1 the difference between the sample statistics and the population mean lies between –2.5 and +2.5 years, whereas in the second, it is between –1.17 and +1.17 years. The gap between the sample statistics and the population mean is reduced in Table 12.2. This reduction is attributed to the increase in the sample size. This, therefore, leads to the second principle:

> **Principle two**—*The greater the sample size, the more accurate will be the estimate of the true population mean.*

The third principle of sampling is particularly important as a number of sampling strategies, such as stratified and cluster sampling, are based on it. To understand this principle, let us continue with the same example but use slightly different data. Suppose the ages of four individuals are markedly different: A = 18, B = 26, C = 32 and D = 40. In other words, we are visualising a population where the individuals with respect to age—the variable we are interested in—are markedly different.

Let us follow the same procedure, selecting samples of two individuals at a time and then three. If we work through the same procedures (described above) we will find that the difference in the average age in the case of samples of two ranges between –7.00 and + 7.00 years and in the case of the sample of three ranges between –3.67 and +3.67. In both cases the range of the difference is greater than previously calculated. This is attributable to the greater difference in the ages of the four individuals—the sampling population. In other words, the sampling population is more heterogeneous in regard to age.

> **Principle three**—*The greater the difference in the variable under study in a population for a given sample size, the greater will be the difference between the sample statistics and the true population mean.*

These principles are crucial to keep in mind when you are determining the sample size needed for a particular level of accuracy, and in selecting the sampling strategy best suited to your study.

Factors affecting the inferences drawn from a sample

The above principles suggest that two factors may influence the degree of certainty about the inferences drawn from a sample:

1 **The size of the sample**—findings based upon larger samples have more certainty than those based on smaller ones. As a rule, *the larger the sample size, the more accurate will be the findings.*
2 **The extent of variation in the sampling population**—the greater the variation in the study population with respect to the characteristics under study for a given sample size, the greater will be the uncertainty. (In technical terms, the greater the standard deviation, the higher will be the standard error for a given sample size in your estimates.) If a population is homogeneous with respect to the characteristics under

study, a small sample can provide a reasonably good estimate, but if it is heterogeneous, you need to select a larger sample to obtain the same level of accuracy. Of course, if all the elements in a population are identical, then the selection of even one will provide an absolutely accurate estimate. As a rule, *the higher the variation with respect to the characteristics under study in the study population, the greater will be the uncertainty for a given sample size.*

Aims in selecting a sample

The aims in selecting a sample are to:

- achieve maximum precision in your estimates within a given sample size;
- avoid bias in the selection of your sample.

Bias in the selection of a sample can occur if:

- sampling is done by a non-random method—that is, if the selection is consciously or unconsciously influenced by human choice;
- the sampling frame—list, index or other population records—which serves as the basis of selection, does not cover the sampling population accurately and completely;
- a section of a sampling population is impossible to find or refuses to co-operate.

Types of sampling

The various sampling strategies can be categorised as follows (Figure 12.2):

- random/probability sampling designs;
- non-random/non-probability sampling designs;
- 'mixed' sampling designs.

To understand these designs, we will discuss each individually.

Random/probability sampling designs

For a sampling design to be called a random or probability sample, it is imperative that each element in the population has an *equal* and *independent* chance of selection in the sample. Equal implies that the probability of selection of each element in the population is the same; that is, the choice of an element in the sample is not influenced by other considerations such as personal preference. The concept of independence means that the choice of one element is not dependent upon the choice of another element in the sampling; that is, the selection or rejection of one element does not affect the inclusion or exclusion of another. To explain these concepts let us return to our example of the class.

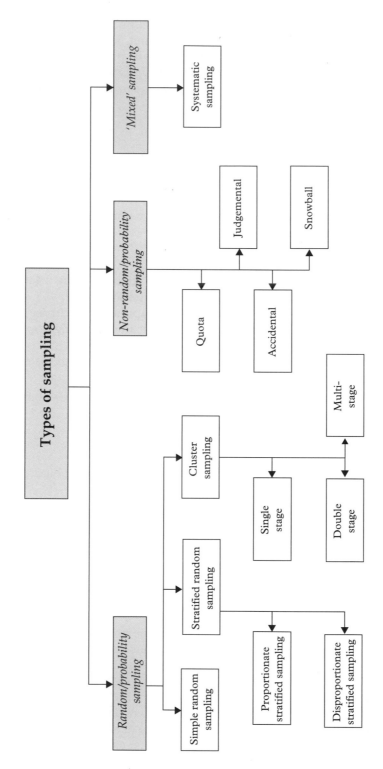

Figure 12.2   Types of sampling

Suppose there are 80 students in the class. Assume 20 of these refuse to participate in your study. You want the entire population of 80 students in your study but as 20 refuse to participate, you can only use a sample of 60 students. The 20 students who refuse to participate could have strong feelings about the issues you wish to explore, but your findings will not reflect their opinions. Their exclusion from your study means that each of the 80 students does not have an equal chance of selection. Therefore, your sample does not represent the total class.

The same could apply to a community. In a community, in addition to the refusal to participate, let us assume that you are unable to identify all the residents living in the community. If a significant proportion of people cannot be included in the sampling population because they either cannot be identified or refuse to participate, then any sample drawn will not give each element in the sampling population an equal chance of being selected in the sample. Hence, the sample will not be representative of the total community.

To understand the concept of an *independent chance of selection*, let us assume that there are five students in the class who are extremely close friends. If one of them is selected but refuses to participate because the other four are not chosen, and you are therefore forced to select either the five or none, then your sample will not be considered an independent sample since the selection of one is dependent upon the selection of others. The same could happen in the community where a small group says that either all of them or none of them will participate in the study. In these situations where you are forced either to include or to exclude a part of the sampling population, the sample is not considered to be independent, and hence is not representative of the sampling population.

A sample can only be considered a random/probability sample and therefore representative of the population under study if both these conditions are met. If not, bias can be introduced into the study.

There are two main advantages of random/probability samples:

- As they represent the total sampling population, the inferences drawn from such samples can be generalised to the total sampling population.
- Some statistical tests based upon the theory of probability can be applied only to data collected from random samples. Some of these tests are important for establishing conclusive correlations.

Methods of drawing a random sample

Of the methods that you can adopt to select a random sample the three most common are:

- **the fishbowl draw**—if your total population is small, an easy procedure is to number each element using separate slips of paper for each element, put all the slips into a box, and then pick them out one by one without looking, until the number of slips selected equals the sample size you decided upon. This method is used in some lotteries.
- **computer program**—there are a number of programs that can help you to select a random sample.

Table 12.3 Selecting a sample using a table for random numbers

	1	2	3	4	5	6	7	8	9	10
1	48461	14952	72619	73689	52059	37086	60050	86192	67049	64739
2	76534	38149	49692	31366	52093	15422	20498	33901	10319	43397
3	70437	25861	38504	14752	23757	29660	67844	78815	23758	86814
4	59584	03370	42806	11393	71722	93804	09095	07856	55589	46820
5	04285	58554	16085	51555	27501	73883	33427	33343	45507	50063
6	77340	10412	69189	85171	29802	44785	86368	02583	96483	76553
7	59183	62687	91778	80354	23512	97219	65921	02035	59487	91403
8	91800	04281	39979	03927	82564	28777	59049	97532	54540	79472
9	12066	24817	81099	48940	69554	55925	48379	12866	41232	21580
10	69907	91751	53512	23748	65906	91385	84983	27915	48491	91068
11	80467	04873	54053	25955	48518	13815	37707	68687	15570	08890
12	78057	67835	28302	45048	56761	97725	58438	91529	24645	18544
13	05648	39387	78191	88415	60269	94880	58812	42931	71898	61534
14	22304	39246	01350	99451	61862	78688	30339	60222	74052	25740
15	61346	50269	67005	40442	33100	16742	61640	21046	31909	72641
16	56793	37696	27965	30459	91011	51426	31006	77468	61029	57108
17	56411	48609	36698	42453	85061	43769	39948	87031	30767	13953
18	62098	12825	81744	28882	27369	88185	65846	92545	09065	22653
19	68775	06261	54265	16203	23340	84750	16317	88686	86842	00879
20	52679	19599	13687	74872	89181	01939	18447	10787	76246	80072
21	84096	87152	20719	25215	04349	54434	72344	93008	83282	31670
22	83964	55937	21417	49944	38356	98404	14850	17994	17161	98981
23	31191	75131	72386	11689	95727	05414	88727	45583	22568	77700
24	30545	68523	29850	67833	05622	89975	79042	27142	99257	32349
25	52573	91001	52315	26430	54175	30122	31796	98842	37600	26025
26	16586	81842	01076	99414	31574	94719	34656	80018	86988	79234
27	81841	88481	61191	25013	30272	23388	22463	65774	10029	58376
28	43563	66829	72838	08074	57080	15446	11034	98143	74989	26885
29	19945	84193	57581	77252	85604	45412	43556	27518	90572	00563
30	79374	23796	16919	99691	80276	32818	62953	78831	54395	30705
31	48503	26615	43980	09810	38289	66679	73799	48418	12647	40044
32	32049	65541	37937	41105	70106	89706	40829	40789	59547	00783
33	18547	71562	95493	34112	76895	46766	96395	31718	48302	45893
34	03180	96742	61486	43305	84183	99605	67803	13491	09243	29557
35	94822	24738	67749	83748	59799	25210	31093	62925	72061	69991
36	04330	60599	85828	19152	68499	27977	35611	96240	62747	89529
37	43770	81537	59527	95674	76692	86420	69930	10020	72881	12532
38	56908	77192	50623	41215	14311	42834	80651	93750	59957	31211
39	32787	07189	80539	75927	75475	73965	11796	72140	48944	74156
40	52441	78392	11733	57703	29133	71164	55355	31006	25526	55790
41	22377	54723	18227	28449	04570	18882	00023	67101	06895	08915
42	18376	73460	88841	39602	34049	20589	05701	08249	74213	25220
43	53201	28610	87957	21497	64729	64983	71551	99016	87903	63875
44	34919	78801	59710	27396	02593	05665	11964	44134	00273	76358
45	33617	92159	21971	16901	57383	34262	41744	60891	57624	06962
46	70010	40964	98780	72418	52571	18415	64362	90637	38034	04909
47	19282	68447	35665	31530	59838	49181	21914	65742	89815	39231
48	91429	73328	13266	54898	68795	40948	80808	63887	89939	47938
49	97637	78393	33021	05867	86520	45363	43066	00988	64040	09803
50	95150	07625	05255	83254	93943	52325	93230	62668	79529	66964

Source: *Statistical Tables*, 3e, by F. James Rohlf and Robert R. Sokal. Copyright © 1969, 1981, 1994 by W.H. Freeman and Company. Used with permission.

- **a table of random numbers**—most books on research methodology and statistics include a table of randomly generated numbers in their appendices (see, for example, Table 12.3). You can select your sample using these tables according to the procedure described in Figure 12.3. The procedure for selecting a sample using a table of random numbers is as follows:

Figure 12.3   The procedure for using a table of random numbers

Step 1   Identify the total number of elements in the study population, for example 50, 100, 430, 795 or 1265. The total number of elements in a study population may run up to four or more digits (if your total sampling population is 9 or less, it is one digit; if it is 99 or less, it is two digits; ...).
Step 2   Number each element starting from 1.
Step 3   If the table for random numbers is on more than one page, choose the starting page by a random procedure. Again, select a column or row that will be your starting point with a random procedure and proceed from there in a predetermined direction.
Step 4   Corresponding to the number of digits to which the total population runs, select the same number, randomly, of columns or rows of digits from the table.
Step 5   Decide on your sample size.
Step 6   Select the required number of elements for your sample from the table. If you happen to select the same number twice, discard it and go to the next. This can happen as the table for random numbers is generated by sampling with replacement.

Let us take an example to illustrate the use of Table 12.3 for random numbers. Let us assume that your sampling population consists of 256 individuals. Number each individual, from 1 to 256. Randomly select the starting page, set of column (1 to 10) or row from the table and then identify three columns or rows of numbers.

Suppose you identify the ninth column of numbers and the last three digits of this column (underlined). Assume that you are selecting 10 per cent of the total population as your sample (25 elements). Let us go through the numbers underlined in the ninth set of columns. The first number is 049 which is below 256 (total population); hence, the 49th element becomes a part of your sample. The second number, 319, is more than the total elements in your population (256); hence, you cannot accept the 319th element in the sample. The same applies to the next element, 758, and indeed the next five elements, 589, 507, 483, 487 and 540. After 540 is 232, and as this number is within the sampling frame, it can be accepted as a part of the sample. Similarly, if you follow down the same three digits in the same column, you select 052, 029, 065, 246 and 161, before you come to the element 029 again. As the 27th element has already been selected, go to the next number, and so on until 25 elements have been chosen. Once you have reached the end of a column, you can either move to the next set of columns or randomly select another one in order to continue the process of selection. For example the 25 elements shown in Table 12.4 are selected from the ninth, tenth and second columns of Table 12.3:

Table 12.4 Selected elements using the table of random numbers

Column Table 12.3	Elements selected				
19	49	232	52	29	65
	246	161	243	61	213
	34	40			
10	63	68	108	72	25
	234	44	211	156	220
	231				
2	149	246			

Different systems of drawing a random sample

There are two ways of selecting a random sample:

- sampling without replacement;
- sampling with replacement.

Suppose you want to select a sample of 20 students out of a total of 80. The first student is selected out of the total class, and so the probability of selection for the first student is 1/80. When you select the second student there are only 79 left in the class and the probability of selection for the second student is not 1/80 but 1/79. The probability of selecting the next student is 1/78. By the time you select the 20th student, the probability of his or her selection is 1/61. This type of sampling is called *sampling without replacement*. But this is contrary to our basic definition of randomisation; that is, each element has an equal and independent chance of selection. In the second system, called *sampling with replacement*, the selected element is replaced in the sampling population and if it is selected again, it is discarded and the next one is selected. If the sampling population is fairly large, the probability of selecting the same element twice is fairly remote.

Specific random/probability sampling designs

There are three commonly used types of random sampling design.

- **Simple random sampling (SRS)**—the most commonly used method of selecting a probability sample. In line with the definition of randomisation, whereby each element in the population is given an equal and independent chance of selection, a simple random sample is selected by the procedure presented in Figure 12.4.

Figure 12.4 The procedure for selecting a simple random sample

Step 1 Identify by a number all elements or sampling units in the population.
Step 2 Decide on the sample size (n).
Step 3 Select (n) using either the fishbowl draw, the table of random numbers or a computer program.

To illustrate, let us again take our example of the class. There are 80 students in the class, and so the first step is to identify each student by a number from 1 to 80. Suppose you decide to select a sample of 20 using the simple random sampling technique. Use either the fishbowl draw, the table for random numbers or a computer program to select the 20 students. These 20 students become the basis of your inquiry.

- **Stratified random sampling**—as discussed, the accuracy of your estimate largely depends on the extent of variability or heterogeneity of the study population with respect to the characteristics that have a strong correlation with what you are trying to ascertain (Principle three). It follows, therefore, that if the heterogeneity in the population can be reduced by some means for a given sample size you can achieve greater accuracy in your estimate. Stratified random sampling is based upon this logic.

   In stratified random sampling the researcher attempts to stratify the population in such a way that the population within a stratum is homogeneous with respect to the characteristic on the basis of which it is being stratified. It is important that the characteristics chosen as the basis of stratification are clearly identifiable in the study population. For example, it is much easier to stratify a population on the basis of gender than on the basis of age, income or attitude. It is also important for the characteristic that becomes the basis of stratification to be related to the main variable that you are exploring. Once the sampling population has been separated into non-overlapping groups you select the required number of elements from each stratum, using the simple random sampling technique. There are two types of stratified sampling: *proportionate* and *disproportionate stratified sampling*. With proportionate stratified sampling, the number of elements from each stratum in relation to its proportion in the total population is selected, whereas in disproportionate stratified sampling, consideration is not given to the size of the stratum. The procedure for selecting a stratified sample is schematically presented in Figure 12.5.

- **Cluster sampling**—simple random and stratified sampling techniques are based on a researcher's ability to identify each element in a population. It is easy to do this if the total sampling population is small, but if the population is large, as in the case of a city, state or country, it becomes difficult and expensive to identify each sampling unit. In such cases the use of cluster sampling is more appropriate.

   Cluster sampling is based on the ability of the researcher to divide the sampling population into groups, called clusters, and then to select

Figure 12.5   The procedure for selecting a stratified sample

Step 1	Identify all elements or sampling units in the sampling population.
Step 2	Decide upon the different strata (k) into which you want to stratify the population.
Step 3	Place each element into the appropriate stratum.
Step 4	Number every element in each stratum separately.
Step 5	Decide the total sample size (n).
Step 6	Decide whether you want to select proportionate or disproportionate stratified sampling and follow the steps below.

Disproportionate stratified sampling	**Proportionate stratified sampling**
Step 7 Determine the number of elements to be selected from each stratum $$= \frac{\text{sample size } (n)}{\text{no. of strata } (k)}$$	**Step 7** Determine the proportion of each stratum in the study population (p) $$= \frac{\text{elements (\#) in each stratum}}{\text{total population size}}$$
Step 8 Select the required number of elements from each stratum with SRS technique	**Step 8** Determine the number of elements to be selected from each stratum $= (\text{sample size}) \times (p)$
	Step 9 Select the required number of elements from each stratum with SRS technique
As this method does not take the size of the stratum into consideration in the selection of the sample, it is called disproportionate stratified sampling.	*As the sample selected is in proportion to the size of each stratum in the population, this method is call proportionate stratified sampling.*

elements within each cluster, using the SRS technique. Clusters can be formed on the basis of geographical proximity or a common characteristic that has a correlation with the main variable of the study (as in stratified sampling). Depending on the level of clustering, sometimes sampling may be done at different levels. These levels constitute the different stages (single, double or multi) of clustering, which will be explained later.

Imagine you want to investigate the attitude of post-secondary students in Australia towards problems in higher education in the country. Higher education institutions are in every state and territory of Australia. In addition, there are different types of institutions, for example universities, universities of technology, colleges of advanced education and technical and further education (TAFE) colleges (Figure 12.6). Within each institution various courses are offered both at undergraduate and postgraduate levels. Each academic course could take three to four years. You can imagine the magnitude of the task. In such situations cluster sampling is extremely useful in selecting a random sample.

The first level of cluster sampling could be at the state or territory level. Clusters could be grouped according to similar characteristics that ensure their comparability in terms of student population. If this is not easy, you may decide to select all the states and territories and then select a sample at the institutional level. For example, with a simple random technique, one institution from each category within each state could be selected (one university, one university of technology, one college of advanced education and one TAFE college). This is based upon the assumption that institutions within a category are fairly similar with regards to student profile. Then, within an institution on a random basis, one or more academic programs could be selected, depending on resources. Within each study program selected, students studying in a particular year could be selected. Further selection of a proportion of students could then occur. The process of selecting a sample in this manner is called ***multi-stage cluster sampling***.

Figure 12.6   The concept of cluster sampling

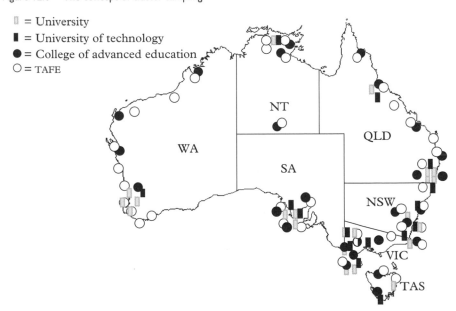

▯ = University
▮ = University of technology
● = College of advanced education
○ = TAFE

Non-random/non-probability sampling designs

Non-probability sampling designs do not follow the theory of probability in the choice of elements from the sampling population. Non-probability sampling designs are used when the number of elements in a population is either unknown or cannot be individually identified. In such situations the selection of elements is dependent upon other considerations. There are four non-random designs, each based on a different consideration, which are commonly used in qualitative and quantitative research:

- quota sampling;
- accidental sampling;
- judgemental or purpose sampling;
- snowball sampling.

Quota sampling

The main consideration directing quota sampling is the researcher's ease of access to the sample population. In addition to convenience, s/he is guided by some visible characteristic, such as gender or race, of the study population that is of interest to him/her. The sample is selected from a location convenient to the researcher, and whenever a person with this visible relevant characteristic is seen that person is asked to participate in the study. The process continues until the researcher has been able to contact the required number of respondents (quota).

Let us suppose that you want to select a sample of 20 male students in order to find out the average age of the male students in your class. You decide to stand at the entrance to the classroom, as this is convenient, and whenever a male student enters the classroom, you ask his age. This process continues until you have asked 20 students their age. Alternatively, you might want to find out about the attitudes of Aboriginal and Torres Strait Islander students towards the facilities provided to them in your university. Stand at a convenient location and whenever you see such a student, collect the required information through whatever method you have adopted for the study.

There are advantages and disadvantages with this design. The advantages are: it is the least expensive way of selecting a sample; you do not need any information, such as a sampling frame, the total number of elements, their location, or other information about the sampling population; and it guarantees the inclusion of the type of people you need. The disadvantages are: as the resulting sample is not a probability one, the findings cannot be generalised to the total sampling population; and the most accessible individuals might have characteristics that are unique to them and hence might not be truly representative of the total sampling population.

Accidental sampling

Accidental sampling is also based upon convenience in accessing the sampling population. Whereas quota sampling attempts to include people possessing an obvious/visible characteristic, accidental sampling makes no such attempt.

This method of sampling is common among market research and newspaper reporters. It has more or less the same advantages and disadvantages as quota sampling. As you are not guided by any obvious characteristics, some people contacted may not have the required information.

Judgemental or purposive sampling

The primary consideration in purposive sampling is the judgement of the researcher as to who can provide the best information to achieve the objectives of the study. The researcher only goes to those people who in his/her opinion are likely to have the required information and be willing to share it.

This type of sampling is extremely useful when you want to construct a historical reality, describe a phenomenon or develop something about which only a little is known.

Snowball sampling

Snowball sampling is the process of selecting a sample using networks. To start with, a few individuals in a group or organisation are selected and the required information is collected from them. They are then asked to identify other people in the group or organisation, and the people selected by them become a part of the sample. Information is collected from them, and then these people are asked to identify other members of the group and, in turn, those identified become the basis of further data collection (Figure 12.7). This process is continued until the required number or a saturation point has been reached, in terms of the information being sought.

This sampling technique is useful if you know little about the group or organisation you wish to study, as you need only to make contact with a few individuals, who can then direct you to the other members of the group. This method of selecting a sample is useful for studying communication patterns, decision making or diffusion of knowledge within a group. There are disadvantages to this technique, however. The choice of the entire sample rests upon the choice of individuals at the first stage. If they belong to a particular faction or have strong biases, the study may be biased. Also, it is difficult to use this technique when the sample becomes fairly large.

Figure 12.7   Snowball sampling

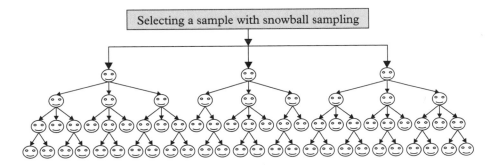

'Mixed' sampling designs

Systematic sampling design

Systematic sampling has been classified under the 'mixed' sampling category because it has the characteristics of both random and non-random sampling designs.

In systematic sampling the sampling frame is first divided into a number of segments called *intervals*. Then, from the first interval, using the SRS technique, one element is selected. The selection of subsequent elements from other intervals is dependent upon the order of the element selected in the first interval. If in the first interval it is the fifth element, the fifth element of each subsequent interval will be chosen. Notice that from the first interval the choice of an element is on a random basis, but the choice of the elements from subsequent intervals is dependent upon the choice from the first, and hence cannot be classified as a random sample. For this reason it has been classified here as 'mixed' sampling. The procedure used in systematic sampling is presented in Figure 12.8.

Figure 12.8   The procedure for selecting a systematic sample

Step 1   Prepare a list of all the elements in the study population (N).
Step 2   Decide on the sample size (n).
Step 3   Determine the *width of the interval* (k) = $\dfrac{\text{total population}}{\text{sample size}}$
Step 4   Using the SRS, select an element from the first interval (nth order).
Step 5   Select the same order element from each subsequent interval.

Although the general procedure for selecting a sample by the systematic sampling technique is described above, one can deviate from it by selecting a different element from each interval with the SRS technique. By adopting this, systematic sampling can be classified under probability sampling designs.

To select a random sample one must have a sampling frame (Figure 12.9). Sometimes this is impossible or obtaining one may be too expensive. However, in real life there are situations when a kind of sampling frame exists, for example records of clients in an agency, enrolment lists of students in a school or university, electoral lists of people living in an area, or records of the staff employed in an organisation. All these can be used as a sampling frame to select a sample with the systematic sampling technique. This convenience of having a 'ready made' sampling frame may be at a price: in some cases it may not truly be a random listing. Mostly these lists are in alphabetical order, based upon a number assigned to a case, or arranged in a way that is convenient to the users of the records. If the 'width of an interval' is large, say, 1 in 30 cases, and if the cases are arranged in alphabetical order, you could preclude some whose surnames start with the same letter or some adjoining letter may not be included at all.

Figure 12.9   Systematic sampling

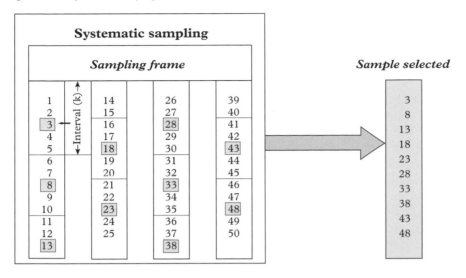

Suppose there are 50 students in a class and you want to select 10 students using the systematic sampling technique. The first step is to determine the width of the interval (50/10 = 5). This means that from every five you need to select one element. Using the SRS technique, from the first interval (1–5 elements), select one of the elements. Suppose you selected the third element. From the rest of the intervals you would select every third element.

The calculation of sample size

'How big a sample should I select?', 'What should be my sample size?' and 'How many cases do I need?' These are the most common questions asked. Basically, it depends on what you want to do with the findings and what type of relationships you want to establish. Your purpose in undertaking research is the main determinant of the level of accuracy required in the results, and this level of accuracy is an important determinant of sample size. However, in qualitative research, as the main focus is to explore or describe a situation, issue, process or phenomenon, the question of sample size is less important. You usually collect data till you think you have reached saturation point in terms of discovering new information. Once you think you are not getting much new data from your respondents, you stop collecting further information. Of course, the diversity or heterogeneity in what you are trying to find out about plays an important role in how fast you will reach saturation point. And remember: *the greater the heterogeneity or diversity in what you are trying to find out about, the greater the number of respondents you need to contact to reach saturation point.* In determining the size of your sample for quantitative studies and in particular for cause-and-effect studies, you need to consider the following:

- At what *level of confidence* do you want to test your results, findings or hypotheses?
- With what *degree of accuracy* do you wish to estimate the population parameters?
- What is the estimated *level of variation* (standard deviation), with respect to the main variable you are studying, in the study population?

Answering these questions is necessary regardless of whether you intend to determine the sample size yourself or have an expert do it for you. The size of the sample is important for testing a hypothesis or establishing an association, but for other studies the general rule is *the larger the sample size, the more accurate will be your estimates*. In practice, your budget determines the size of your sample. Your skills in selecting a sample, within the constraints of your budget, lie in the way you select your elements so that they effectively and adequately represent your sampling population.

To illustrate this procedure let us take the example of a class. Suppose you want to find out the average age of the students within an accuracy of 0.5 of a year; that is, you can tolerate an error of half a year on either side of the true average age. Let us also assume that you want to find the average age within half a year of accuracy at 95 per cent confidence level; that is, you want to be 95 per cent confident about your findings.

The formula (from statistics) for determining the confidence limits is:

$$\hat{x} = \bar{x} \pm (t_{0.05})\frac{\sigma}{\sqrt{\eta}}$$

where

$\hat{x}$ = estimated value of the population mean
$\bar{x}$ = average age calculated from the sample
$t_{0.05}$ = value of t at 95 per cent confidence level

$\frac{\sigma}{\sqrt{\eta}}$ = standard error

σ = standard deviation
η = sample size
$\sqrt{}$ = square root

If we decide to tolerate an error of $1/2$ years, that means:

$$\bar{x} \pm (t_{0.05})\frac{\sigma}{\sqrt{\eta}}$$

$$\underbrace{\qquad\qquad}$$
$$= 0.5$$
$$= \bar{x} \pm 0.5$$

in other words we would like $\left[(t_{0.05})\frac{\sigma}{\sqrt{\eta}}\right] = 0.5$

or $(1.96^\star)\,\frac{\sigma}{\sqrt{\eta}} = 0.5$ (value of $t_{0.05} = 1.96$)

$$\therefore \sqrt{\eta} = \frac{1.96 \times \sigma}{0.5}$$

*t-value from the following table

Level	0.02	0.10	0.05	0.02	0.01	0.001
t-value	1.282	1.645	1.960	2.326	2.576	3.291

There is only one unknown quantity in the above equation, that is σ.

Now the main problem is to find the value of σ without having to collect data. This is the biggest problem in estimating the sample size. Because of this it is important to know as much as possible about the study population.

The value of σ can be found by one of the following:

1 guessing;
2 consulting an expert;
3 obtaining the value of σ from previous comparable studies; or
4 carrying out a pilot study to calculate the value.

Let us assume that σ is 1 year.

$$\therefore \sqrt{\eta} = \frac{1.96 \times 1}{0.5} = 3.92$$

$$\therefore \eta = 15.37, \text{ say, } 16$$

Hence, to determine the average age of the class at a level of 95 per cent accuracy (assuming $\sigma = 1$ year) with $1/2$ year of error, a sample of at least 16 students is necessary.

Now assume that instead of 95 per cent, you want to be 99 per cent confident about the estimated age, tolerating an error of $1/2$ year.

$$\sqrt{\eta} = \frac{2.576 \times 1}{0.5}$$

$$= 5.15$$

$$\therefore \eta = 26.54, \text{ say, } 27$$

Hence, if you want to be 99 per cent confident and are willing to tolerate an error of $1/2$ year, you need to select a sample of 27 students. Similarly, you can calculate the sample size with varying values of σ. Remember the golden rule: *the greater the sample size, the more accurately your findings will reflect the 'true' picture.*

SUMMARY

In this chapter you have learnt about sampling, the process of selecting a few elements from a sampling population. Sampling, in a way, is a trade-off between accuracy and resources. Through sampling you *make an estimate* about the information of interest. You do not find the true population mean.

Sampling is guided by three principles. One of the most important principles of sampling is that the greater the sample size, the more accurate will be the estimate of the true population mean, given that everything else remains the same. The inferences drawn from a sample can be affected by both the size of the sample and the extent of variation in the sampling population.

Sampling designs can be classified as random/probability sampling designs, non-random/non-probability sampling designs and 'mixed' sampling designs. For a sample to be called a random sample, each element in the study population must have an equal and independent chance of selection. Three random designs were discussed: simple random sampling, stratified random sampling and cluster sampling. The procedures for selecting a sample using these designs were detailed step by step. The use of the fishbowl technique, the table of random numbers, and specifically designed computer programs are three commonly used methods of selecting a probability sample.

There are four non-probability sampling designs: quota, accidental, judgemental and snowball. Each is used for a different purpose and in different situations.

Systematic sampling is classified under the 'mixed' category as it has the properties of both probability and non-probability sampling designs.

The last section of the chapter described determinants of, and procedures for, calculating sample size. Although it might be slightly more difficult for the beginner, it was included to make you aware of the determinants involved as questions relating to this area are so commonly asked. In qualitative research, the question of sample size is less important, as your aim is to explore, not quantify, the extent of variation for which you are guided by reaching saturation point in terms of new findings.

STEP V

WRITING A RESEARCH PROPOSAL

CHAPTER 13
Writing a research proposal

CHAPTER
thirteen

Writing a research
proposal

The research proposal

All research endeavours in every academic and professional field are preceded by a research proposal. It informs your academic supervisor or potential provider of a research contract of your conceptualisation of the total research process that you propose to undertake, and examines its suitability and validity. In any academic field, your research proposal will go through a number of committees for approval. Unless it is approved by all of them, you will not be able to start your research. Hence, it is important for you to study closely what constitutes a research proposal.

Both for qualitative and quantitative research studies you need to write a research proposal. Both do have a similar structure. However, their main difference is in proposed procedures and methodologies for undertaking the research endeavour. Hence, this chapter is appropriate for both types of research proposal.

Certain requirements for a research proposal may vary from university to university, within a university from discipline to discipline, but what is outlined here will satisfy most requirements. You should therefore be selective regarding what is needed in your situation.

A research proposal is an overall plan, scheme, structure and strategy designed to obtain answers to the research questions or problems that constitute your research project. A research proposal should outline the various tasks you plan to undertake to fulfil your research objectives, test hypotheses or obtain answers to your research questions. It should also state your reasons for undertaking the study. Broadly, a research proposal's main function is *to detail the operational plan for obtaining answers to your research questions. In doing so it ensures and reassures the reader of the validity of the methodology for obtaining answers to your research questions accurately and objectively.*

In order to achieve this function, a research proposal must tell you, your research supervisor and reviewers the following information about your study:

- *what* you are proposing to do;
- *how* you plan to proceed;
- *why* you selected the proposed strategy.

Contents of a research proposal

A research proposal should contain the following information about your study:

- an introduction, including a brief *literature review*;
- *theoretical framework* that underpins your study;
- *conceptual framework* which constitutes the basis of your study;
- *objectives* or *research questions* of your study;
- *hypotheses* to be tested, if applicable;
- *study design* that you are proposing to adopt
- *setting* for your study;

- *research instrument(s)* you are planning to use;
- *sampling design* and *sample size*;
- *ethical issues* involved and how you propose to deal with them;
- *data-processing procedures*;
- *proposed chapters* of the report;
- *problems* and *limitations* of the study;
- proposed *time-frame* for the project.

A research proposal should communicate the purpose and plan of the research in such a way that it:

- enables you to return to the proposal for your own guidance in decision making at different stages of the research process;
- convinces your research supervisor or a reviewer that your proposed methodology is meritorious, valid, appropriate and workable in terms of obtaining answers to your research questions or objectives.

Universities and other institutions may have differing requirements regarding the style and content of a research proposal. Requirements may also vary within an institution, from discipline to discipline or from supervisor to supervisor. (The guidelines set out in this chapter therefore provide a framework within which a research proposal should be written.)

Your proposal should follow the suggested guidelines and be written in an academic style. It must contain appropriate references in the body of the text and a bibliography at the end. Your survey of the relevant literature should cover major publications on the topic. The *theoretical frame* for your study must emerge from this literature review and must have its grounding in empirical evidence. As a rule, the literature review includes:

- a conceptual framework, and theoretical and empirical information about the main issues under study;
- some of the major research findings relating to your topic, research questions raised in the literature, and gaps identified by previous researchers.

Your literature review should also raise issues relating to the methodology you are proposing. For example, it may examine how other studies operationalised the major variables of relevance to your study and may include a critique of methodology relevant to your study. The critiques of methods and procedures should be included under their respective headings. For example, a critique of the sampling design you adopt should be included under 'sampling' or a critique to the study design should be discussed under 'study design'.

Note that the suggested outline does not contain a section entitled 'survey of the literature' or 'literature review'. This is because references to literature should be integrated with your arguments conceptually rather than chronologically. Literature should be reviewed under main themes that emerge from your reading of the literature. Issues to do with research methodology and problems pertinent to the various aspects of research procedures should be discussed under their respective headings. For example, issues pertaining to the study design under 'study design', issues relating to sampling under 'sampling', and literature pertaining to the research instrument under the 'measurement procedure'.

In suggesting this format it is assumed that you are acquainted reasonably well with research methodology and an academic style of writing. That is, you know how to write a set of objectives or construct a hypothesis, you are familiar with the various study designs, and you can construct a research instrument and cite a reference.

The pages that follow outline a framework for a research proposal. The contents under each heading may vary markedly from discipline to discipline and according to the academic level of the student (BA Hons, MA, PhD).

Each section of the proposed outline for a research proposal is divided into two parts:

1 a suggested title for the section and an outline of its contents;
2 examples outlining contents for the section—the same three examples of research projects, each taken from a different discipline, are used as illustration in each section.

Preamble/introduction

The proposal should start with an introduction to include some of the information listed below. Remember that some of the contents suggested in this section may not be relevant to certain studies; so use your discretion in selecting only what is pertinent to your study. In writing this section, the literature review (see Chapter 3 on reviewing the literature) is of central importance as it serves two main functions:

1 It acquaints you with the available literature in the area of your study, thereby broadening your knowledge base.
2 It provides you with information on methods and procedures other people have used in similar situations and tells you what works and what does not.

The type, extent and quality of a literature review are mostly dependent upon the academic level for which you are writing the proposal. The contents of this section may also vary greatly according to the subject area under study.

Start with a very broad perspective of the main subject area, before gradually narrowing the focus to the central problem under investigation. In doing so, cover the following aspects of your study area:

- an overview of the main area under study;
- a historical perspective (development, growth, etc.) pertinent to the study area;
- philosophical or ideological issues relating to the topic;
- trends in terms of prevalence, if appropriate;
- major theories, if any;
- the main issues, problems and advances in the subject area under study;
- important theoretical and practical issues relating to the central problem under study;
- the main findings relating to the core issue(s).

Three examples of possible topics for the preamble/introduction for a research proposal follow.

Example A

Suppose that you are conducting a study to investigate the impact of immigration on the family. The preamble/introduction should include a brief description of the following:

- The origins of migratory movements in the world.
- General theories developed to explain migratory behaviour.
- The reasons for migration.
- Current trends in migration (national and state).
- The impact of immigration on family roles and relationships (e.g. on husband and wife, on children and parents, on parental expectations of children etc.).
- Occupational mobility.
- etc.

Example B

Suppose your research project is to conduct a study of the attitudes of foster carers towards foster payment in … (name of the place/state/country). The preamble/introduction would include the following:

- The origins of foster placement, the philosophy of foster care, a historical overview of foster care and changes over the years.
- Reasons for foster care and changes over time.
- The origins of foster placement in … (the country in which you are conducting your study).
- The effects of foster placement on children and parents.
- Policies with respect to foster care in … (the region).
- The origins of foster care in … (the region).
- Policies with respect to foster care in … (the region).
- Administrative procedures for foster care in … (the region).
- The training of foster parents in … (the region)
- The role and responsibility of foster parents.
- etc.

Example C

Suppose that you plan to study the relationship between academic achievement and social environment. The preamble/introduction would include the following:

- The role of education in our society.
- Major changes in the philosophy of education over time.
- Factors affecting attitudes towards education.
- The development of education in … (country).
- Trends in education participation rates in … (country) with particular reference to the region in which the study is being carried out.
- Changing educational values.
- Role of parents and peers in academic achievement.
- Impact of social environment on academic achievement.
- etc.

The problem

Having provided a broad introduction to the area under study, now focus on issues relating to its central theme, identifying some of the gaps in the existing body of knowledge. Identify some of the main unanswered questions. Here some of the main research questions that you would like to answer through your study should also be raised, and a rationale for each should be provided. Knowledge gained from other studies and the literature about the issues you are proposing to investigate should be an integral part of this section. Specifically, this section should:

- identify the issues that are the basis of your study;
- specify the various aspects of/perspectives on these issues;
- identify the main gaps in the existing body of knowledge;
- raise some of the main research questions that you want to answer through your study;
- identify what knowledge is available concerning your questions, specifying the differences of opinion in the literature regarding these questions if differences exist;
- develop a rationale for your study with particular reference to how your study will fill the identified gaps.

The following examples outline the topics that you should include in the section entitled 'The problem'.

Example A

- What settlement process does a family go through after immigration?
- What adjustments do immigrants have to make?
- What types of change can occur in family members' attitudes? (Theory of acculturation etc.).
- What is the possible impact of settlement on family roles and relationships?
- In terms of impact, what specific questions do you want to answer through the study? What does the literature say about these questions? What are the different viewpoints on these issues? What are your own ideas about these questions?
- What do you think will be the relevance of the findings of your study to the existing body of knowledge and to your profession?
- How will the findings add to the body of knowledge and be useful to professionals in your field?
- etc.

Example B

- What are the broad issues, debates, arguments and counter-arguments regarding foster-care payment?
- What are the attitudes of foster parents to the amount, mode and form of payment and what does the literature say about these issues?

- What are the different viewpoints/perspectives regarding payment for foster care?
- What main questions will your study answer?
- How will your findings help in policy formulation and program development?
- etc.

Example C

- What theories have been developed to explain the relationship between academic achievement and social environment?
- What is the relationship between educational achievement and social environment: what theoretical model will be the basis of your study?
- What do previous theories and research have to say regarding the components of the theoretical model and academic achievement, for example the relationship between academic achievement and:
  −the self-esteem and aspirations/motivation of a student;
  −peer-group influence;
  −parental involvement and its relationship with their socioeconomic status;
  −the motivation, and interest of students in the subject;
  −employment prospects;
  −relationship with a teacher
  −etc.

Objectives of the study

In this section include a statement of both your study's main and subobjectives (see Chapter 4). Your main objective indicates the central thrust of your study whereas the subobjectives identify the specific issues you propose to examine.

The objectives of the study should be clearly stated and specific in nature. Each subobjective should delineate only one issue. Use action-oriented verbs such as 'to determine', 'to find out' and 'to ascertain' in formulating subobjectives, which should be numerically listed. If the objective is to test a hypothesis, you must follow the convention of hypothesis formulation in wording the specific objectives.

Example A

Main objective:
  To ascertain the impact of immigration on the family.

Subobjectives:

1 To determine the impact of immigration on husband/wife roles as perceived by immigrants.
2 To find out the impact of immigration on marital relations.

3 To ascertain perceived changes in parental expectations of children's academic and professional achievement.
4 To determine perceived changes of attitude towards marriage in the study population.

Example B

Main objective:

To determine the opinion of foster carers about the form and extent of foster payment they feel they should receive for taking care of a foster child.

Subobjectives:

1 To determine the form and mode of payment for taking care of a foster child.
2 To identify the factors that foster parents believe should be the basis for determining the rate of payment for fostering a child.
3 To determine the relationship, if any, between the socioeconomic–demographic characteristics of foster parents and their views on payment.

Example C

Main objective:

To examine the relationship between academic achievement and social environment.

Subobjectives:

1 To find out the relationship, if any, between self-esteem and a student's academic achievement at school.
2 To ascertain the association between parental involvement in a student's studies and his/her academic achievement at school.
3 To examine the links between a student's peer group and academic achievement.
4 To explore the relationship between academic achievement and the attitude of a student towards teachers.

Hypotheses to be tested

A hypothesis is a statement of your assumptions about the prevalence of a phenomenon or about a relationship between two variables that you plan to test within the framework of the study (see Chapter 6). If you are going to test hypotheses, list them in this section.

When formulating a hypothesis you have an obligation to draw conclusions about it in the text of the report. Hypotheses have a particular style of formulation. You must be acquainted with the correct way of wording them. In a study you may have as many hypotheses as you want to test. However, it is *not* essential to have a hypothesis in order to undertake a study—you can conduct a perfectly satisfactory study without formulating a hypothesis.

Example A

H_1 = In most cases there will be a change in husband/wife roles after immigration.

H_2 = In a majority of cases there will be a change in parents' expectations of their children.

H_i = etc.

Example B

H_1 = Most people become foster parents because of their love of children.

H_2 = A majority of foster parents would like to be trained to care for foster children.

H_i = etc.

Example C

H_1 = A student's self-esteem and academic achievement at school are positively correlated.

H_2 = The greater the parental involvement in a student's studies, the higher the academic achievement.

H_3 = A student's attitude towards teachers is positively correlated with his/her academic achievement in that subject.

H_i = etc.

Study design

Describe the study design (for details see Chapter 8) you plan to use to answer your research questions. (For example, say whether it is a case study, descriptive, cross-sectional, before-and-after, experimental or non-experimental design.) Identify the strengths and weaknesses of your study design.

Include details about the various logistical procedures you intend to follow while executing the study design. One characteristic of a good study design is that it explains the details with such clarity that, if someone else wants to follow the proposed procedure, s/he will be able to do exactly as you would have done. Your study design should include information about the following:

- Who makes up the study population?
- Can each element of the study population be identified? If yes, how?
- Will a sample or the total population be studied?
- How will you get in touch with the selected sample?
- How will the sample's consent to participate in the study be sought?
- How will the data be collected (e.g. by interview, questionnaire or observation)?

- In the case of a mailed questionnaire, to what address should the questionnaire be returned?
- Are you planning to send a reminder regarding the return of questionnaires?
- How will confidentiality be preserved?
- How and where can respondents contact you if they have queries?

Example A

The study is primarily designed to find out from a cross-section of immigrants from ..., ... and ... (names of the countries) the perceived impact of immigration on family roles. Initial contact with the ethnic associations for these countries will be made through the elected office bearers to obtain a list of members. Five immigrants will be selected from the list at random, and will be contacted by phone to explain the purpose of the study and its relevance, and to seek their agreement to participate in the study. Those who give their consent will be interviewed at their homes or any other convenient place. To select a further sample, a snowball sampling technique will be used until the desired sample size is obtained.

Example B

The study design is cross-sectional in nature, being designed to find out from a cross-section of foster parents their opinions about foster payment. All foster parents currently registered with the Department ... (name of the office) constitute the study population. From the existing records of this department it seems that there are 457 foster parents in ... (name of the region). As it is impossible for the researcher, within the constraints of time and money, to collect information from all the foster parents, it is proposed to select a sample of 50 per cent of the study population with the proposed sampling strategy. The questionnaire, with a supporting letter from the department, will be sent with a prepaid envelope. The respondents will be requested to return the questionnaire by ... (date). The letter from the researcher attached to the questionnaire will explain the objectives and relevance of the study, assure the respondents of anonymity, and give them the option of not participating in the study if they do not wish to. A contact number will be provided in case a respondent has any questions. In the case of a low response rate (less than 25 per cent), a reminder will be sent to respondents.

Example C

It is proposed that the study will be carried out in two government high schools in the metropolitan area. The principals of the schools most accessible to the researcher will be contacted to explain the purpose of the study and the help needed from the school, and to seek their permission for the students to participate in the study. As the constraints of time and resources do not permit the researcher to select more than two schools, negotiations with other schools will cease when two schools agree to participate in the study.

It is proposed to select year 9 students as the academic achievement of students in years 8 and 10 could be affected by factors unique to them. Year 8 students may be experiencing anxiety as a result of having just made the transition to a new system. The motivation of students in year 10 could be affected by their being at the stage in their education where they must decide if they will continue on at school.

In order to control the variance attributable to the gender of a student it is proposed to select only male students.

Once the principal of a school agrees to allow the study to be carried out, the researcher will brief the teacher in charge about the study and its relevance, and will arrange a date and time for administering the questionnaire.

When the students are assembled ready to participate in the study, the researcher will explain its purpose and relevance, and then distribute the questionnaire. The researcher will remain in the class to answer any questions the students might have.

The setting

Briefly describe the organisation, agency or community in which you will conduct your study. If the study is about a group of people, highlight some of the salient characteristics of the group (e.g. its history, size, composition and structure) and draw attention to any available relevant information.

If your research concerns an agency, office or organisation, include the following in your description:

• the main services provided by the agency, office or organisation;
• its administrative structure;
• the type of clients served;
• information about the issues that are central to your research.

If you are studying a community, briefly describe some of the main characteristics, such as:

• the size of the community;
• a brief social profile of the community (i.e. the composition of the various groups within it);
• issues of relevance to the central theme of your study.

Note that due to the nature of the content, it would be difficult to provide examples.

Measurement procedures

This section should contain a discussion of your instrument (see Chapters 9 and 10) and the details of how you plan to operationalise your *major* variables (Chapter 5).

To start with, justify your choice of research tool, highlighting its strengths and pointing out its weaknesses. Then outline the major segments of your research tool and their relevance to the main objectives of the study. If you are using a standard instrument, briefly discuss the availability of evidence on its reliability and validity. If you adapt or modify it in any way, describe and explain the changes you have made.

You should also discuss how you are going to operationalise the major concepts. For example, if measuring effectiveness, specify how it will be measured. If you plan to measure the self-esteem of a group of people, mention the main indicators of self-esteem and the procedures for its measurement (e.g. the Likert or Thurstone scale, or any other procedure).

Ideally you should attach a copy of the research instrument to your proposal. Note that due to the nature of the content, it would be difficult to provide examples for this section.

Ethical issues

All academic institutions are particular about any ethical issues that research may have. To deal with them, all institutions have some form of policy on ethics. You need to be acquainted with your institution's policy. It is imperative that you identify any ethical issues, and describe how you propose to deal with them in your proposal. You need to look at the ethical issues particularly from the viewpoint of your respondents, and in case of any potential 'harm', psychologically or otherwise, you need to detail the mechanism in place to deal with it.

Sampling

Under this section of the proposal include the following (consult Chapter 12 on sampling):

- the size of the sampling population (if known), and from where and how this information will be obtained;
- the size of the sample you are planning to select, and your reasons for choosing this size;
- an explanation of the sampling design you are planning to use in the selection of the sample (simple random sampling, stratified random sampling, quota sampling etc.).

Example A

Because a lack of information as to the exact location of migrant families makes it difficult to use a probability sampling design, it is proposed that the researcher will employ a snowball-sampling technique. The researcher will make the initial contact with five families who have emigrated from ... (name of the country) during the past seven to ten years, who are either known to him/her or on the basis of the information obtained from the office bearers of the formal associations representing the migrant groups. From each respondent the researcher will obtain names and addresses of other immigrants who have come from the same country during the same period. The respondents thus identified will then be interviewed and asked to identify other respondents for the researcher. This process will continue until the researcher has interviewed 70 respondents.

Example B

Because of the constraints of time and resources it is proposed to select 50 per cent of the foster parents currently registered (457) with the department using the systematic random sampling technique. Every other foster parent registered with the department will be selected, thus 229 individuals will constitute the sample for the study.

Example C

The selection of schools will be done primarily through quota sampling. Schools will be selected on the basis of their geographical proximity to the researcher. The researcher will prepare a list of schools, in rank order, of accessibility. Once two schools agree to participate in the study, negotiations with other schools will cease.

All year 9 male students will constitute the study population. It is expected that the sample will not exceed 100 students.

Analysis of data

In general terms, describe the strategy you intend to use for data analysis (Chapter 15). Specify whether the data will be analysed manually or by computer. For computer analysis, identify the program and the statistical procedures you plan to perform on the data. Also identify the main variables for cross-tabulation.

Example A

Frequency distributions in terms of:

- age;
- education;
- occupation;
- number of children;
- duration of immigration;
- etc.

Cross-tabulations:
Impact of husband/wife roles

- age;
- number of children;
- education;
- occupation;
- etc.

Example B

Frequency distributions in terms of:

- age;
- income;
- education;
- occupation;
- marital status;
- duration of foster care;
- number of foster children;
- etc.

Cross-tabulations:
Attitude towards foster payment

- age;
- number of children;
- education;
- occupation;
- etc.

Statistical tests to be applied:

- Chi square;
- regression analysis;
- etc.

Example C

Frequency distributions in terms of:

- age;
- parents' occupation;
- parents' educational levels;
- students' occupational aspirations;
- parental involvement in students' studies;
- self-esteem;
- peer-group influence;
- number of hours spent on studies;
- etc.

Cross-tabulations:
Academic achievement

- peer-group influence;
- parental involvement in students' studies;
- self-esteem;
- occupational aspirations;
- attitude towards teachers;
- etc.

Structure of the report

As clearly as possible, state how you intend to organise the final report (see Chapter 17). In organising your material for the report, the specific objectives of your study are of immense help. Plan to develop your chapters around the main themes of your study. The title of each chapter should clearly communicate the main thrust of its contents.

The first chapter, possibly entitled 'Introduction', should be an overall introduction to your study, covering most of your project proposal and pointing out deviations, if any, from the original plan.

The second chapter should provide some information about the study population itself—that is, some of its socioeconomic–demographic character-istics. The main aim of this chapter is to give readers some background on the population from which you collected the information. The second chapter, therefore, may be entitled, 'Socioeconomic–demographic characteristics of the study population' or 'The study population' or any other title that communicates this theme to readers. Titles for the rest of the chapters will vary from study to study but, as mentioned, each chapter should be written around a main theme. Although the wording of chapter titles is an individual choice, each must communicate the main theme of the chapter. In developing these themes the specific objectives of the study should be kept in the forefront of your mind.

Example A

It is proposed that the report will be divided into the following chapters:

Chapter 1:   Introduction
Chapter 2:   The socioeconomic–demographic characteristics of the
             study population
Chapter 3:   The impact on husband/wife roles
Chapter 4:   The impact on marital relations
Chapter 5:   The impact on expectations of children
Chapter 6:   The impact on attitudes towards marriage
Chapter 7:   Summary, conclusions and recommendations

Example B

The dissertation will be divided into the following chapters:

Chapter 1:   Introduction
Chapter 2:   A profile of the study population
Chapter 3:   Foster carers' perceptions of their role
Chapter 4:   Attitudes of foster carers towards foster-care payment
Chapter 5:   The preferred method of payment
Chapter 6:   General comments made by respondents about foster care
Chapter 7:   Summary, conclusions and recommendations

Example C

The report will have the following chapters:

Chapter 1:   Introduction
Chapter 2:   The study population
Chapter 3:   Occupational aspirations, self-esteem and academic
             achievement
Chapter 4:   The extent of parental involvement and academic
             achievement
Chapter 5:   Peer-group influence and academic achievement
Chapter 6:   Academic achievement and student attitudes towards
             teachers
Chapter 7:   Summary, conclusions and recommendations

Problems and limitations

This section should list problems you thought you might encounter concerning, for example, the availability of data, securing permission from the agency/organisation to carry out the study, obtaining the sample, or any other aspect of the study.

You will not have unlimited resources and as this may be primarily an academic exercise, you might have to do less than an ideal job. However, it is important to be aware of—and communicate—any limitations that could affect the validity of your conclusions and generalisations.

Here, *problems* refer to difficulties relating to logistical details, whereas *limitations* designate structural problems relating to methodological aspects of the study. In your opinion the study design you chose may not be the best but you might have had to adopt it for a number of reasons. This is classified as a limitation of the study. This is also true for sampling or measurement procedures. Such limitations should be communicated to readers.

Appendix

As an appendix, attach your research instrument and a list of references.

Work schedule

You must set yourself dates as you need to complete the research within a certain time-frame. List the various operational steps you need to undertake and indicate against each the date by which you aim to complete that task. Remember to keep some time towards the end as a 'cushion' in case the research process does not go as smoothly as planned. Develop a chart as shown in Table 13.1.

Table 13.1 Developing a time-frame for your study

To be completed by

(Weeks or months)

Tasks (Any tasks which you consider important)	1	2	3	4	5	6	7	8	9	10	11	12	13	14	15
Proposal writing	↑		▲												
Instrument construction		↑		▲											
Data collection					↑		▲								
Coding									▲						
Data analysis										↑	▲				
Report/first										↑			▲		
Report/final											↑			▲	
Typing												↑			▲

SUMMARY

A research proposal details the operational plan for obtaining answers to research questions. It must tell your supervisor and others what you propose to do, how you plan to proceed and why the chosen strategy has been selected. It thus assures readers of the validity of the methodology used to obtain answers accurately and objectively.

The guidelines set out in this chapter provide only a framework within which a research proposal should be written and assume that you are acquainted reasonably well with research methodology and an academic style of writing. The contents of your proposal are arranged under the following headings: preamble/introduction, the problem, objectives of the study, hypotheses to be tested, study design, setting, measurement procedures, sampling, analysis of data, structure of your report, and problems and limitations.

The 'preamble' or 'introduction' introduces the main area of the study. To start with, the literature review is broad and then it gradually narrows to the specific problem you are investigating. The theoretical framework should be a part of this section. The next section, 'the problem', details the specific problem under study. The research questions for which you are planning to find answers are raised in this section. 'Objectives of the study' contains your main objectives and your subobjectives. Hypotheses, if any, should be listed in the section 'hypotheses to be tested'. The logistical procedures you intend to follow are detailed under 'study design'. 'The setting' consists of a description of the organisation or community in which you plan to conduct your study. The procedure for obtaining information and the measurement of major variables are explained in 'the measurement procedure' section. You need to write about ethical issues that your study might have and how you propose to deal with them. How you will select your sample is described under 'sampling'. The procedure for data analysis is discussed under 'data analysis'. The way you plan to structure your report is outlined under 'structure of the report'. Anticipated problems in conducting the study and limitations with its design are described under 'problems and limitations'. As an appendix to your proposal attach a copy of the research instrument and a list of the references.

A work schedule provides a time-frame for your study.

STEP VI

COLLECTING DATA

CHAPTER 14
Considering ethical issues
in data collection

CHAPTER
fourteen

Considering
ethical issues
in data collection

Ethics

All professions are guided by a code of ethics that has evolved over the years to accommodate the changing ethos, values, needs and expectations of those who hold a stake in the professions. Some professions are more advanced than others in terms of the level of development of their code of ethics. Some have very strict guidelines, monitor conduct effectively and take appropriate steps against those who do not abide by the guidelines.

Most professions have an overall code of conduct that also governs the way they carry out research. In addition, many research bodies have evolved a code of ethics separately for research. Medicine, epidemiology, business, law, education, psychology and other social sciences have well-established codes of ethics for research.

Let us first examine what we mean by 'ethics' or 'ethical behaviour'. According to the *Collins Dictionary* (1979: 502), ethical means 'in accordance with principles of conduct that are considered correct, especially those of a given profession or group'. The keywords here, 'principles of conduct' and 'considered correct', raise certain questions:

- What are these principles of conduct?
- Who determines them?
- In whose judgement must they be considered correct?

Closely related questions are:

- Are there universal principles of conduct that can be applied to all professions?
- Do these change with time?
- Should they?
- What happens when a professional does not abide by them?

The subject of ethics needs to be considered in the light of these questions.

The way each profession serves society is continuously changing in accordance with society's needs and expectations and with the technology available for the delivery of a service. The ethical codes governing the manner in which a service is delivered also need to change. What has been considered ethical in the past may not be so judged at present, and what is ethical now may not remain so in the future. Any judgement about whether a particular practice is ethical is made on the basis of the code of conduct prevalent at that point in time.

As the service and its manner of delivery differ from profession to profession, no code of conduct can be uniformly applied across all professions. Each profession has its own code of ethics, though there are commonalities. If you want guidelines on ethical conduct for a particular profession, you need to consult the code of ethics adopted by that profession or discipline.

'What are these principles of conduct?' is the most important question as it addresses the issue of the contents of ethical behaviour in a profession. As the code of conduct varies from profession to profession, it is not possible to provide a universal answer to this question. However, in research, any dilemma stemming from a moral quandary is a basis of ethical conduct.

There are certain behaviours in research—such as causing harm to individuals, breaching confidentiality, using information improperly and introducing bias—that are considered unethical in any profession.

The next question is: In whose judgement must a code of conduct be considered correct? Who decides whether a particular practice is wrong? If a procedure is carried out wrongly, what penalties should be imposed? It is the overall body of professionals or government organisations that collectively develops a professional code of conduct and forms a judgement as to whether or not it is being followed.

As mentioned, most professions have established an overall code of ethics and also a code of ethics for conducting research in their respective fields. As this book is designed for researchers in the social sciences, we will examine ethical issues in general and issues that are applicable to most social science disciplines.

Stakeholders in research

There are many stakeholders in a research activity; so it is important to look at ethical issues in relation to each one of them. The various stakeholders are:

1 the participants or subjects;
2 the researcher;
3 the funding body.

Participants or subjects to be considered as stakeholders depend on the profession. In the fields of medicine, public health, epidemiology and nursing, these are patients and non-patients who become part of a study, information-collection exercise, experiment or drug trial, and service managers and planners who contribute information for a research study.

In the social sciences, the participants include individuals, groups and communities providing information to help a researcher to gain understanding of a phenomenon, situation, issue or interaction. In social work and psychology, participants include clients as well as non-clients of an agency from whom information is collected to find out the magnitude of a problem, the needs of a community or the effectiveness of an intervention; and service providers, social workers and psychologists, when they provide information for a study. In business, consumers as well as non-consumers of a product provide information about consumption patterns and behaviour. In education, subjects include students, teachers and perhaps the community at large who participate in educational research activities.

Similarly, in any discipline in which a research activity is undertaken, those from whom information is collected or those who are studied by a researcher become participants of the study.

The researcher is in the second category of the above list of stakeholders. Anyone who collects information for a specific purpose, adhering to the accepted code of conduct, is a researcher. S/he may represent any academic discipline.

The organisation responsible for funding a research activity falls into the third category of stakeholders above. Most research is carried out using funds provided by business organisations, service institutions (government, semi-government or voluntary), research bodies and/or academic institutions. The funds are given for specific purposes. The funding body may have a vested interest in the research it is sponsoring, and this could affect the way the research is conducted or the way the report is written.

Each category of stakeholders in a research activity may have different interests, perspectives, purposes, aims and motivations that could affect the way in which research activity is carried out and the way results are communicated and used. Because of this, it is important to ensure that research is not affected by the self-interest of any party and is not carried out in a way that harms any party. Accordingly, ethical conduct in research concerning issues relating to different stakeholders should be examined under separate categories.

Ethical issues concerning research participants

There are many ethical issues in relation to participants of a research activity.

Collecting information

One could ask, why should a respondent give any information to a researcher? What right does a researcher have to knock at someone's door or to send out a questionnaire? Is it ethical to disturb an individual, even if you ask permission before asking questions? Why should a person give you his/her time? Your request for information may create anxiety or put pressure on a respondent. Is this ethical?

But the above questions display a naive attitude. The author believes that if this attitude had been adopted, there would have been no progress in the world. Research is required in order to improve conditions. Provided any piece of research is likely to help society directly or indirectly, it is acceptable to ask questions, if you first obtain the respondents' informed consent. Before you begin collecting information, you must consider the relevance and usefulness of the research you are undertaking and be able to convince others of this also. If you cannot justify the relevance of the research you are conducting, you are wasting your respondents' time, which is unethical.

Seeking consent

In every discipline it is considered unethical to collect information without the knowledge of participants, and their expressed willingness and informed consent. Seeking informed consent 'is probably the most common method in medical and social research' (Bailey 1978: 384). Informed consent implies that subjects are made adequately aware of the type of information you want from them, why the information is being sought, what purpose it will be put to, how they are expected to participate in the study, and how it will directly or indirectly affect them. It is important that the consent should also be voluntary and without pressure of any kind. Schinke and Gilchrist write:

> Under standards set by the National Commission for the Protection of Human Subjects, all informed-consent procedures must meet three criteria: participants must be competent to give consent; sufficient information must be provided to allow for a reasoned decision; and consent must be voluntary and uncoerced. (1993: 83)

Competency, according to Schinke and Gilchrist, 'is concerned with the legal and mental capacities of participants to give permission' (1993: 83). For example, some very old people, those suffering from conditions that exclude them from making informed decisions, people in crisis, people who cannot speak the language in which research is being carried out, people who are dependent upon you for a service and children are not considered to be competent.

Providing incentives

Is it ethical to provide incentives to respondents to share information with you? Some researchers provide incentives to participants for their participation in a study, feeling this to be quite proper as participants are giving their time. Others think that the offering of inducements is unethical.

In the author's experience most people do not participate in a study because of incentives, but because they realise the importance of the study. Therefore, giving a small gift after having obtained your information, as a token of appreciation, is in the author's opinion not unethical. However, giving a present before data collection is unethical.

Seeking sensitive information

Information sought can pose an ethical dilemma in research. Certain types of information can be regarded as sensitive or confidential by some people and thus an invasion of privacy. Asking for this information may upset or embarrass a respondent. However, if you do not ask for the information, it may not be possible to pursue your interest in the area and contribute to the existing body of knowledge.

For most people, questions on sexual behaviour, drug use and shoplifting are intrusive. Even questions on marital status, income and age may be considered to be an invasion of privacy by some. In collecting data you need to be careful about the sensitivities of your respondents.

The dilemma you face as a researcher is whether you should ask sensitive and intrusive questions. In the author's opinion it is not unethical to ask such questions provided that you tell your respondents the type of information you are going to ask clearly and frankly, and give them sufficient time to decide if they want to participate, without any major inducement.

The possibility of causing harm to participants

Is the research going to harm participants in any way? Harm includes:

> not only hazardous medical experiments but also any social research that might involve such things as discomfort, anxiety, harassment, invasion of privacy, or demeaning or dehumanising procedures' (Bailey 1978: 384).

When you collect data from respondents or involve subjects in an experiment, you need to examine carefully whether their involvement is likely to harm them in any way. If it is likely to, you must make sure that the risk is minimal. Minimum risk means that the extent of harm or discomfort in the research is not greater than that ordinarily encountered in daily life. If the way information is sought creates anxiety or harassment, you need to take steps to prevent this.

Maintaining confidentiality

Sharing information about a respondent with others for purposes other than research is unethical. Sometimes you need to identify your study population to put your findings into context. In such a situation you need to make sure that at least the information provided by respondents is kept anonymous. It is unethical to identify an individual respondent. Therefore, you need to ensure that after the information has been collected, its source cannot be known. In certain types of study you might need to visit respondents repeatedly, in which case you will have to identify them until the completion of your visits. If you are doing research for someone else, you need to make sure that confidentiality is maintained by this party as well.

Ethical issues relating to the researcher

Avoiding bias

Bias on the part of the researcher is unethical. Bias is different from subjectivity. Subjectivity, as mentioned earlier is related to your educational background, training and competence in research, and your philosophical perspective. Bias is a deliberate attempt either to hide what you have found in your study, or to highlight something disproportionately to its true existence. It is the bias that is unethical and not the subjectivity.

Provision or deprivation of a treatment

Both the provision and deprivation of a treatment may pose an ethical dilemma for you as a researcher. When testing an intervention or a treatment, a researcher usually adopts a control experiment design. In such studies, is it ethical to provide a study population with an intervention or treatment that has not yet been conclusively proven effective or beneficial? But if you do not test a treatment/intervention, how can you prove or disprove its effectiveness or benefits? On the other hand, you are providing an intervention that may not be effective. Is this ethical? Is it ethical to deprive the control group of a treatment even if it may prove to be only slightly effective? And beyond the issue of control groups, is it ethical to deprive people who are struggling for life of the possible benefit, however small it may be, which may be derived from a drug that is only under trial? As a researcher you need to be aware of these ethical issues.

There are no simple answers to these dilemmas. Ensuring informed consent, 'minimum risk' and frank discussion as to the implications of participation in the study will help to resolve ethical issues.

Using inappropriate research methodology

A researcher has an obligation to use appropriate methodology in conducting a study. It is unethical to use a method or procedure you know to be inappropriate (e.g. selecting a highly biased sample, using an invalid instrument or drawing wrong conclusions).

Incorrect reporting

To use an appropriate methodology, but to report the findings in a way that changes or slants them to serve your own or someone else's interest, is unethical.

Inappropriate use of the information

How will the information obtained from respondents be used by the researcher? The use of information in a way that directly or indirectly adversely affects respondents is unethical. Can information be used to adversely affect the study population? If so, how can the study population be protected? As a researcher you need to consider and resolve these issues. Sometimes it is possible to harm individuals in the process of achieving benefits for organisations. An example would be a study to examine the feasibility of restructuring an organisation. Restructuring may be beneficial to the organisation as a whole but may be harmful to some individuals. Should you ask respondents for information that is likely to be used against them? If you do so, the information may be used against them and if you do not, the organisation may not be able to derive the benefits of restructuring. In the author's opinion, it is ethical to ask questions provided you tell respondents of the potential use of the information, including the possibility of it being used against some of them, and you let them decide if they want to participate.

Ethical issues regarding the sponsoring organisation

Restrictions imposed by the sponsoring organisation

Most research in the social sciences is carried out using funds provided by sponsoring organisations for a specific purpose. The funds may be given to develop a program or evaluate it; to examine its effectiveness and efficiency; to study the impact of a policy; to test a product; to study the behaviour of a group or community; or to study a phenomenon, issue or attitude. Sometimes there may be direct or indirect controls exercised by sponsoring organisations. They may select the methodology, prohibit the publication of 'what was found' or impose other restrictions on the research that may stand in the way of obtaining and disseminating accurate information. Both the imposition and acceptance of these controls and restrictions are unethical, as they constitute interference and could amount to the sponsoring organisation tailoring research findings to meet its vested interests.

The misuse of information

How is the sponsoring body going to use the information? How is this likely to affect the study population? Sometimes sponsoring organisations use research as a pretext for obtaining management's agenda. It is unethical to let your research be used as a reason for justifying management decisions.

SUMMARY

This chapter is designed to make you aware of the ethical issues to be considered when conducting research. How you resolve them depends upon you, and the conditions under which you are working.

Being ethical means adhering to the code of conduct that has been evolved over the years for an acceptable professional practice. For most professions ethical codes in research are an integral part of their overall ethics, though some research bodies have evolved their own codes.

Ethical issues in research can be looked at as they relate to participants, researchers and sponsoring organisations. With regard to participants, ethical considerations concern the following: collecting information; seeking consent; providing incentives; seeking sensitive information; the possibility of causing harm to participants; and maintaining confidentiality. With regard to the researcher, areas of ethical concern include the following: introducing bias; providing and depriving individuals of treatment; using unacceptable research methodology; inaccurate reporting; and the inappropriate use of information. Ethical considerations in relation to sponsoring organisations concern restrictions imposed on research designs and the possible use of findings.

STEP VII

PROCESSING DATA

CHAPTER
fifteen

Processing data

If you were actually doing a research study, you would by now have reached a stage where you have either extracted or collected the required information. The next step is what to do with this information. How do you find the answers to your research questions? How do you prove or disprove your hypothesis if you had one? How do you make sense of the information collected? How should the information be analysed to achieve the objectives of your study? To answer these questions you need to go through a series of steps that constitute the core of data processing (Figure 15.1).

Irrespective of the method of data collection, the information collected is called *raw data* or simply *data*. The first step in processing your data is to ensure that the data are 'clean'—that is, free from inconsistencies and incompleteness. This process of 'cleaning' is called *editing*.

Editing data collected through structured inquiries (quantitative studies)

Editing consists of scrutinising the completed research instruments to identify and minimise, as far as possible, errors, incompleteness, misclassification and gaps in the information obtained from the respondents. Sometimes even the best investigators can:

- forget to ask a question;
- forget to record a response;
- wrongly classify a response;
- write only half a response;
- write illegibly.

In the case of a questionnaire, similar problems can crop up. These problems to a great extent can be reduced simply by:

- checking the contents for completeness;
- checking the responses for internal consistency.

The way you check the contents for completeness depends upon the way the data have been collected. In the case of an interview, just checking the interview schedule for the above problems may improve the quality of the data. It is good practice for an interviewer to take a few moments to peruse responses for possible incompleteness and inconsistencies. In the case of a questionnaire, again, just by carefully checking the responses some of the problems may be reduced. There are several ways of minimising such problems:

- **by inference**—certain questions in a research instrument may be related to one another and it might be possible to find out the answer to one question from the answer to another. Of course, you must be careful about making such inferences or you may introduce new errors into the data.
- **by recall**—if the data are collected by means of interviews, sometimes it might be possible for the interviewer to recall a respondent's answers. Again, you must be extremely careful.

Figure 15.1   Steps in data processing

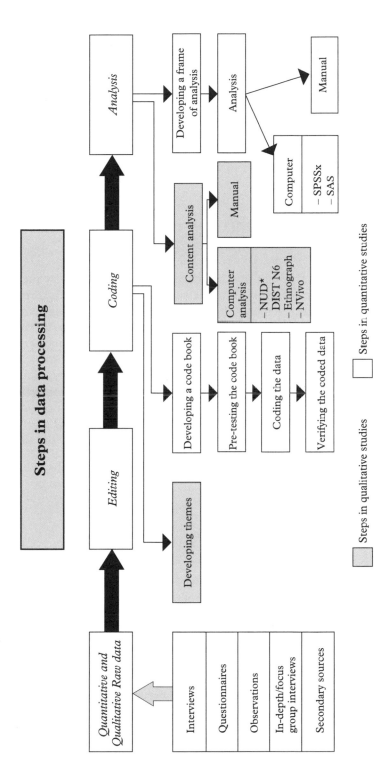

- **by going back to the respondent**—if the data have been collected by means of interviews or the questionnaires contain some identifying information, it is possible to visit or phone a respondent to confirm or ascertain an answer. This is, of course, expensive and time-consuming.

There are two ways of editing the data:

1 examine answers to one question or variable at a time;
2 examine answers to all questions at the same time that is, examine all the responses given by a respondent.

The author prefers the second method as it provides a total picture of the responses, which also helps you to assess their internal consistency.

Editing data collected through unstructured interviewing

If you collected data through unstructured interviewing (e.g. by means of in-depth interview, focus group interviews, narratives or oral histories) its editing is more difficult, as the methods mentioned above are inappropriate for the purpose. However, it is possible that you may be able to go through your notes to identify if something does not make sense. In such an event, you may be able to recall the context and correct the contents, but be careful in doing so. Another way of ensuring accuracy is to transcribe the interviews and send them back to their respective respondents for confirmation and approval. Validation of the information by a respondent is an important aspect of collecting data through unstructured interviews. It ensures accuracy of contents and helps in removing ambiguities in meanings and inferences drawn by you as a researcher.

Coding data: introduction

Having 'cleaned' the data, the next step is to code it. The method of coding is largely dictated by two considerations:

1 the way a variable has been measured (measurement scale) in your research instrument (e.g., if a response to a question is descriptive, categorical or quantitative);
2 the way you want to communicate the findings about a variable to your readers.

For coding, the first level of distinction is whether a set of data is qualitative or quantitative in nature. For qualitative data a further distinction is whether the information is descriptive in nature (e.g. a description of a service to a community, a case history) or is generated through discrete qualitative categories. For example, the following information about a respondent is in discrete qualitative categories: income—above average, average, below average; gender—male, female; religion—Christian, Hindu,

Muslim, Buddhist, etc.; or attitude towards an issue—strongly favourable, favourable, uncertain, unfavourable, strongly unfavourable. Each of these variables is measured either on a *nominal* or an *ordinal* scale. Some of them could also have been measured on a *ratio* or an *interval* scale. For example, income can be measured in dollars (ratio scale), or an attitude towards an issue can be measured on an interval or a ratio scale. The way you proceed with the coding depends upon the measurement scale used in the measurement of a variable and whether a question is open-ended or closed-ended.

In addition, the type of statistical procedures that can be applied to a set of information to a large extent depends upon the measurement scale on which a variable was measured in the research instrument. For example, you can find out different statistical descriptors such as mean, mode and median if income is measured on a ratio scale, but not if it is measured on an ordinal or a nominal scale. It is extremely important to understand that the way you are able to analyse a set of information is dependent upon the measurement scale used in the research instrument for measuring a variable. It is therefore important to visualise—particularly at the planning stage when constructing the research instrument—the way you are going to communicate your findings.

How you can analyse information obtained in response to a question depends upon how a question was asked, and how a respondent answered it. In other words, it depends upon the measurement scale on which a response can be measured/classified. If you study answers given by your respondents in response to a question, you will realise that almost all responses can be classified into one of the following three categories:

- quantitative responses;
- categorical responses (which may be quantitative or qualitative);
- descriptive responses (which are invariably qualitative).

For the purpose of analysis, quantitative and categorical responses need to be dealt with differently from descriptive ones. Quantitative and categorical information go through a process that is primarily aimed at transforming the information into numerical values, called **codes**, so that the information can be easily analysed, either manually or by computers. On the other hand, descriptive information first goes through a process called **content analysis**, whereby you identify main themes that emerge from the descriptions given by respondents in answer to questions. Having identified the main themes, there are three ways that you can deal with them: (1) you can examine verbatim responses and integrate them with the text of your report to either support or contradict your argument; (2) you can assign a code to each theme and count how frequently each has occurred; and (3) you can combine both methods to communicate your findings. This is your choice, and is based on your impression of the preference of your readers. Hence, coding of data—the process of assigning a numerical value to each response category—is described separately under the following headings:

- Coding quantitative/categorical (qualitative and quantitative) data;
- Coding descriptive/qualitative data.

Coding quantitative/categorical (qualitative and quantitative) data

For coding quantitative/categorical (qualitative and quantitative) data you need to go through the following steps:

- developing a code book;
- pre-testing code book;
- coding the data;
- verifying the coded data.

Developing a code book

A code book provides a set of rules for assigning numerical values to answers obtained from respondents. Let us take an example. Figure 15.2 lists some questions taken from a questionnaire used in a survey conducted by the author in Western Australia to ascertain the impact of occupational redeployment on an individual. The questions selected should be sufficient to serve as a prototype for developing a code book, as they cover the various issues involved in the process.

To develop a code book to prepare data for computer analysis, it is important to know a little about the working of computers and the program being used. Briefly, there are three types of computer: mainframe, macro and personal. There are many statistical and other programs (software) that can be used with certain types of computer (depending upon the operating system for which the software is designed). The type of statistical procedures you can apply to your data are dependent not only upon the purpose of the analysis, the way you want to communicate your findings to the reader and your knowledge of statistical procedures, but also on the capabilities of the software. For almost all programs, data are entered in a specified format. It is, therefore, important to know what format is required for your program.

There are two formats for data entry: 'fixed' and 'free'. In this chapter we will be using the fixed format to illustrate how to develop a code book. The fixed format stipulates that a piece of information obtained from a respondent is entered in a specific column. Each column has a number and the 'Col. no.' in the code book refers to the column in which a specific type of information is to be entered. The information about an individual is thus entered in a row(s) comprising these columns. Previously computers allowed for 80 columns per record (in each row) but nowadays one can enter the information about an individual in as many as 256 columns. If the information for an individual respondent exceeds 80 or 256 columns, you need to use the second record (or second row). As the width of a computer monitor is 80 characters, you must restrict yourself to only 80 columns per record if you want to see the complete data set on your screen.

Figure 15.2   Example of questions from a survey

1 Please indicate:
   (a) Your current age in completed years: _____
   (c) Your marital status: (Please tick)
      Currently married _____
      Living in a de facto relationship _____
      Separated _____
      Divorced _____
      Never married _____

2 (b) If tertiary/university, please specify the level achieved and area of study.
      (Please specify all postgraduate qualifications.)

Level of achievement	Area of study: e.g. engineering, accounting
Associate diploma	
Diploma	
Bachelor	
Graduate diploma	
Masters	
PhD	

11 What, in your opinion, are the main differences between your jobs prior
    to and after redeployment?

    _____
    _____
    _____

12 We would like to know your perception of the two jobs *before* and *after*
    redeployment with respect to the following aspects of your job. Please
    rate them on a five-point scale using the following guide:

    5 = extremely satisfied, 4 = very satisfied, 3 = satisfied, 2 = dissatisfied,
    1= extremely dissatisfied

Before redeployment					Areas	After redeployment				
1	2	3	4	5		1	2	3	4	5
					Job status					
					Job satisfaction					
					Motivation to work					
					Interest in the job					
					Self-esteem					
					Professional competence					
					Peer interaction					
					Morale					
					Work environment					
					Social interaction					

For a beginner it is important to understand the structure of a code book (Table 15.1), which is based on the responses given to the questions listed in Figure 15.2.

Table 15.1 An example of a code book

Col. no.	Q. no.	Variable name	Response pattern	Code
1	2	3	4	5
1–3	S. no.	ID	Actual serial number	Code actual
4	Record no.	RNO	First record	1
			Second record	2
			Third record	3
5	1(a)	Age	20–24	1
			25–29	2
			30–34	3
			35–39	4
			40–44	5
			45–49	6
			No response	9
6	1(c)	MS	Currently married	1
			Living in a de facto relationship	2
			Separated	3
			Divorced	4
			Never married	5
			No response	9
	2(b)	TEDU	Assoc. Dip.	1
			Diploma	2
			Bachelors	3
			Grad. Dip.	4
			Masters	5
			PhD	6
			Not applicable	8
			No response	9
7		TEDU1	Same as in TEDU	Code
8		TEDU2	Same as in TEDU	as in
9		TEDU3	Same as in TEDU	TEDU
		STUDY	Behavioural Sciences	1
			Business	2
			Economics/Commerce	3
			Communication	4
			Engineering	5
			Geography	6
			History	7
			Graphics	8
			Librarianship	9
			Nursing	10
			Performing Arts	11
			Secretarial	12
			Social Work	13
			Psychology	14
			Education	15
			Chartered Acct.	16
			Zoology	17
			Anthropology	18
			Social Sciences	19
			Public/Health Admin.	20

(Continued on next page)

Table 15.1—*Continued*

Col. no.	Q. no.	Variable name	Response pattern	Code
1	*2*	*3*	*4*	*5*
			English	21
			Audio–visual Aids Education	22
			Not Applicable	88
			No response	99
10–11	2(b)	STUDY 1	Same as in STUDY	Code
12–13		STUDY 2	Same as in STUDY	as in
				STUDY
14–15		STUDY 3	Same as in STUDY	
	11	DIFWK	Lack of job satisfaction	
			–current job	01
			–previous job	02
			Less responsibility	
			–current job	03
			–previous job	04
			Low morale	
			–current job	05
			–previous job	06
			Lack of recognition of hard work	
			–current job	07
			–previous job	08
			Skills irrelevant	
			–current job	09
			–previous job	10
			Repetitious nature	
			–current job	11
			–previous job	12
			Job more segmented	
			–current job	13
			–previous job	14
			Reduction in occup. status	15
			Greater involvement in total process	
			–current job	16
			–previous job	17
			More restricted duties	
			–current job	18
			–previous job	19
			Less flexibility	
			–current job	20
			–previous job	21
			More people contact	
			–current job	22
			–previous job	23
			Less people contact	
			–current job	24
			–previous job	25
			More responsibility	
			–current job	26
			–previous job	27

(Continued on next page)

Table 15.1—*Continued*

Col. no. 1	Q. no. 2	Variable name 3	Response pattern 4	Code 5
			Better work environment	
			−current job	28
			−previous job	29
			Better work morale	
			−current job	30
			−previous job	31
			Working in a team	
			−current job	32
			−previous job	33
			Work as an individual	
			−current job	34
			−previous job	35
			Lack of job security	
			−current job	36
			−previous job	37
			Current job full–time	38
			Better career prospects	
			−current job	39
			−previous job	40
			No commonality	41
			Different working conditions	42
			Change in occup. status (not specified)	43
			High occup. level	
			−current job	44
			−previous job	45
			More job security in present job	46
			More professional environment in	
			−current job	47
			−previous job	48
			Different skills to learn in current job	49
			Higher workload	
			−current job	50
			−previous job	51
			Less supervision in	
			−current job	52
			−previous job	53
			Current job more relevant to my training	54
			Current job more rewarding	55
			Better morale in current job	56
			Greater variety of duties in	
			−current job	57
			−previous job	58
			Current job more rewarding	59
			Better morale in	
			−current job	60

(Continued on next page)

Table 15.1—*Continued*

Col. no. 1	Q. no. 2	Variable name 3	Response pattern 4	Code 5
			Less variety of tasks in current job	61
			Fewer skills required in	
			–current job	62
			–previous job	63
			Change in job title	64
			Previous job very demanding	65
			Opportunity to use initiative in previous job	66
			Current job does not require initiative	67
			Different skills required in current job	68
			No career prospects	
			–current job	69
			–previous job	70
			More professional environment in current job	71
			Different skills to learn in current job	72
			Different working conditions	73
			Change in occup. status (change not specified)	74
			Change in job resp. (change not specified)	75
			Current job is more structured	76
			Now part of the team	77
			No change	78
			Irrelevant response	79
			Other	80
			Not applicable	88
			No response	99
16–17	11	DIFWK1	Same as in DIFWK	code as
18–19		DIFWK2	Same as in DIFWK	in
20–21		DIFWK3	Same as in DIFWK	DIFWK
22–23		DIFWK4		
24–25		DIFWK5		
			Extremely dissatisfied	1
			Dissatisfied	2
	12	BEAFTER	Satisfied	3
			Very satisfied	4
			Extremely satisfied	5
			Same as in BEAFTER	
26		JOBSTA	Same as in BEAFTER	Code as
27		JOBSTB	Same as in BEAFTER	in BEAFTER
28		JOBSATA	Same as in BEAFTER	Code as
29		JOBSATB	Same as in BEAFTER	in BEAFTER
			and so on	

In Table 15.1, *column 1* refers to the columns in which a particular piece of information is to be entered. Allocation of columns in a fixed format is extremely important as when you write a program you need to specify the column in which a particular piece of information is entered so that the computer can perform the required procedures.

Column 2 identifies the question number in the research instrument for which the information is being coded. This is primarily to identify coding with the question number in the instrument.

Column 3 refers to the name of the variable. Each variable in a program is given a unique name so that the program can carry out the requested statistical procedures. Usually there are restrictions on the way you can name a variable (e.g. the number of characters you can use to name a variable and whether you use the alphabet or numerals). You need to check your program for this. It is advisable to name a variable in such a way that you can easily recognise it from its name.

Column 4 lists the responses to the various questions. Developing a response pattern for the questions is the most important, difficult and time-consuming part of developing a code book. The degree of difficulty in developing a response pattern differs with the types of questions in your research instrument (open- or closed-ended). If a question is closed-ended, the response pattern has already been developed as part of the instrument construction and all you need to do at this stage is to assign a numerical value to each response category. In terms of analysis, this is one of the main advantages of closed-ended questions. If a closed-ended question includes 'other' as one of the response categories, to accommodate any response that you may not have listed when developing the instrument, you should analyse the responses and assign them to non-overlapping categories in the same way as you would do for open-ended questions. Add these to the already developed response categories and assign each a numerical value.

If the number of responses to a question is less than nine, you need only one column to code the responses, and if it is more than nine but less than 99, you need two columns (Column 1 in the code book). But if a question asks respondents to give more than one response, the number of columns assigned should be in accordance with the number of responses to be coded. If there are, say, eight possible responses to a particular question and a respondent is asked to give three responses, you need three columns to code the responses to the question. Let us assume there are 12 possible responses to a question. To code each response you need two columns and, therefore, to code three responses you need six columns.

The coding of open-ended questions is more difficult. Coding of open-ended questions requires the response categories to be developed first through a process called ***content analysis***. One of the easier ways of analysing open-ended questions is to select a number of interview schedules/questionnaires randomly from the total completed interview schedules or questionnaires received. Select an open-ended question from one of these schedules or questionnaires and write down the response(s) on a sheet of paper. If the person has given more than one response, write them separately on the same sheet. Similarly, from the same questionnaire/schedule select another open-ended question and write down the responses given on a separate sheet. In the same way you can select other open-ended questions and write down the response(s). Remember that the responses to each question should be written on a separate sheet. Now select another questionnaire/interview schedule and go through the same process, adding response(s) given for the same question on the sheet for that question. Continue the process until you feel that the responses are being repeated and you are getting no or very few new ones—that is, when you reached a saturation point.

Now, one by one, examine the responses to each question to ascertain the similarities and differences. If two or more responses are similar in meaning though not necessarily in language, try to combine them under one category. Give a name to the category that is descriptive of the responses. Remember, when you code the data you code categories, *not* responses *per se*. It is advisable to write down the different responses under each category in the code book so that, while coding, you know the type of responses you have grouped under a category. In developing these categories there are three important considerations:

1 The categories should be *mutually* exclusive. Develop non-overlapping categories. A response should not be able to be placed within two categories.
2 The categories should be *exhaustive*; that is, almost every response should be able to be placed within one of the categories. If too many responses cannot be so categorised, it is an indication of ineffective categorisation. In such a situation you should examine your categories again.
3 The use of the '*other*' category, effectively a 'waste basket' for those odd responses that cannot be put into any category, must be kept to the absolute minimum because, as mentioned, it reflects the failure of the classification system. This category should not include more than 5 per cent of the total responses and should not contain any more responses than any other category.

Column 5 lists the actual codes of the code book that you decide to assign to a response. You can assign any numerical value to any response so long as you do not repeat it for another response within the same question. Two responses to questions are repeated commonly: 'not applicable' and 'no response'. You should select a number that can be used for these responses for all or most questions. For example, responses such as 'not applicable' and 'no response' could be given a code of 8 and 9 respectively, even though the responses to a question may be limited to only 2 or 3. In other words, suppose you want to code the gender of a respondent and you have decided to code female = 1 and male = 2. For 'no response', instead of assigning a code of 3, assign a code of 9. This suggestion helps in remembering codes, which will help to increase your speed in coding.

To explain the coding process, let us take the questions listed in the example in Figure 15.2. We will take each question one by one to detail the process.

Question 1(a)

This is an open-ended quantitative question. In questions like this it is important to determine the range of responses—the respondent with the lowest and the respondent with the highest age. To do this, go through a number of questionnaires/interview schedules. Once the range is established, divide it into a number of categories. The categories developed are dependent upon a number of considerations such as the purpose of analysis, the way you want to communicate the findings of your study and whether the findings are going to be compared with those of another study. Let us assume that the range in the study is 23 to 49 years and assume that you develop the following categories to suit your purpose: 20–24, 25–29, 30–34, 35–39, 40–44 and 45–49. If your range is correct you should need no other categories. Let us assume that you decide to code 20–24 =1, 25–29 =2, 30–34 =3 and so on. To accommodate 'no response' you decide to assign a code of 9. Let us assume you decided to code the responses to this question in column 5 of the code sheet.

Question 1(c)

This is a closed-ended categorical question; that is, the response pattern is already provided. In these situations you just need to assign a numerical value to each category. For example, you may decide to code 'currently married' = 1, 'living in a de facto relationship' = 2, 'separated' = 3, 'divorced' = 4 and 'never married' = 5. You may add 'no response' as another category and assign it with a code of 9. The response to this question is coded in column 6 of the code sheet.

Question 2(b)

In this question a respondent is asked to indicate the area in which s/he has achieved a tertiary qualification. The question asks for two aspects: 1) Level of achievement, which is categorical, and 2) Area of study, which is open-ended. Also, a person may have more than one qualification which makes it a **multiple response question**. In such questions both aspects of the question are to be coded. In this case, this means the level of achievement (e.g. associate diploma, diploma) and the area of study (e.g. engineering, accounting). When coding multiple responses, decide the maximum possible number of responses to be coded. Let us assume you code a maximum number of three levels of tertiary education. (This would depend upon the maximum number of levels of achievement identified by the study population.) First code the levels of achievement TEDU (TEDU: T = tertiary and EDU = education; the naming of the variable—'level of achievement'—in this manner is done for easy identification) and then the area of study, STUDY (the variable name given to the 'area of study' = STUDY). In the above example, let us assume that you decided to code three levels of achievement. To distinguish them from each other we call the first level TEDU1, the second TEDU2 and the third TEDU3, and decide to code them in columns, 7, 8, and 9 respectively. Similarly, the names given to the three areas of STUDY are STUDY1, STUDY2 and STUDY3 and we decide to code them in columns 10–11, 12–13 and 14–15. The codes (01 to 23) assigned to different qualification are listed in the code book. If a respondent has only one qualification, the question of second and third qualification is not applicable and you need to decide a code for 'not applicable'. Assume you assigned a code of 88. 'No response' would then be assigned a code of 99 for this question.

Question 11

This is an open-ended question. To code this you need to go through the process of content analysis as explained earlier. Within the scope of this chapter it is not possible to explain the details but response categories that have been listed are based upon the responses given by 109 respondents to the survey on occupational redeployment in Western Australia. In coding questions like this, on the one hand you need to keep the variation in the respondents' answers and on the other, you want to break them up into meaningful categories to identify the commonalities. Because this question is asking respondents to identify the differences between their jobs before and after redeployment, for easy identification let us assume this variable was named DIFWK (DIF = difference and WK = work). Responses to this question are listed in Figure 15.3. These responses have been selected at random from the questionnaires returned.

A close examination of the above responses reveals that a number of themes are common, for example: 'learning new skills in the new job'; 'challenging tasks are missing from the new position'; 'more secure in the present job'; 'more interaction in the present job'; 'less responsibility'; 'more variety'; 'no difference'; 'more satisfying'. There are many similar themes that hold for both the before and after jobs. Therefore, we developed these themes for 'current job' and 'previous job'.

One of the main differences between qualitative and quantitative research is the way responses are used in the report. In qualitative research the responses are normally used either verbatim or are organised under certain themes and the actual responses are provided to substantiate them.

In quantitative research the responses are examined, common themes are identified, the themes are named (or categories are developed), and the responses given by respondents are classified under these themes. The data are then analysed to determine the frequency of the themes. It is also possible to analyse the themes in relation to some other characteristics such as age, education and income of the study population.

The code book lists the themes developed on the basis of responses given. As you can see, many categories may result. The author's advice is not to worry about this as categories can always be combined later if required. The reverse is impossible unless you go back to the raw data.

Let us assume you want to code up to five responses to this question and that you have decided to name these five variables as DIFWK1, DIFWK2, DIFWK3, DIFWK4 and DIFWK5. Let us also assume that you have coded them in columns 16–17, 18–19, 20–21, 22–23 and 24–25 respectively.

Figure 15.3   Some selected responses to the open-ended question (no. 11) in Figure 15.2

Respondent 3
    'Hours now FT: totally different skills required; deal with public; busier, more structured day and duties; now a part of the team instead of an independent worker.'

Respondent 20
    'That I am happy and made to feel as though I am a valuable part of a team.'

Respondent 41
    'This one is great, other one was lousy due to mismanagement, poor morale and feelings that dedication and hard work counted for nothing. Department of ... is well managed and morale is good and the graphic design work is fun and I am supported by my supervisors and subordinates.'

Respondent 48
'Before	*After*
15 hours per week	*24 hours per week*
Monday to Friday	*Very satisfactory*
On the go the whole time	*Dealing with the public*

(Continued on next page)

> No sitting
> Dealings with the public

> Dealing with severe psychiatric
> patients can be very stressful.

Respondent 52
'No difference.'

Respondent 54
'My substantive position has been the same before and after the redeployment, but before the redeployment I was acting as Project Manager (level 5) and after being redeployed I was assigned to programming duties (level e).'

Respondent 63
'This position has more day-to-day administration (it includes corporate services, finance, PR, IT, etc).'

Respondent 69
'Had to find my own job.'

Respondent 72
'The job I was doing I looked after the needs of a workshop where in this job I process files and deliver them.'

Respondent 78
'Challenging tasks are missing from the new position now that I am familiar with it. Many routine activities (that I have been glad to learn in terms of career development) but that I am becoming bored with. My previous job was much more difficult and interesting than this one.'

Respondent 79
'I am more secure in my present job and it is better paid as I work longer hours now. I only worked 6 ½ hours as a tea attendant.'

Respondent 81
'My previous job required me to be involved in the whole area of government/ community and non-government requiring assistance in relation to settlement needs of migrants. My current position does not provide job satisfaction, particularly in relation to the offenders that I currently deal with.'

Respondent 97
'Less responsibility, more specific job, restricted job.'

Respondent 105
'More variety, more flexibility, more responsibility in the present job, but less confidence, more caution and some resentment.'

Question 12

This is a very structured question asking respondents to compare on a five-point ordinal scale their level of satisfaction with various areas of their job before and after redeployment. As we are gauging the level of satisfaction before and after redeployment, respondents are expected to give two responses to each area. In this example let us assume you have used the name JOBSTA for job status after redeployment (JOB = job, ST = status and A = after redeployment) and JOBSTB for before redeployment, (JOB = job, ST = status and B = before redeployment). Similarly, for the second area, job satisfaction, you have decided that the variable name, JOBSATA (JOB = job, SAT = satisfaction and A = after) will stand for the level of job satisfaction after redeployment and JOBSATB will stand for the level before redeployment. Other variable names have been similarly assigned. In this example the variable, JOBSTA, is entered in column 26, JOBSTB in column 27 and so on.

Pre-testing code book

Once a code book is designed, it is important to pre-test it for any problems before you code your data. A pre-test involves selecting a few questionnaires/interview schedules and actually coding the responses to ascertain any problems in coding. It is possible that you may not have provided for some responses and therefore will be unable to code them. Change your code book, if you need to, in the light of the pre-test.

Coding the data

Once your code book is finalised, the next step is to code the raw data. There are three ways of doing this:

1 coding on the questionnaires/interview schedule itself, if space for coding was provided at the time of constructing the research instrument;
2 coding on separate code sheets that are available for purchase;
3 coding directly into the computer using a program (SPSSx).

To explain the process of coding let us take the same questions that were used in developing the code book. We select three questionnaires at random from a total of 109 respondents (Figures 15.4, 15.5, 15.6). Using the code book as a guide, we code the information from these sheets on to the coding sheet (Figure 15.7). Let us examine the coding process by taking respondent 3 (Figure 15.4).

Respondent 3

The total number of respondents is more than 99 and this is the third questionnaire so 003 was given as the identification number which is coded in columns 1–3 (Figure 15.7). Because it is the first record for this respondent, 1 was coded in column 4. This respondent is 49 years of age and falls in the category 45–49, which was coded as 6. As the information on age is entered in column 5, 6 was coded in this column of the code sheet. The marital status of this person is 'divorced', hence 4 was coded in column 6. This person has a bachelors degree in librarianship. The code chosen for a bachelors degree is 3, which was entered in column 7. Three tertiary qualifications have been provided for, and as this person does not have any other qualifications, TEDU2 and TEDU3 are not applicable, and therefore a code of 8 is entered in columns 8 and 9. This person's bachelors degree is in librarianship for which code 09 was assigned and entered in columns 10–11. Since there is only one qualification, STUDY2 and STUDY3 are not applicable; therefore, a code of 88 was entered in columns 12–13 and 14–15. This person has given a number of responses to question no. 11 (DIFWK), which asks respondents to list the main differences between their jobs before and after redeployment. In coding such questions much caution is required.

Figure 15.4   Some questions from a survey—respondent 3

RESPONDENT = 3
1   Please indicate:
     (a) Your current age in completed years: _____49_____
     (c) Your marital status: (Please tick)
         Currently married _____
         Living in a de facto relationship _____
         Separated _____
         Divorced __✓__
         Never married _____

2(b) If tertiary/university, please specify the level achieved and area of study.
     (Please specify all postgraduate qualifications.)

Level of achievement	Area of study: e.g. engineering, accounting
Associate diploma	
Diploma	
Bachelor	*Librarianship*
Graduate diploma	
Masters	
PhD	

11 What, in your opinion, are the main differences between your jobs prior
    to and after redeployment?

'Hours -now F.T', 'Totally different skills required', 'Now deal with public',
'Busier , more structured day and duties', 'Now part of the team instead of
independent worker'

12 We would like to know your perception of the two jobs *before* and *after*
    redeployment with respect to the following aspects of your job. Please rate
    them on a five-point scale, using the following guide:

    5 = extremely satisfied, 4 = very satisfied, 3 = satisfied, 2 = dissatisfied,
    1 = extremely dissatisfied

Before redeployment					Areas	After redeployment				
1	2	3	4	5		1	2	3	4	5
			✓		Job status					✓
			✓		Job satisfaction					✓
			✓		Motivation to work					✓
			✓		Interest in the job					✓
			✓		Self-esteem					✓
			✓		Professional competence				✓	
			✓		Peer interaction					✓
			✓		Morale				✓	
			✓		Work environment				✓	
				✓	Social interaction			✓		

Figure 15.5   Some questions from a survey—respondent 59

RESPONDENT = 59
1   Please indicate:
    (a) Your current age in completed years: _____45_____
    (c) Your marital status: (Please tick)
        Currently married _____✓_____
        Living in a de facto relationship _____
        Separated _____
        Divorced _____
        Never married _____

2(b) If tertiary/university, please specify the level achieved and area of study.
    (Please specify all postgraduate qualifications.)

Level of achievement	Area of study: e.g. engineering, accounting
Associate diploma	
Diploma	
Bachelor	*Behavioural Sciences*
Graduate diploma	
Masters	
PhD	

11 What, in your opinion, are the main differences between your jobs prior
    to and after redeployment?

    _____*'Less Responsibility', 'More specific jobs'*_____
    _____*'Restricted scope'.*_____
    _____

12 We would like to know your perception of the two jobs *before* and *after*
    redeployment with respect to the following aspects of your job. Please rate
    them on a five-point scale using the following guide:

    5 = extremely satisfied, 4 = very satisfied, 3 = satisfied, 2 = dissatisfied,
    1 = extremely dissatisfied

Before redeployment					Areas	After redeployment				
1	2	3	4	5		1	2	3	4	5
			✓		Job status		✓			
			✓		Job satisfaction			✓		
			✓		Motivation to work		✓			
				✓	Interest in the job			✓		
				✓	Self-esteem			✓		
				✓	Professional competence			✓		
				✓	Peer interaction				✓	
				✓	Morale		✓			
				✓	Work environment			✓		
			✓		Social interaction				✓	

Figure 15.6   Some questions from a survey—respondent 81

RESPONDENT = 81

1   Please indicate:
    (a) Your current age in completed years: _____42_____
    (c) Your marital status: (Please tick)
        Currently married ____✓____
        Living in a de facto relationship _____
        Separated _____
        Divorced _____
        Never married _____

2(b) If tertiary/university, please specify the level achieved and area of study.
      (Please specify all postgraduate qualifications.)

Level of achievement	Area of study: e.g. engineering, accounting
Associate diploma	
Diploma	
Bachelor	Social Work
Graduate diploma	
Masters	
PhD	

11 What, in your opinion, are the main differences between your jobs prior
    to and after redeployment?

*'My previous job required me to be involved in the whole area of government/
community and non-government requiring assistance in relation to settlement
needs of migrants. My current position does not provide job satisfaction,
particularly in relation to the offenders that I currently deal with.'*

12 We would like to know your perception of the two jobs *before* and *after*
    redeployment with respect to the following aspects of your job. Please rate
    them on a five-point scale using the following guide:

    5 = extremely satisfied, 4 = very satisfied, 3 = satisfied, 2 = dissatisfied,
    1 = extremely dissatisfied

Before redeployment					Areas	After redeployment				
1	2	3	4	5		1	2	3	4	5
		✓			Job status		✓			
			✓		Job satisfaction		✓			
				✓	Motivation to work			✓		
			✓		Interest in the job		✓			
			✓		Self-esteem		✓			
		✓			Professional competence		✓			
		✓			Peer interaction			✓		
			✓		Morale		✓			
			✓		Work environment		✓			
		✓			Social interaction		✓			

Figure 15.7 An example of coded data on a code sheet

Program

Programmer | | Date

Fortran S

Column groups: *Identification number* / Statement Number (Cont.) — *Marital status* — *Study area* — *Difference in work* — *Level of satisfaction*

Annotations: *Record no.*, *Age*, *Achievement level*

1	2	3	4	5	6	7	8	9	10	11	12	13	14	15	16	17	18	19	20	21	22	23	24	25	26	27	28	29	30	31	32	33	34	35	36	37	38	39	40
	0	3	1	6	4	3	8	8	0	9	8	8	8	8	2	2	6	9	9	7	7	8	3	8	5	4	5	4	5	4	5	4	5	4					
	0	5	9	1	6	1	3	8	8	0	1	8	8	8	8	0	3	1	8	7	7	8	8	8	8	2	4	3	4	2	4	3	5	3	5					
	0	8	1	1	5	1	2	8	8	1	3	8	8	8	8	1	7	0	1	8	8	8	8	8	8	2	3	2	3	3	5	2	4	2	4					

Examine the responses named DIFWK1, DIFWK2, DIFWK3, DIFWK4 and DIFWK5, to identify the codes that can be assigned. A code of 22 (now deal with public) was assigned to one of the responses, which we enter in columns 16–17. The second difference, DIFWK2, was assigned a code of 69 (totally different skill required), which is coded in columns 18–19.

DIFWK3 was assigned a code of 77 (current job more structure) and coded in columns 20–21. Similarly, the fourth (DIFWK4) and the fifth (DIFWK5) difference in the jobs before and after redeployment are coded as 78 (now part of the team instead of independent worker) and 38 (hours—now full time), which are entered in columns 22–23 and 24–25 respectively. Question 12 is extremely simple to code. Each area of a job has two columns, one for before and the other for after. Job status (JOBST) is divided into two variables, JOBSTA for a respondent's level of satisfaction after redeployment and JOBSTB for his/her level before redeployment. JOBSTA is entered in column 26 and JOBSTB in column 27. For JOBSTA the code, 5, (as marked by the respondent) is entered in column 26 and the code for JOBSTB, 4, is entered in column 27. Other areas of the job before and after redeployment are similarly coded.

The other two examples are coded in the same manner. The coded data are shown in Figure 15.7. In the process of coding you might find some responses that do not fit your predetermined categories. If so, assign them a code and add these to your code book.

Verifying the coded data

Once the data is coded, select a few research instruments at random and record the responses to identify any discrepancies in coding. Continue to verify coding until you are sure that there are no discrepancies. If there are discrepancies, re-examine the coding.

Coding descriptive/qualitative data

Whether or not you code descriptive data depends upon how you plan to communicate the findings of your study. For analysing qualitative data, as just mentioned, you need to go through a process called **content analysis**. Content analysis means analysis of the contents of an interview in order to identify the main themes that emerge from the responses given by your respondents. This process involves a number of steps:

Step 1   **Identify the main themes**. You need to carefully go through descriptive responses given by your respondents to each question in order to understand the *meaning* they communicate. From these responses you develop broad themes that reflect these meanings. You will notice that people use different words and language to express themselves. It is important for you to select the wording of your themes in a way that accurately represents the meaning of the responses categorised under a theme. These themes become the basis for analysing the text of unstructured interviews.

Step 2   **Assign codes to the main themes**. Whether or not you assign a code to a main theme is dependent upon whether or not you want to count the number of times a theme has occurred in an interview. If you decide to count these themes you should, at random, select a few responses to an open-ended question and identify the main themes. You continue to identify these themes from the same question till you have reached saturation point. Write these themes and assign a code to each of them, using numbers or keywords.

Step 3   **Classify responses under the main themes**. Having identified the themes, the next step is to go through the transcripts of all your interviews and classify the responses under the different themes. You can also use a computer program such as Ethnograph, NUD*DIST N6, NVivo, XSight for undertaking this thematic analysis. You will benefit by learning one of these programs if your data are suitable for such analysis.

Step 4   **Integrate themes and responses into the text of your report**. Having identified responses that fall within different themes, the next step is to integrate them into the text of your report. How you integrate them into your report is mainly your choice. Some people, while discussing the main themes that emerged from their study, use verbatim responses to keep the feel of the responses. There are others who count how frequently a theme has occurred, and then provide a sample of the responses. It entirely depends upon the way you want to communicate the findings to your readers.

Developing a frame of analysis for quantitative studies

Although a framework of analysis needs to evolve continuously while writing your report, it is desirable to broadly develop it before analysing the data. A frame of analysis should specify:

- which variables you are planning to analyse;
- how they should be analysed;
- what cross-tabulations you need to work out;
- which variables you need to combine to construct your major concepts or to develop indices (in formulating a research problem concepts are changed to variables—at this stage change them back to concepts);
- which variables are to be subjected to which statistical procedures.

To illustrate, let us take the example from the survey used in this chapter.

Frequency distributions

Frequency distributions group respondents into the subcategories into which a variable can be divided. Unless you are not planning to use answers to some of the questions, you should have a frequency distribution for all the variables. Each variable can be specified either separately or collectively in the frame of analysis. To illustrate they are identified here separately by the names used in the code book. For example frame of analysis should include frequency distribution for the following variables:

- AGE;
- MS;
- TEDU (TEDU1, TEDU2, TEDU3—multiple responses, to be collectively analysed);
- STUDY (STUDY1, STUDY2, STUDY3—multiple responses, to be collectively analysed);
- DIFWK (DIFWK1, DIFWK2, DIFWK3, DIFWK4, DIFWK5—multiple responses, to be collectively analysed);
- JOBSTA, JOBSTB;
- JOBSATA, JOBSATB;
- MOTIVA, MOTIVB.
- etc.

Cross-tabulations

Cross-tabulations analyse two variables, usually independent and dependent or attribute and dependent, to determine if there is a relationship between them. The subcategories of both the variables are cross-tabulated to ascertain if a relationship exists between them. Usually, the absolute number of respondents, and the row and column percentages, give you a reasonably good idea as to the possible association.

In the study we cited as an example in this chapter, one of the main variables to be explained is the level of satisfaction with the 'before' and 'after' jobs after redeployment. We developed two indices of satisfaction:

1 satisfaction with the job before redeployment (SATINDB);
2 satisfaction with the job after redeployment (SATINDA).

Differences in the level of satisfaction can be affected by a number of personal attributes such as the age, education, training and marital status of the respondents. Cross-tabulations help to identify which attributes affect the levels of satisfaction. Theoretically, it is possible to correlate any variables, but it is advisable to be selective or an enormous number of tables will result. Normally only those variables you think have an effect on the dependent variable should be correlated. The following cross-tabulations are an example of the basis of a frame of analysis. You can specify as many variables as you want.

SATINDA and SATINDB by:

- AGE;
- MS;

- TEDU;
- STUDY;
- DIFWK.

These determine whether job satisfaction before and after redeployment is affected by age, marital status, education and so on.

SATINDA by:

- SATINDB.

This ascertains whether there is a relationship between job satisfaction before and after redeployment.

Constructing the main concepts

There may be places in a research instrument where you look for answers through a number of questions about different aspects of the same issue, for example the level of satisfaction with jobs before and after redeployment (SATINDB and SATINDA). In the questionnaire there were ten aspects of a job about which respondents were asked to identify their level of satisfaction before and after redeployment. The level of satisfaction may vary from aspect to aspect. Though it is important to know respondents' reactions to each aspect, it is equally important to gauge an overall index of their satisfaction. You must therefore ascertain, before you actually analyse data, how you will combine responses to different questions.

In this example the respondents indicated their level of satisfaction by selecting one of the five response categories. A satisfaction index was developed by assigning a numerical value—the greater the magnitude of the response category, the higher the numerical score—to the response given by a respondent. The numerical value corresponding to the category ticked was added to determine the satisfaction index. The satisfaction index score for a respondent varies between 10 and 50. The interpretation of the score is dependent upon the way the numerical values are assigned. In this example the higher the score, the higher is the level of satisfaction.

Statistical procedures

Regression analysis:

- SATINDA and SATINDB.

Multiple regression analysis:

- SATINDA with AGE, EDUCATION, MS.
- SATINDB with AGE, EDUCATION, MS.

ANOVA:

Similarly, it may be necessary to think about and specify the different variables to be subjected to the various statistical procedures. There are a number of user-friendly programs such as SPSSx and SAS that you can easily learn.

Developing a frame of analysis for qualitative studies

For qualitative studies, the most important consideration in developing the frame of analysis is your preference for a particular style of writing. If you want to communicate the frequency of various themes, you need to analyse your data that achieves counting of different themes, but on the other hand, if you choose to write the text on the basis of verbatim responses, you need to accordingly analyse the data.

Analysing data

Coded data can be analysed manually or with the help of a computer. If the number of respondents is reasonably small, there are not many variables to analyse, and you are neither familiar with a relevant computer program nor wish to learn one, you can manually analyse the data. However, manual analysis is useful only for calculating frequencies and for simple cross-tabulations. In addition, if you want to carry out statistical tests, they have to be calculated manually. However, the use of statistics depends upon your expertise and desire/need to communicate the findings in a certain way.

Be aware that manual analysis is extremely time-consuming. The easiest way to analyse data manually is to code it directly onto large graph paper in columns in the same way as you would enter it into a computer. On the graph paper you do not need to worry about the column number. Detailed headings can be used or question numbers can be written on each column to code information about the question (Figure 15.8).

Figure 15.8   Manual analysis using graph paper

ID	Age	MS	Education			Study area			Difference in work					Status		Satisfaction	
			1	2	3	1	2	3	1	2	3	4	5	Before	After	Before	After
03	6	4	3	8	8	09	88	88	22	69	77	78	38	5	4	5	4
59	6	1	3	8	8	01	88	88	03	18	77	88	88	2	4	3	4
81	5	1	2	8	8	13	88	88	17	01	88	88	88	2	3	2	4

To manually analyse data (frequency distributions), count various codes in a column and then decode them. For example, age from Figure 15.8, 5 = 1, 6 = 2. This shows that out of the three respondents, one was between 40 and 44 years of age and the other two were between 45 and 49. Similarly, responses for each variable can be analysed. For cross-tabulations two columns must be read simultaneously to analyse responses in relation to each other.

If you want to analyse data using a computer, you should be familiar with the appropriate program. You should know how to create a data file, how to use the procedures involved, what statistical tests to apply and how to interpret them. Obviously in this area knowledge of computers and statistics plays an important role.

The role of computers in research

Knowledge of computers and the relevant programs is extremely important and ultimately saves time. Data can be analysed with the help of computers even for qualitative and descriptive information. Computers primarily help to save labour in manual data analysis and in the calculation of descriptive and inferential statistics. Computers are tools that increase your speed, handle complicated statistical and mathematical procedures, print the report, display the analysed data and present them graphically. They are designed to perform extremely complicated procedures, which otherwise could be very time-consuming, in an extremely short time.

While computers are designed to help, a good understanding of them is required to be able to benefit from them. The time spent in learning about computers is ultimately worthwhile, whether you classify yourself as a qualitative or quantitative researcher.

The role of statistics in research

The role of statistics in research is sometimes exaggerated. Statistics have a role only when you have collected the required information, adhering to the requirements of each operational step of the research process. Once data are collected you encounter two questions:

1 How do I organise these data to understand them?
2 What do they mean?

In a way, the answer to the first question forms the basis for the second. Statistics can play a very important role in answering your research questions.

From individual responses, particularly if there are many, it becomes extremely difficult to understand the patterns in the data, so it is important for the data to be summarised. Some simple statistical measures such as percentages, means, standard deviations and co-efficients of correlations can reduce the volume of data, making it easier to understand. In computing summary measures certain information is lost and therefore misinterpretation is possible. Hence, caution is required when interpreting data.

Statistics play a vital role in understanding the relationship between variables, particularly when there are more than two. With experience, it is easy to 'read' the relationship between two variables from a table, but not to quantify this relationship. Statistics help you to ascertain the strength of a relationship. They confirm or contradict what you read from a piece of information, and provide an indication of the strength of the relationship and the level of confidence that can be placed in findings. When there are more than two variables, statistics are also helpful in understanding the interdependence between them, and their contribution to a phenomenon or event.

Indirectly, knowledge of statistics helps you at each step of the research process. Knowledge of the problems associated with data analysis, the types of statistical test that can be applied to certain types of variable, and knowledge of the calculation of summary statistics in relation to the measurement scale used play an important role in a research endeavour. However, you can also carry out a perfectly valid study without using any statistical procedures. This depends upon the objectives of your study.

SUMMARY

In this chapter you have learnt about processing data. Irrespective of the method of data collection, qualitative or quantitative, the information is called 'raw data' or simply 'data'. The processing of data includes all operations undertaken from when a set of data is collected until it is ready to be analysed either manually or by a computer. The process of data processing starts with data editing, which is basically 'cleaning' your data. The coding of data, which entails developing a code book, pre-testing it, coding *per se* and verifying the coded data, is the next step. This chapter has discussed the process of developing a code book and has provided a prototype for it. How to develop codes for open-ended and closed-ended questions has been described in detail. The chapter has also guided you through the steps of coding data by taking an example from a survey.

Though the development of a frame of analysis continues until you have finished the report, it helps immensely in data analysis to develop this before you begin analysing data. In the frame of analysis the type of analysis to be undertaken (e.g. frequency distribution, cross-tabulation), and the statistical procedures to be applied should be specified.

Computers primarily help by saving labour. Their application in handling complicated statistical and mathematical procedures, word processing, displaying and graphic presentation of the analysed data save time and increase speed. Statistics are desirable but not essential for a study. The extent of their application depends upon the purpose of the study. Statistics primarily help you to make sense of data, 'read' the data, explore relationships and interdependence between variables, ascertain the magnitude of an existing relationship or interdependence and place confidence in your findings.

CHAPTER
sixteen

Displaying data

Having analysed the data, the next task is to present findings effectively to readers. The main purpose of using data-display techniques is to make the findings clear and easily understood. There are many ways of presenting information. The choice of a particular method should be determined primarily by your impressions/knowledge of your likely readership's familiarity with the topic and with research and statistics. If your readers are likely to be familiar with 'reading' data, you can use complicated methods of data display; if not, it is wise to keep to simple techniques. Although there are many ways of displaying data, this chapter is limited to the more commonly used ones. There are many computer programs that can help you with this task.

Tables

Structure

Tables are the most common method of presenting analysed data. 'Tables offer a useful means of presenting large amounts of detailed information in a small space' (*The Chicago Manual of Style* 1993: 321). It is, therefore, essential for beginners to know about their structure and types. Figure 16.1 shows the structure of a table.

A table has five parts:

1 **Title**—this normally indicates the table's number and describes the type of data it contains. It is important to give each table its own number as you will need to refer to the tables when interpreting and discussing the data. The tables should be numbered sequentially as they appear in the text. The procedure for numbering tables is a personal choice. If you are writing an article, simply identifying tables by number is sufficient. In the case of a dissertation or a report, one way to identify a table is by the chapter number followed by the sequential number of the table in the chapter—the procedure adopted in this book. The main advantage of this procedure is that if it becomes necessary to add or delete a table when revising the report, the table numbers for that chapter only, rather than for the whole report, will need to be changed.

   The description accompanying the table number must clearly specify the contents of that table. In the description identify the variables about which information is contained in the table, for example 'Respondents by age' or 'Attitudes towards uranium mining'. If a table contains information about two variables, the dependent variable should be identified first in the title, for example 'Attitudes towards uranium mining [dependent variable] by gender [independent variable]'.

2 **Stub**—the subcategories of a variable, listed along the y-axis (the left-hand column of the table). According to *The McGraw-Hill Style Manual* (Longyear 1983: 97), 'The stub, usually the first column on the left, lists the items about which information is provided in the horizontal rows to the right.' *The Chicago Manual of Style* (1993: 331) describes the stub as: 'a vertical listing of categories or individuals about which information is given in the columns of the table'.

3 **Column headings**—the subcategories of a variable, listed along the x-axis (the top of the table). In univariate tables (tables displaying

information about one variable) the column heading is usually the 'number of respondents' and/or the 'percentage of respondents' (Tables 16.1 and 16.2). In bivariate tables (tables displaying information about two variables) it is the subcategories of one of the variables displayed in the column headings (Table 16.3).

4 **Body**—the cells housing the analysed data.

5 **Supplementary notes or footnotes**—there are four types of footnote: source notes; other general notes; notes on specific parts of the table; and notes on the level of probability (*The Chicago Manual of Style*: 333). If the data are taken from another source, you have an obligation to acknowledge this. The source should be identified at the bottom of the table, and labelled by the word 'Source:' as in Figure 16.1. Similarly, other explanatory notes should be added at the bottom of a table.

Figure 16.1   The structure of a table

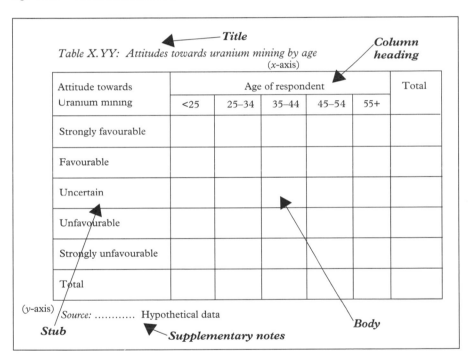

Table 16.1   Respondents by age (frequency table for one population—hypothetical data)

Age	No. of respondents
<20 years	2 (2.0)
20–24	12 (12.0)
25–29	22 (22.0)
30–34	14 (14.0)
35–39	17 (17.0)
40–44	10 (10.0)
45–49	11 (11.0)
50–54	9 (9.0)
55+00	3 (3.0)
Total	100 (100.0)

Note: Figures in parentheses are percentages

Table 16.2   Respondents by age (frequency table comparing two populations—hypothetical data)

Age	Population A	Population B
<20	2 (2.0)	1 (0.6)
20–24	12 (12.0)	17 (10.9)
25–29	22 (22.0)	23 (14.7)
30–34	14 (14.0)	18 (11.5)
35–39	17 (17.0)	26 (16.7)
40–44	10 (10.0)	16 (10.3)
45–49	11 (11.0)	18 (11.5)
50–54	9 (9.0)	27 (17.3)
55+	3 (3.0)	10 (6.4)
No response	0 (0.0)	0 (0.0)
Total	100 (100.0)	156 (99.9*)

Note: Figures in parentheses are percentages (*rounding error)

Table 16.3   Respondents by attitude towards uranium mining and age (cross-tabulation—hypothetical data)

Attitude towards uranium mining	Age					
	<25	25–34	35–44	45–54	55+	Total
Strongly favourable	(0.0)* 0 (0.0)@	(5.5) 2 (12.5)@	(14.8) 4 (25.0)@	(35.0) 7 (43.6)@	(100.0) 3 (18.6)@	16 (100.0)@
Favourable	(0.0)* 0 (0.0)	(8.3) 3 (25.0)	(18.5) 5 (41.7)	(20.0) 4 (33.3)	(0.0) 0 (0.0)	12 (100.0)
Uncertain	(0.0)* 0 (0.0)	(0.0) 0 (0.0)	(7.4) 2 (33.3)	(20.0) 4 (66.7)	(0.0) 0 (0.0)	6 (100.0)
Unfavourable	(14.3)* 2 (20.0)	(19.4) 7 (70.0)	(3.7) 1 (10.0)	(0.0) 0 (0.0)	(0.0) 0 (0.0)	10 (100.0)
Strongly unfavourable	(85.7)* 12 (21.4)	(66.7) 24 (42.9)	(55.6) 15 (26.8)	(25.0) 5 (8.9)	(0.0) 0 (0.0)	56 (100.00
Total	(100.0)* 14	(100.0) 36	(100.0) 27	(100.0) 20	(100.0) 3	(100.0) 100

* = Column percentage; @ = Row percentage

Types of tables

Depending upon the number of variables about which information is displayed, tables can be categorised as univariate (containing information about one variable, e.g, Tables 16.1 and 16.2), also called frequency tables; bivariate (containing information about two variables, e.g. Table 16.3), also called cross-tabulations; or polyvariate/multivariate (containing information about more than two variables, e.g. Table 16.4).

Table 16.4   Attitude towards uranium mining by age and gender (hypothetical data)

Attitude towards uranium mining	Number of respondents										Total		
	<25		25–34		35–44		45–54		55+				
	F	M	F	M	F	M	F	M	F	M	F	M	T
Strongly favourable	0	0	1	1	3	1	5	2	3	–	12	4	16
Favourable	0	0	1	2	3	2	3	1	0	0	7	5	12
Uncertain	0	0	0	0	1	1	2	2	0	0	3	3	6
Unfavourable	1	1	4	3	1	0	0	0	0	0	6	4	10
Strongly unfavourable	4	8	17	7	8	7	2	3	0	0	31	25	56
Total	5	9	23	13	16	11	12	8	3	0	59	41	100

Types of percentages

The ability to interpret data accurately and to communicate findings effectively are important skills for a researcher. For accurate and effective interpretation of data, you may need to calculate other measures such as percentages, cumulative percentages or ratios. It is also sometimes important to apply other statistical procedures to data. The use of percentages is a common procedure in the interpretation of data. There are three types of percentage: 'row', 'column' and 'total'. It is important to understand the relevance, interpretation and significance of each. Let us take some examples.

Tables 16.1 and 16.2 are univariate or frequency tables. In any univariate table, percentages calculate the magnitude of each subcategory of the variable out of a constant number (100). Such a table shows what would have been the expected number of respondents in each subcategory had there been 100 respondents. Percentages in a univariate table play a more important role when two or more samples or populations are being compared (Table 16.2). As the total number of respondents in each sample or population group normally varies, percentages enable you to standardise them against a fixed number (100). This standardisation against 100 enables you to compare the magnitude of the two populations within the different sub-categories of a variable.

In a cross-tabulation such as in Table 16.3, the subcategories of both variables are examined in relation to each other. To make this table less congested, we have collapsed the age categories shown in Table 16.1. For such tables you can calculate three different types of percentage: row, column and total.

- **Row percentage**—calculated from the total of *all* the subcategories of one variable that are displayed along a row in different columns, in relation to only *one* subcategory of the other variable. For example, in Table 16.3 figures in parentheses marked with @ are the row percentages calculated out of *the total* (16) of all age subcategories of the variable age in relation to only one subcategory of the second variable (i.e. those who hold a strongly favourable attitude towards uranium mining)—in other words, one subcategory of a variable displayed on the stub by all the subcategories of the variable displayed on the column heading of a table. Out of those who hold a strongly unfavourable attitude towards uranium mining, 21.4 per cent are under the age of 25 years, none is above the age of 55 and the majority (42.9 per cent) are between 25–34 years of age (Table 16.3). This row percentage has thus given you the variation in terms of age among those who hold a strongly unfavourable attitude towards uranium mining. It has shown how the 56 respondents who hold a strongly unfavourable attitude towards uranium mining differ in age from one another. Similarly, you can select any other subcategory of the variable (attitude towards uranium mining) to examine its variation in relation to the other variable, age.

- **Column percentage**—in the same way, you can hold age at a constant level and examine variations in attitude. For example, suppose you want to find out differences in attitude among 25–34 year-olds towards uranium mining. The age category 25–34 (column) shows that of the 36 respondents, 24 (66.7 per cent) hold a strongly unfavourable attitude while only two (5.5 per cent) hold a strongly favourable attitude towards uranium mining. You can do the same by taking any subcategory of the variable age, to examine differences with respect to the different subcategories of the other variable (attitudes towards uranium mining).
- **Total percentage**—this standardises the magnitude of each cell; that is, it gives the percentage of respondents who are classified in the subcategories of one variable in relation to the subcategories of the other variable. For example, what percentage do those who are under the age of 25 years, and hold a strongly unfavourable attitude towards uranium mining, constitute of the total population?

It is possible to sort data for three variables. Table 16.4 (percentages not shown) examines respondents' attitudes in relation to their age and gender. As you add more variables to a table it becomes more complicated to read and more difficult to interpret, but the procedure for interpreting it is the same.

The introduction of the third variable, *gender*, helps you to find out how the observed association between the two subcategories of the two variables, age and attitude, is distributed in relation to gender. In other words, it helps you to find out how many males and females constitute a particular cell showing the association between the other two variables. For example, Table 16.4 shows that of those who have a strongly unfavourable attitude towards uranium mining, 24 (42.9 per cent) are 25–34 years of age. This group comprises 17 (70.8 per cent) females and 7 (29.2 per cent) males. Hence, the table shows that a greater proportion of female than male respondents between the ages of 25 and 34 hold a strongly unfavourable attitude towards uranium mining. Similarly, you can take any two subcategories of age and attitude and relate these to either subcategory (male/female) of the third variable, gender.

Graphs

Statistical data not only require careful analysis but also attractive display for easier understanding and communication. One of the choices you need to make is whether a set of information is best presented as a table, a graph or as text. The main objective of a graph is to present data in a way that is easy to understand and interpret, and interesting to look at. Your decision to use a graph should be based mainly on this consideration. 'A graph is based entirely on the tabled data and therefore can tell no story that cannot be learnt by inspecting a table. However, graphic representation often makes it easier to see the pertinent features of a set of data' (Minium 1978: 45).

Graphs can be constructed for every type of data—quantitative and qualitative—and for any type of variable (measured on a nominal, ordinal, interval or ratio scale). There are different types of graph, and your decision to use a particular type should be made on the basis of the measurement scale used in the measurement of a variable. It is equally important to keep in mind the measurement scale when it comes to interpretation. It is not uncommon to find people misinterpreting a graph and drawing wrong conclusions simply because they have overlooked the measurement scale used in the measurement of a variable.

When constructing a graph of any type it is important to be acquainted with the following points:

- A graphic presentation is constructed in relation to two axes: horizontal and vertical. The horizontal axis is called the 'abscissa', or more commonly, the x-axis, and the vertical axis is called the 'ordinate', or more commonly, the y-axis (Minium: 45).
- If a graph is designed to display only one variable, it is customary, but not essential, to represent the subcategories of the variable along the x-axis and the frequency or count of that subcategory along the y-axis. The point where the axes intersect, is considered as the zero point for the y-axis. When a graph presents two variables, one is displayed on each axis and the point where they intersect is considered as the starting or zero point.
- A graph, like a table, should have a title that describes its contents. The axes should be labelled also.
- A graph should be drawn to an appropriate scale. It is important to choose a scale that enables your graph to be neither too small nor too large, and your choice of scale for each axis should result in the axes being roughly proportionate to one another. Sometimes, to fit the spread of the scale (when it is too spread out) on one or both axes, it is necessary to break the scale and alert readers by introducing a break (usually two slanting parallel lines) in the axes.
- As mentioned, the type of graph you choose depends upon the type of data you are displaying. For categorical variables you can construct only bar charts, histograms or pie charts, whereas for continuous variables, in addition to the above, line or trend graphs can also be constructed. The number of variables shown in a graph are also important in determining the type of graph you can construct.

The histogram

A histogram consists of a series of rectangles drawn next to each other without any space between them, each representing the frequency of a category or subcategory (Figure 16.2). Their height is in proportion to the frequency they represent. The height of the rectangles may represent the absolute or proportional frequency or the percentage of the total. As mentioned, a histogram can be drawn for both categorical and continuous variables. When interpreting a histogram you need to take into account whether it is representing categorical or continuous variables. Figure 16.2a, b and c shows two histograms, using data from Tables 16.1 and 16.4.

Figure 16.2a Two-dimentional histogram

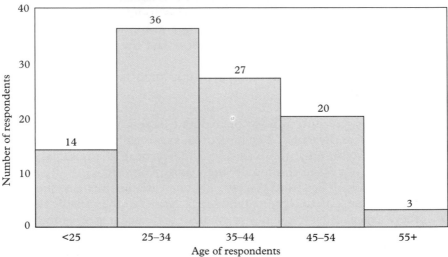

Figure 16.2b Three-dimensional histogram

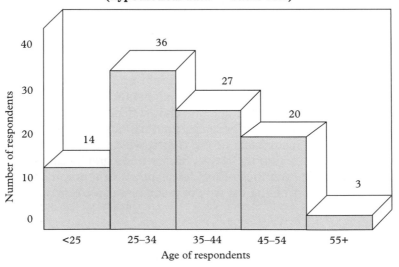

Figure 16.2c Two-dimensional histogram with two variables

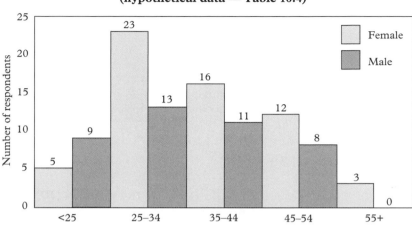

The bar chart

The bar chart or diagram is used for displaying categorical data (Figure 16.3). A bar chart is identical to a histogram, except that in a bar chart the rectangles representing the various frequencies are spaced, thus indicating that the data are categorical. The bar diagram is used for variables measured on nominal or ordinal scales. The discrete categories are usually displayed along the x-axis and the number or percentage of respondents, on the y-axis. However, as illustrated, it is possible to display the discrete categories along the y-axis. The bar diagram is an effective way of visually displaying the magnitude of each subcategory of a variable.

The stacked bar chart

A stacked bar chart is similar to a bar chart except that in the former each bar shows information about two or more variables stacked onto each other vertically (Figure 16.4). The sections of a bar show the proportion of the variables they represent in relation to one another. The stacked bars can be drawn only for categorical data.

The 100 per cent bar chart

The 100 per cent bar chart (Figure 16.5) is very similar to the stacked bar chart. The only difference is that in the former the subcategories of a variable for a particular bar total 100 per cent and each bar is sliced into portions in relation to their proportion out of 100.

Figure 16.3   Bar charts

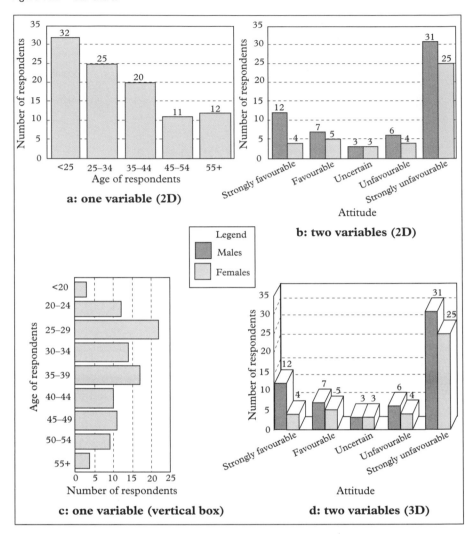

The frequency polygon

The frequency polygon is very similar to a histogram. A frequency polygon is drawn by joining the midpoint of each rectangle at a height commensurate with the frequency of that interval (Figure 16.6). One problem in constructing a frequency polygon is what to do with the two categories at either extreme. To bring the polygon line back to the x-axis, imagine that the two extreme categories have an interval similar to the rest and assume the frequency in these categories to be zero. From the midpoint of these intervals, you extend the polygon line to meet the x-axis at both ends. A frequency polygon can be drawn using either absolute or proportionate frequencies.

Figure 16.4   The stacked bar chart

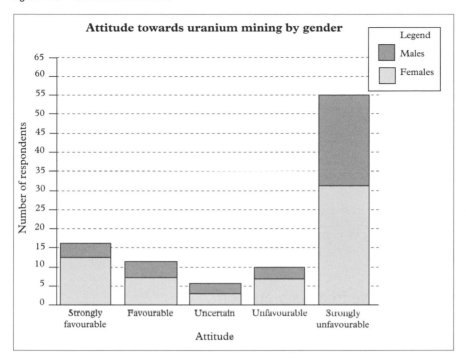

Figure 16.5   The 100 per cent bar chart

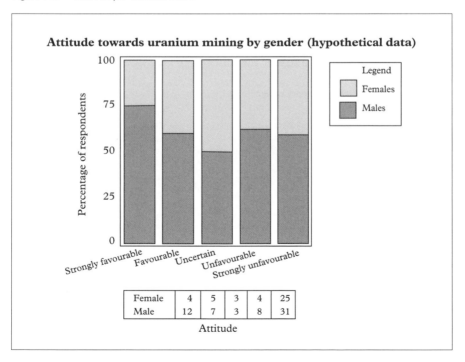

Figure 16.6   The frequency polygon

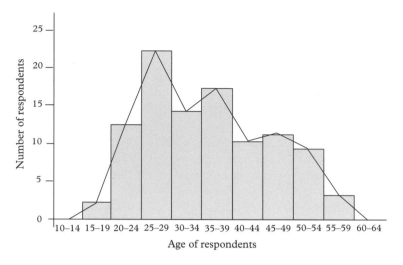

The cumulative frequency polygon

The cumulative frequency polygon or cumulative frequency curve (Figure 16.7) is drawn on the basis of cumulative frequencies. The main difference between a frequency polygon and a cumulative frequency polygon is that the former is drawn by joining the midpoints of the intervals, whereas the latter is drawn by joining the end points of the intervals because cumulative frequencies interpret data in relation to the upper limit of an interval. As a cumulative frequency distribution tells you the number of observations less than a given value and is usually based upon grouped data, to interpret a frequency distribution the upper limit needs to be taken.

Figure 16.7   The cumulative frequency polygon

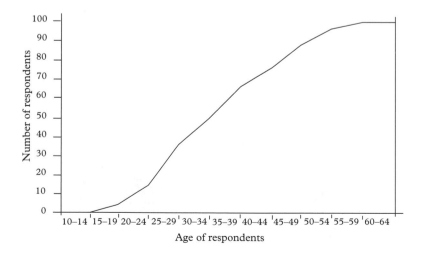

The stem-and-leaf display

The stem-and-leaf display is an effective, quick and simple way of displaying a frequency distribution (Figure 16.8). The stem-and-leaf for a frequency distribution running into two digits is plotted by displaying digits 0 to 9 on the left of the *y*-axis, representing the tens of a frequency. The figures representing the units of a frequency (i.e. the right-hand figure of a two digit frequency) are displayed on the right of the *y*-axis. Note that the stem-and-leaf display does not use grouped data but absolute frequencies. If the display is rotated 90 degrees in an anti-clockwise direction, it becomes a histogram. With this technique some of the descriptive statistics relating to frequency distribution, such as the mean, the mode and the median, can easily be ascertained; however, the procedure of their calculation is beyond the scope of this book. Stem-and-leaf displays are also possible for frequencies running into three and four digits (100s and 1000s).

Figure 16.8 The stem-and-leaf display

1	89
2	00011122222223344555556667777788899
3	001112223333334455556667777889
4	112223333444555566779
5	000113355667

The pie chart

The pie chart is another way of representing data graphically (Figure 16.9), this time as a circle. There are 360 degrees in a circle, and so the full circle can be used to represent 100 per cent, or the total population. The circle

Figure 16.9 Two- and three-dimensional pie charts

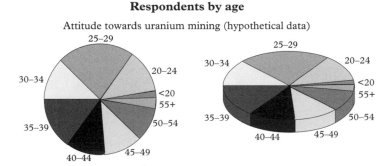

Respondents by age

Attitude towards uranium mining (hypothetical data)

or pie is divided into sections in accordance with the magnitude of each sub-category, and so each slice is in proportion to the size of each subcategory of a frequency distribution. The proportions may be shown either as absolute numbers or as percentages. Manually, pie charts are more difficult to draw than other types of graph because of the difficulty in measuring the degrees of the pie/circle. They can be drawn for both qualitative data and variables measured on a continuous scale but grouped into categories.

The line diagram or trend curve

A set of data measured on a continuous interval or a ratio scale can be displayed using a line diagram or trend curve. A trend line can be drawn for data pertaining to both a specific time (e.g. 1975, 1976, 1977) or a period (e.g. 1965–69, 1970–74, 1975–79). If it relates to a period, the midpoint of each interval at a height commensurate with each frequency—as in the case of a histogram—is marked as a dot. These dots are then connected with straight lines to examine trends in a phenomenon. If the data pertain to exact time, a point is plotted at a height commensurate with the frequency. These points are then connected with straight lines. A line diagram is a useful way of visually conveying the changes when long-term trends in a phenomenon or situation need to be studied, or the changes in the subcategory of a variable is measured on an interval or a ratio scale (Figure 16.10). Trends plotted as a line diagram are more clearly visible than in a table. For example, a line diagram would be useful for illustrating trends in birth or death rates, and changes in population size.

Figure 16.10 The line diagram or trend curve

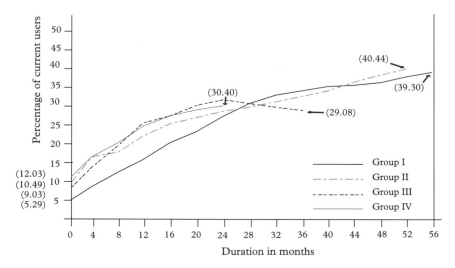

The area chart

For variables measured on an interval or a ratio scale, information about the subcategories of a variable can also be presented in the form of an area chart. It is plotted in the same way as a line diagram with the area under each line shaded to highlight the magnitude of the subcategory in relation to other subcategories. Thus an area chart displays the area under the curve in relation to the subcategories of a variable. For example, Figure 16.11 shows the number of male and female respondents by age.

Figure 16.11   The area chart

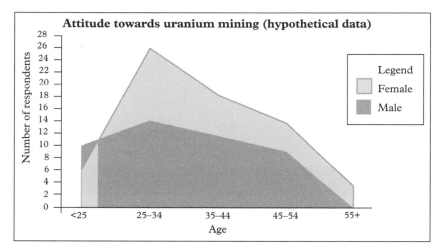

The scattergram

When you want to show visually how one variable changes in relation to a change in the other variable, a scattergram is extremely effective.

For a scattergram, both the variables must be measured either on interval or ratio scales and the data on both the variables need to be available in absolute values for each observation. Data for both variables are taken in pairs and displayed as dots in relation to their values on both axes. Let us take the data on age and income for ten respondents of a hypothetical study in Table 16.5. Figure 16.12 shows the relationship between age and income based upon hypothetical data. You cannot develop a scattergram for categorical variables.

Table 16.5   Age and income data

Respondent	Income	Age
A	25 500	24
B	46 000	50
C	30 500	36
D	55 000	45
E	27 000	29
F	35 000	38
G	40 000	37
H	52 000	48
I	47 000	41
J	38 000	47

Figure 16.12 The scattergram

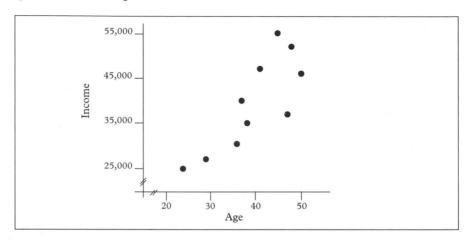

SUMMARY

Research findings are usually conveyed to readers as text. However, there are times when a piece of information can be better communicated in the form of a table or graph. These do not give readers any more information but they communicate it clearly. What you use should be determined by what you think will be easiest for readers to understand. Tables have the advantage of containing a great deal of information in a small space, whilst graphs make it easy for readers to absorb information at a glance.

Ideally, a table should have five parts: title, stub, column headings, body and supplementary notes or footnotes. Depending upon the number of variables about which information in a table is stored, there are three types of table: univariate (frequency), bivariate (cross-tabulation) and polyvariate.

To interpret a table, simple arithmetic procedures such as percentages, cumulative frequencies, or ratios can be used. You can also calculate simple descriptive statistical procedures such as the mean, the mode, the median, the chi-square test, the t-test, and the coefficient of correlation. If you have statistical knowledge, advanced statistics can be applied.

While there are many types of graphs, the common ones are: the histogram, the bar diagram, the stacked bar chart, the 100 per cent bar chart, the frequency polygon, the stem-and-leaf display, the pie chart, the line or trend diagram, the area chart and the scattergram. Which is used depends upon your purpose and the measurement scale used to measure the variable(s) being displayed. Some graphs are difficult to draw but several computer programs are capable of this.

STEP VIII

WRITING A
RESEARCH REPORT

CHAPTER 17
Writing a research report

CHAPTER
seventeen

Writing a
research report

Research writing in general

The last step in the research process is writing the research report. Each step of the process is important for a valid study, as negligence at any stage will affect all of the study, not just that part. In a way, this last step is the most crucial as it is through the report that the findings of the study and their implications are communicated to your supervisor and readers. Most people will not be aware of the amount and quality of work that has gone into your study: while much hard work and care may have been put into every stage of the research, all readers see is the report. Therefore, the whole enterprise can be spoiled if the report is not well-written. As Burns writes, 'extremely valuable and interesting practical work may be spoiled at the last minute by a student who is not able to communicate the results easily' (1994: 229).

In addition to your understanding of research methodology, the quality of the report depends upon such things as your written communication skills and clarity of thought, your ability to express thoughts in a logical and sequential manner, and your knowledge base of the subject area. Another important determinant is your experience in research writing: the more experience you acquire, the more effective you will become in writing a research report. The use of statistical procedures will reinforce the validity of your conclusions and arguments as they enable you to establish if an observed association is due to chance or otherwise (i.e. whether a relationship is spurious or non-spurious) and indicate the strength of an association so readers can place confidence in your findings. The use of graphs to present the findings, though not essential, will make the information more easily understood by readers. Whether or not graphs are used depends entirely upon the purpose for which the findings are to be used.

The main difference between research and other writing is in the degree of control, rigorousness and caution required. Research writing is controlled in the sense that you need to be extremely careful about what you write, the words you choose, the way ideas are expressed, and the validity and verifiability of the bases for the conclusions you draw. What most distinguishes research writing from other writing is the high degree of intellectual rigour required. Research writing must be absolutely accurate, clear, free of ambiguity, logical and concise. Assumptions as to the knowledge of readers about the study must be avoided. Bear in mind that you must be able to defend whatever you write should anyone challenge it. Do not use ornamental and superficial language. Even the best researchers make a number of drafts before writing up their final one, so be prepared to undertake this task.

Referencing

The report should follow an academic style of referencing. There are four referencing systems from which to choose (Butcher 1981: 226) and you need to adopt the one that is acceptable to your university and academic discipline. 'The first of these is used in most general books, the second mainly in science and social science books; the third and fourth less frequently' (Butcher 1981: 167). The four referencing systems are:

1 The short-title system;
2 The author–date system;
3 The reference by number system;
4 The author–number system.

Writing a bibliography

Again, there are several well-established systems for writing a bibliography and your choice is dependent upon the preference of the discipline and university. In the social sciences some of the most commonly used ones are (Longyear 1983: 83):

- the Harvard system;
- the American Psychological Association system;
- the American Medical Association system;
- the McGraw-Hill system;
- the Modern Languages Association system;
- the footnote system.

To learn about these systems and styles, consult the references provided at the end of this book or consult your library.

Developing an outline

Before you start writing your report, it is a good practice to develop an outline (chapterisation). This means deciding how you are going to divide your report into different chapters and planning what will be written in each one. In developing chapterisation, the subobjectives of the study provide immense guidance. Develop the chapters around the main themes of your study. Depending upon the importance of a theme, either devote a complete chapter to it or combine it with related themes to form one chapter. The title of each chapter should be descriptive of the main theme, communicate its main thrust, and be clear and concise.

The first chapter of your report, possibly entitled, 'Introduction', should be a general introduction to the study, covering most of your project proposal and pointing out the deviations, if any, from the original plan. This chapter covers all the preparatory tasks undertaken prior to conducting the study, such as the literature review, the theoretical framework, the objectives of the study, study design, the sampling strategy and the measurement procedures. An example is the study on foster-care payments referred to in earlier chapters. This chapter could be written around the following subheadings:

Chapter I   Introduction

- Introduction
- The development of foster care
- Foster care in Australia
- Foster care in Western Australia
- The department of community services
- The out-of-home and community care program
- Current trends in foster-care placement in Western Australia
- Becoming a foster carer
- Foster-care subsidies
- Issues regarding foster-care payment
- Rationale for the study
- Objectives of the study
- Study design
- Sampling
- Measurement procedure
- Problems and limitations
- Working definitions

The second chapter should provide information about your study population. Here, the relevant social, economic and demographic characteristics of the study population should be described. This chapter serves two purposes.

1 It provides readers with some background information about the population from which you collected the information so they can relate the findings to the type of population studied.
2 It helps to identify the variance within a group; for example, you may want to examine how the level of satisfaction of the consumers of a service changes with their age, gender or education.

The second chapter, therefore, could be entitled 'Socioeconomic–demographic characteristics of the study population' or just 'The study population'. This chapter could be written around the following sub-headings:

Chapter II   The study population

- Introduction
- Respondents by age (Information obtained in response to the question on age should be presented here. Consult 'Writing about a variable', the next section of this chapter.)
- Respondents by gender (Follow the suggestions made under 'Writing about a variable' (p. 269) for the rest of the variables.)
- Marital status of the study population
- Ethnicity of respondents
- Study population by number of children
- Annual average income of the study population
- Study population by type of dwelling
- etc.

The title and contents of subsequent chapters depend upon what you have attempted to describe, explore, examine, establish or prove in your study. As the content of each project is different, these chapters will be different. As indicated earlier, the title of each chapter should reflect the main thrust of its contents.

The outline should specify the subsections of the chapter. These subsections should be developed around the different aspects of the theme being discussed in the chapter. If you plan to correlate the information obtained from one variable with another, specify the variables. Plan the sequence for discussion of the variables. In deciding this, keep in mind the linkage and logical progression between the sections. This does not mean that the proposed outline cannot be changed when writing the report—it is possible for it to be significantly changed. However, an outline, even if extremely rough, will be of immense help to you. Again, let us take the study on foster-care payment as an example:

Chapter III Attitudes towards the present level of payment for foster
care

- Introduction
- Attitudes towards adequacy of payment for foster care (Responses to questions on the adequacy of foster-care payment should be presented here.)
  - adequacy by age (Cross-tabulation, i.e. responses to the question on adequacy of foster-care payment are examined in relation to the responses to questions on age.)
  - adequacy by marital status (Cross-tabulation, i.e. responses to the question on adequacy of foster-care payment are examined in relation to the responses to question on marital status.)
  - adequacy by income of the family (Cross-tabulation, i.e. responses to the question on adequacy of foster-care payment are examined in relation to the responses to questions on income.)
- Aspects of foster care not covered by the payment
- Major costs borne by foster carers
- Effects of the current level of payment on the family
- Reasons for increasing the payment
- Proposed level of payment
  - proposed level by income of the family
- Conclusions

Note: Cross-tabulations can be included for any variable where appropriate.

Writing about a variable

Having developed a chapter outline, the next step is to start writing. Though the way researchers organise their writing is extremely individualised, the following guidelines and format may prove helpful for beginners.

When writing about the information obtained in response to a question (variable), write as if you were providing answers to the following questions.

- Why did you think it important to study the variable? What effects, in your opinion, may this variable have on the main variable you are explaining? (*This is where you provide your own rationale for studying the variable.*)
- In the case of a cross-tabulation, what relationships have other studies found between the variables you are analysing? (*This is where the literature review is integrated into the findings of the study.*)
- What did you expect to find out in terms of the relationship between the two variables? (*If you have formulated a hypothesis, state it here.*)
- What has your study found out? (*Provide the hard data from your study here, either as tables, graphs or text.*)
- What do the data show? (*Interpret the findings of your analysis.*)
- What conclusions can you draw? How do the conclusions drawn from your study compare with those from similar studies in the past? Does your study support or contradict them?
- What explanation can you provide for the findings of your study?

The above is only a suggested format for ordering your thoughts, not a list of subheadings. You may wish to change the suggested order to make the reading more interesting. Below is an example of writing about a variable, 'Adequacy of payment for foster care' from Chapter 13.

- Why did you think it important to find out if foster-care payments are adequate? What effects, in your opinion, could the adequacy or otherwise of payment for foster care have on the quality of foster care?
- What have other studies in your literature review said about the adequacy of foster-care payments?
- What did you expect to find out from your study population in terms of their feelings about the adequacy of foster-care payments? If you formulated a hypothesis, you should specify that here. For example, H_i = *Most foster parents would consider the current level of foster-care payments to be adequate.*
- What did you find out about the adequacy of foster-care payments? What proportion of the study population said it was adequate? What proportion said it was inadequate? Provide a table or graph showing the distribution of respondents by their response to the question regarding the adequacy of foster-care payments.
- What do your data show about the adequacy of foster-care payments? What are the main findings of your study? How do these findings compare with those of other studies you reviewed in your literature review? Does your study support or contradict them?
- What conclusions can you draw about the adequacy of the amount of payment for foster care?
- What explanation can you provide for the observed findings? Why do you think those who said that foster payments are either adequate or inadequate feel that way?

In the suggested format in writing about information obtained from questions, notice that the literature review is integrated with the findings and conclusions. The extent of the integration of literature with findings mostly depends upon the level at which you are writing your dissertation (Honours, Masters or PhD)—the higher the level, the more extensive the literature review and its integration with your findings need to be and the more careful and confident you need to be about your conclusions.

The suggested format is organised around the main themes of the study. There are other formats. Some researchers write everything under one heading, 'The findings'. This format is appropriate for a research paper, because it is short, but not for a research report or dissertation. Other writers follow the same order as in the research instrument; for example, findings are discussed under each question. The reader needs to continuously refer to the instrument for each question. This format does not explain the content at the beginning and should not be followed.

SUMMARY

In a way, writing your report is the most crucial step in the research process as it communicates the findings to your research supervisor and readers. A badly written report can spoil all the hard work you have put into your research study.

Styles of research writing vary but all research reports must be written clearly and concisely. Furthermore, scientific writing requires intellectual rigour and there are certain obligations in terms of accuracy and objectivity. Reports can be written in different formats and this chapter has suggested one that research students have found to be helpful.

There are different ways of referencing and of writing a bibliography. You need to select the system that is acceptable to your discipline and university.

Before you start writing the research report, develop an outline of the different chapters and their contents. The chapters should be written around the main themes of the study, for which your subobjectives are of immense help. When providing specific information about a variable, the write-up should integrate the rationale for studying the variable; the literature review; the hypothesis, if any; findings; conclusions drawn; and possible explanations for the findings.

The suggested format can be described as *thematic writing*—writing organised around the significant themes of your study. Within a theme the information is provided in an integrated manner following a logical progression of thought.

CHAPTER
eighteen

Research
methodology and
practice evaluation

Research methodology and practice evaluation are integrally related. Practice evaluation relies very heavily on the techniques, methods and skills of research methodology. For an evaluator it is imperative to be also a good researcher. As this book is primarily written for newcomers to research and for practitioners in human services who are increasingly being asked to provide evidence of the effectiveness of their practice, it is only appropriate that this edition includes a chapter that briefly outlines evaluation research and its relationship with research methodology.

Over the past few decades evaluation research has gained greater prominence and has developed rapidly, both in its applications and methodological developments. Scarcity of resources, emergence of a need to be accountable for effective and efficient delivery of services, realisation that consumers have the right to know about the quality of the service they are receiving, and the onset of an era of economic rationalism have all contributed to the rapid development of evaluation research. Though it relies very heavily on the contents of research methodology *per se*, evaluation research is now considered to be a self-defined discipline in its own right, with its own literature, techniques and skills. Methods and models of evaluation have now been applied to almost every field of knowledge in our society. Evaluators are being engaged to evaluate many of the social, economic, health, education and political programs.

The very first question that may come to your mind, as a beginner is: What is evaluation research? Evaluation may have a different meaning in different situations and, also, it may be understood differently by different people. It is, therefore, important for you to understand the various perspectives on and, aspects of, evaluation, so that when you come upon it you can define its meaning for your situation.

What is evaluation?

If you go through the literature on evaluation research, you will come across many different definitions. Below are some definitions that have been selected to highlight the various dimensions of evaluation. According to Rossi, Freeman & Lipsey (1999:4): 'Program evaluation is the use of social research procedures to systematically investigate the effectiveness of social interventions programs'.

Quoted by Stufflebeam & Shinkfield (1985:3), the definition of the Joint Committee on Standards for Education Evaluation is: 'Evaluation is the systematic assessment of the worth and merit of some objects'.

According to Marvin C. Alkin & Lewis C. Solomon (1983:14):

> Evaluation is a process of ascertaining the decision areas of concern, selecting appropriate information, and collecting and analysing information in order to report summary data useful to decision makers in selecting among alternatives.

According to Rutman (1980:17), 'Program evaluation refers to the use of research methods to measure the effectiveness of operative programs'. In another book, edited by Rutman (1977:16), he also defines evaluation as:

Evaluation research is, first and foremost, a process of applying scientific procedures to accumulate reliable and valid evidence in the manner and the extent to which specific activities produce particular effects or outcomes.

If you critically examine these definitions, you will notice that in the evaluation process (as in research methodology) there are certain properties such as validity, reliability and thoroughness. And both processes are designed to collect and analyse information in order to answer research questions. In evaluation research, research questions mainly revolve around various aspects of an intervention, program or practice, whereas in general research they may relate to any aspect or issue of concern or significance. Evaluation research, therefore, is primarily concerned with a critical examination of such aspects as the appropriateness, effectiveness and efficiency of an intervention. Issues relating to efficiency and effectiveness in relation to the costs and benefits of an intervention are also an integral part of evaluation studies. See Figure 18.1.

Figure 18.1   The concept of evaluation

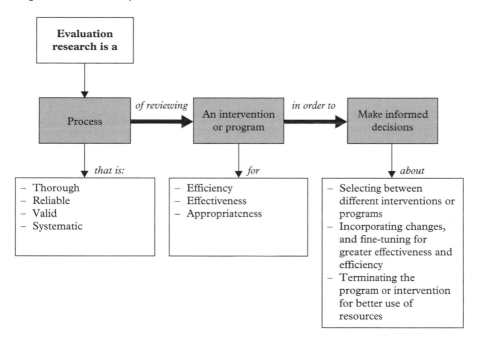

Why evaluation?

Suppose you are working in a human service agency. At some point in the course of your work, questions may come to your mind about the appropriateness of your service, its effectiveness, why some people like or benefit from it and others do not, how it can be improved, what sort of workload a service provider can carry, and what the cost of delivering the service is. Consumers and administrators of your service may ask you similar questions. You can obtain answers to these questions in a number of ways, ranging from gathering anecdotal evidence to undertaking a systematic study, adhering to the principles of scientific inquiry. Evaluation methodology, which (as mentioned) is based upon research methodology, is one way of finding answers to such questions.

You may come across professionals with differing attitudes towards evaluation. Some attach immense importance to it, while others consider it to be not as important because they think of themselves as solely the providers of a service. Whether or not you become involved in evaluating your practice, is dependent upon your interest in examining the practice and upon the demands placed on you by others. However, as a beginner in research methodology, you need to be aware of the importance of evaluation and of the links between it and research methodology. Also, you need to appreciate the significance of evaluation in critically examining a practice for greater efficiency and effectiveness. Even as a service provider you need to be familiar with how your clinical skills can benefit from evaluation processes. Specifically:

- You have a professional and ethical responsibility to provide a good quality of service to your clients. To ensure its effectiveness and efficiency, you need to assess your practice. Knowledge of evaluation research will help you to assess your practice objectively or help you to communicate with an evaluator knowledgeably and professionally about evaluation issues.
- While you, as a professional, have an obligation to provide an effective service to your clients, your clients, on the other hand, have a right to know the quality of the service they are receiving from you. In this age of consumerism, your clients can demand evidence of the quality of your service. In the modern era of consumerism, the emphasis is not only on providing a service but also on how well it is delivered to consumers. In most service professions the concept of so-called evidence-based practice is growing at a very rapid rate.
- When you are dependent upon outside funding for providing a service, you usually need to provide evidence of the effectiveness of your service for renewal of funding. Nowadays almost every funding body uses evaluation reports as the basis of funding decisions. Quite often an evaluation report from an independent evaluator is required. For effective communication with an outside evaluator, knowledge of evaluation will go a long way.
- Because of the paucity of resources and a greater emphasis on economic rationalism nowadays, there is a growing demand on service providers to demonstrate that the service they are providing is worth the expenditure, and people are getting value for money. Critical examination through evaluation of your service will help you to demonstrate the worth and value of your service.
- How do consumers view your service? What do the consumers of your service feel about it? What do they see as the positive aspects of your service? What, in their opinion, are the negative aspects? How can your service be improved upon? Is your service really helping those for whom it was designed? Is it achieving its objectives? In what ways is it benefiting

your clients? To answer such questions you need to evaluate your practice.

- How expensive is your service? What is the cost of providing the service to clients? Is this cost justified? Is the money being well spent?

In the final two points above are some of the questions that you need to answer as a service provider. Skills in evaluation research can help you to answer these questions with greater confidence, objectivity and validity.

Intervention-development-evaluation process

To know the evaluation process for an intervention, it is important that you also understand how it is linked to development of an intervention. The intervention-development-evaluation model is divided into four phases (Figure 18.2):

1 needs assessment;
2 intervention/program development;
3 intervention/program execution;
4 intervention/program evaluation.

Figure 18.2   The intervention-development-evaluation model

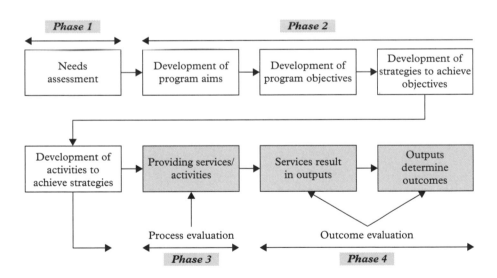

The development of an intervention usually starts with an assessment of the needs of a community, group or people living in a geographical area (phase 1). Based upon the needs, the aims and objectives for a program are developed to meet these needs which in turn become the basis of developing a conceptual intervention program. This conceptual construction is primarily based on previous experiences, understanding of the problem area, knowledge about how others have dealt with the problem in other places, and/or the opinion of the experts in the area. In the development of this conceptual model, particular attention is given to the formulation of strategies to achieve the objectives of the program. Next, the precise activities needed to achieve these strategies are identified. Procedures for undertaking these activities are then drawn up. These activities and procedures constitute the contents of a program (phase 2). Of course, they may need to be streamlined, modified or otherwise changed in the light of experience. Sometimes, a conceptual-intervention-model is first 'tested' out as a feasibility study to identify problems and modifications before launching on a full scale. Having fine-tuned the intervention contents, it is executed in accordance to the proposed plan (phase 3). Services/activities constitute program *inputs*, which result in intervention *outputs*, which in turn produce *outcomes/impacts*. Outputs are the direct products of a program's activities and are usually measured in terms of volume of tasks accomplished. Outcomes are benefits or changes in individuals or populations that can be attributed to the inputs of a program. They may manifest as cognitive and/or non-cognitive changes. These may relate to values, attitudes, knowledge, behaviour, change in a situation or any other aspect that came about in an individual following the introduction of a program. The majority of the evaluations are around either outputs or outcomes (phase 4).

Let us take an example: random breath testing. In RBT the outputs include the number of people tested; the number of awareness campaigns organised; the number of newspaper and television advertisements placed; the number of community forums held; and the number of police officers employed for the task of breath testing. The desired outcomes—the changes sought in people's behaviour and the situation—may include reduction in alcohol-related road accidents and deaths, and a reduction in the number of people caught driving under the influence of alcohol.

Let us take another example: counselling service for couples with marital problems. In this example the outputs are the number of sessions with couples and the number of couples seen. The outcomes might be a reduction in the conflicts; greater marital stability with a beneficial effect on the couple's children; a positive effect on work, productivity and income; increased satisfaction with life in general; or smooth separation by the couple from each other.

Perspectives in the classification of evaluation studies

The various types of evaluation can be looked at from two perspectives:

- The *focus of the evaluation*;
- The *philosophical base* that underpins an evaluation.

It is important to remember that these perspectives are *not* mutually exclusive. All evaluations categorised from the viewpoint of *focus of evaluation* have a *philosophical base* underpinning them, and so can be classified from within this perspective as well.

For example, an *impact/outcome evaluation* from the focus-of-evaluation point of view can *also* be classified as *goal-centred evaluation* from the philosophical perspective. In an outcome evaluation (classified from the focus-of-evaluation perspective), you can explore either the way an intervention has impacted on the study population, or you can seek to determine outcomes by establishing whether or not the program has achieved its intended objective. If the evaluation is from the focus perspective, it is classified as an impact/outcome evaluation, and if the focus is from the philosophical perspective, it is also classified as a *goal-centred evaluation*. Again, if you determine the impact of a program/intervention by asking what clients/consumers perceive its effects to have been on them, this is also classified as a *client-centred evaluation* from a philosophical perspective. If you examine every aspect of a program with regard to its outcome, process and any other aspect, this is categorised as a *holistic evaluation*. Finally, every type of evaluation, process or outcome can be classified as an *improvement-oriented evaluation* from the philosophical perspective as the ultimate aim of any evaluation is to improve an intervention/program. To avoid confusion between the two perspectives, an integrated picture is provided in Figure 18.3.

Figure 18.3   Perspectives in the classification of evaluation studies

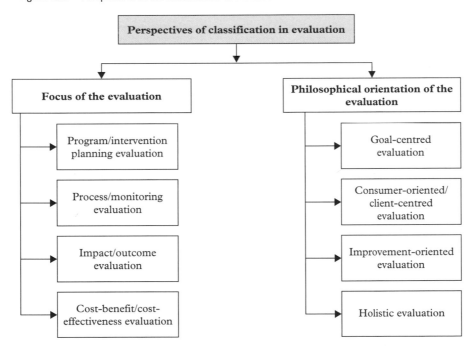

Types of evaluation from a *focus* perspective

From the perspective of the focus of evaluation there are four types of evaluation: *program/intervention planning*, *process/monitoring*, *impact/outcome*, and *cost benefit/cost-effectiveness*. Each type addresses a main and significantly different issue. *Evaluation for planning* addresses the issue of establishing the need for a program or intervention; *process evaluation*'s emphasis is on the evaluation of the process in order to enhance the efficiency of the delivery system; the measurement of outcomes is the focus of an *outcome evaluation*; and the central aim of a *cost-benefit evaluation* is to put a price tag on an intervention in relation to its benefits. Hence, from this perspective, the classification of an evaluation is primarily dependent upon its focus.

It is important for you to understand the different evaluation questions each is designed to answer. Table 18.1 will help you to understand the application of each type of evaluation.

Table 18.1   Types of evaluation from the perspective of its focus and the questions they are designed to answer

Type of evaluation	*Focus of evaluation*	*Main issue for evaluation*	*Questions to be answered*
Program/intervention planning evaluation	Planning for program/ intervention	*Need* for a program/ intervention	– Is there a need for the proposed program/intervention? – If yes, what is its extent? – Who is eligible to receive the service? – What services should be provided and how? – Who should provide the service(s)? – What is the geographical distribution of the target population? – How should the success or failure of the program/ intervention be assessed? – Where should the services be located? – What are the training needs?
Process/monitoring evaluation	Service delivery	*Efficiency* of the service delivery	– What are the problems with the way the service is being delivered? – How can service delivery be improved? – How satisfied are clients with the way the service is being delivered? – Do staff need additional training? – How satisfied are service providers with the service delivery manner? *(Table continues next page)*

Table 18.1 *Continued*

Type of evaluation	Focus of evaluation	Main issue for evaluation	Questions to be answered
Impact/outcome evaluation	Outcomes/ effectiveness	*Effectiveness* of a program/ intervention	– What are the outputs of the program? – What are the outcomes, both direct and indirect, of the program? – How has the program affected clients? – To what extent has the program achieved the objectives set out at the planning stage? – How satisfied are clients with the benefits from the service? – How satisfied are service providers with the intervention outcomes?
Cost-benefit/ cost-effectiveness evaluation	Cost-effectiveness	*Cost* of delivering the service	– What is the cost of delivering the service? – Do the effects justify the cost? – Do benefits justify the cost? – As compared to others, what is the cost of per unit of service?

Evaluation for planning a program/intervention

In many situations it is desirable to examine the feasibility of starting a program/intervention by evaluating the nature and extent of a chosen problem. Actually, this type of study evaluates of the problem *per se*: its nature, extent and distribution. Specifically, evaluation for program/ intervention planning includes:

- estimating of the extent of the problem—in other words, estimating how many people are likely to need the intervention;
- delineating the characteristics of the people and groups who are likely to require the intervention;
- identifying the likely benefits to be derived from the intervention;
- developing a method of delivering the intervention;
- developing program contents: services, activities and procedures;
- identifying training needs for service delivery and developing training material;
- estimating the financial requirements of the intervention;
- developing evaluation indicators for the success or failure of the intervention and fixing a time-line for evaluation.

There are a number of methods for evaluating the extent and nature of a problem, and for devising a service-delivery manner. The choice of a particular method should depend upon the financial resources available, the time at your disposal and the level of accuracy required in your estimates. Some of the methods are:

- **Community need-assessment surveys**—need-assessment surveys are quite prevalent to determine the extent of a problem. You use your research skills to undertake a survey in the relevant community to ascertain the number of people who will require a particular service. The number of people requiring a particular service can be extrapolated using the demographic information about the community and results from your community sample survey. If done properly, a need-assessment survey can give you a reasonably accurate estimate of the needs of a community or the need for a particular type of service. However, you must keep in mind that surveys are not cheap to undertake.
- **Community forums**—conducting community forums is another method to find out the extent of the need for a particular service. However, it is important to keep in mind that community forums suffer from a problem in that participants are self-selected; hence, the picture provided may not be accurate. In a community forum not everyone will participate and those who do may have a vested interest for or against the service. If, somehow, you can make sure that all interest groups are represented in a community forum, it can provide a reasonable picture of the demand for a service. Community forums are comparatively cheap to undertake but you need to examine the usefulness of the information for your purpose. With community forums you cannot ascertain the number of people who may need a particular service, but you can get some indication of the demand for a service and different prevalent community perspectives with respect to the service.
- **Social indicators**—making use of social indicators, in conjunction with other demographic data, if you have information about them, is another method. However, you have to be careful that these indicators have a high correlation with the problem/need and are accurately recorded. Otherwise, the accuracy of the estimates will be affected.
- **Service records**—There are times when you may be able to use existing service records to identify the unmet needs for a service. For example, if an agency is keeping a record of the cases where they have not been able to provide a service for lack of resources, you may be able to use it to estimate the number of people who are likely to need that service.
- **Focus groups of potential service consumers, service providers and experts**—you can also use focus groups made up of consumers, service providers and experts to establish the need for a service.

Community surveys and social indicators tend to be quantitative, whereas the others tend to be qualitative. Thus they give you different types of information. Service records provide an indication of the gap in service and are not reflective of its need.

It is important to remember that all these methods, except the community needs survey, provide only an indication of the demand for a service in a community. You have to determine how accurately you need to estimate the potential number of users to start a service. A community survey will provide you with the most accurate figures but it could put a strain on the resources. Also, keep in mind that use of multiple methods will produce more accurate estimates.

Process/monitoring evaluation

Process evaluation, also known as monitoring evaluation, focuses on the manner of delivery of a service in order to identify issues and problems concerning delivery manner. It also identifies ways of improving service delivery procedures for a better and more efficient service. Specifically, process evaluation is used for:

- determining whether or not the delivery of a service is consistent with the original design specifications and, if not, for identifying the reasons and justifications for non-compliance;
- identifying changes needed in the delivery manner for greater coverage and efficiency;
- ascertaining, when an intervention has no impact, whether this is because of the intervention itself or the manner in which it is being delivered;
- determining whether or not an intervention is reaching the appropriate target population.

Process evaluation includes evaluating the:

- extent of participation of the target population;
- delivery manner of a program/intervention.

Evaluating the participation of the target population in turn involves: (i) ascertaining the appropriateness of the clients for the service in question; and (ii) establishing the total number of clients and the dropout rate among them. Evaluating the service delivery manner, in the same way, includes two tasks: (i) examining the procedures used in providing the service; and (ii) examining the issues relating to the accessibility of the service to potential clients (Figure 18.4).

Figure 18.4   Aspects of process evaluation

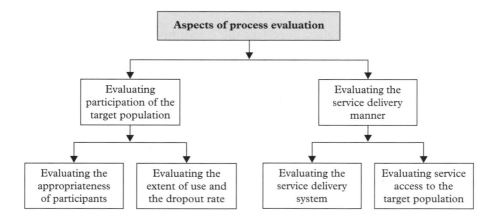

Evaluating participation of the target population

In an evaluation study designed to examine the process of delivering an intervention, it is important to examine the appropriateness of the users of the service because, sometimes, some people use a service even though they do not strictly fall within the inclusion criteria. In other words, in evaluation studies it is important to determine not just the number of users, but whether or not they are eligible users. To determine the appropriate use of an intervention is an integral part of an evaluation.

It is also important to ascertain the total number of users of a program/intervention because it provides an indication of the need for a service, and to find out the number of dropouts because this establishes the extent of the rejection of the service for any reason. There are a number of procedures for evaluating the participation of a target population in an intervention.

- **Percentage of users**—the acceptance of a program by the target population is one of the important indicators of a need for it—the higher the acceptance, the greater the need for the intervention. Some judge the desirability of a program by the number of users alone. Hence, as an evaluator, you can examine the total number of users and, if possible, calculate this as a percentage of the total target population. However, you should be careful using the percentage of users in isolation as an indicator of the popularity of a program. People may be unhappy and dissatisfied with a service; yet use it simply because there is no other option available to them. If used with other indicators, such as consumer satisfaction or in relation to evidence of the effectiveness of a program, it can provide a better indication of its acceptance.
- **Percentage of eligible users of a service**—service records usually contain information on service users that may include data on their eligibility for the service. An analysis of this information will provide you with a percentage of eligible users of the service—the higher the percentage of eligible users, the more positive the evaluation.

$$\frac{\text{no. of eligible users} \times 100}{\text{no. of total users}} = \text{Percentage of eligible users}$$

You can also undertake a survey of the consumers of a service in order to ascertain the percentage of eligible users.

- **Percentage of dropouts**—the dropout rate from a service is reflective of the satisfaction level of consumers with the program. A higher rate indicates either inappropriate service content or flaws in the way it is being delivered: it does not establish whether the problem is with the delivery manner or the intervention content. However, the figure will provide you with an overall indication of the level of satisfaction of consumers with the service: the higher the dropout rate, the higher the level of dissatisfaction, either with the contents of a service (its relevance to the needs of the population) or the way it is being delivered.

$$\frac{\text{no. of dropouts from a program} \times 100}{\text{no. of total program acceptors*}} = \text{Dropout rate}$$

*Acceptors are ever-users of a service.

- **Survey of the consumers of a service**—if service records do not include data regarding client eligibility for a service, you can undertake a survey of ever-users/acceptors of the service to ascertain their eligibility for the service. From the ever-users surveyed, you can also determine the dropout rate among them. In addition, you can find out many other aspects of the evaluation, such as client satisfaction, problems and issues with the service, or how to improve its efficiency and effectiveness. How well you do this survey is dependent upon your knowledge of research methodology and availability of resources.
- **Survey of the target population**—target population surveys, in addition to providing information about the extent of appropriate use of a service, also provide data on the extent of acceptance of a service among those for whom it was designed. The proportion of people who have accepted an intervention can be calculated as follows:

$$\frac{\text{no. of ever-users of the service} \times 100}{\text{no. of eligible individuals surveyed}} = \text{Acceptance of a service}$$

- **Survey of dropouts**—dropouts are an extremely useful source of information for identifying ways of improving an intervention. These are the people who have gone through an intervention, have experienced both positives and negatives, and have then decided to withdraw. Talking to them can provide you with their first-hand experience of the program. They are the people who can provide you with information on possible problems, either with the content of an intervention or the way it has been delivered. They are also an excellent source of suggestions on how to improve a service. A survey, focus group discussion or in-depth interviews can provide valuable information about the strengths as well as weaknesses of a program. Issues raised by them and suggestions made may become the basis for improving that intervention.
- **Survey of non-users of a service**—whereas a group of dropouts can provide extremely useful information about the problems with an intervention, non-users are important in understanding why some, for whom the program was designed, have not accepted it. Choose any method, quantitative or qualitative, to collect information from them. Of course it could be a problem to identify the non-users in a community.

Evaluating service delivery manner

There are situations when a program may not have achieved its intended goals. In such situations, there are two possible causes: the content of the intervention and the way it is being delivered. It is to make sure that an intervention is being delivered effectively that you undertake process evaluation. It involves identifying problems with the way a service is being delivered to consumers or finding ways of improving the delivery system. Evaluating the delivery manner of a program is a very important aspect of process evaluation. There are a number of issues in delivering a service that may impact upon its delivery manner and process evaluation considers them. Some of the issues are:

* the delivery manner *per se*;
* the contents of the service and its relevance to the needs of consumers;
* the adequacy and quality of training imparted to service providers to enable them to undertake various tasks;
* staff morale, motivation and interest in the program, and ways of enhancing these;
* the expectations of consumers;
* resources available and their management;
* issues relating to access to services by the target population;
* ways of further improving the delivery of a service.

A process evaluation aims at studying some or all of these issues. There are a number of strategies that are used in process evaluation. The purpose for which you are going to use the findings should determine whether you adopt a quantitative or qualitative approach. Considerations that determine the use of qualitative or quantitative methods in general also apply in evaluation studies. There are a number of methods used in undertaking process evaluation.

* **Opinion of consumers**—one of the best indicators of the quality of a service is how the consumers of that service feel about it. They are best placed to identify problems in the delivery manner, to point out its strengths and weaknesses, and to tell you how the service can be improved to meet their needs. Simply by gathering the experiences of consumers with respect to utilisation of a service you can gain valuable information about its strengths and weaknesses. Consumer surveys give you an insight into what the consumers of a service like and do not like about a service. In the present age of consumerism it is important to take their opinions into consideration when designing, delivering or changing a service.

    If you want to adopt a qualitative approach to evaluation, you can use in-depth interviewing, focus group discussions and/or target population forums as ways of collecting information about the issues mentioned above. If you prefer to use a quantitative approach you can undertake a survey, giving consideration to all the aspects of quantitative research methodology including sample size and its selection, and methods of data collection. Keep in mind that qualitative methods will provide you with a diversity of opinions and issues but will not tell you the extent of that diversity. If you need to determine the extent of these issues, you should combine qualitative and quantitative approaches.
* **Opinions of service providers**—equally important in process evaluation studies are the opinions of those engaged in providing a service. Service providers are fully aware of the strengths and weaknesses of the way in which a program is being delivered. They are also well-informed about what could be done to improve inadequacies. As an evaluator, you will find invaluable information from service providers for improving the efficiency of a service. Again, you can use qualitative

or quantitative methods for data collection and analysis.

- **Time-and-motion studies**—time-and-motion studies, both quantitative and qualitative, can provide important information about the delivery process of a service. The dominant technique involves observing the users of a service as they go through the process of using it. You, as an evaluator, passively observe each interaction and then draw inferences about the strengths and weaknesses of service delivery.

  In a qualitative approach to evaluation you mainly use observation as a method of data collection, whereas in a quantitative approach you develop more structured tools for data collection (even for observation) and subject the data to appropriate statistical analysis in order to make inferences.

- **Functional analysis studies**—analysis of the functions performed by service providers is another approach people use in the search for increased efficiency in service delivery. An observer, with expertise in program content and the process of delivering a service, follows a client as s/he goes through the process of receiving it. The observer keeps note of all the activities undertaken by the service provider, with the time spent on each of them. Such observations become the basis for judging the desirability of an activity as well as the justification for the time spent on it, which then becomes the basis of identifying 'waste' in the process.

  Again, you can use qualitative or quantitative methods of data collection. You can adopt very flexible methods of data collection or highly structured ones. You should be aware that observations can be very structured or unstructured. The author was involved in a functional analysis study which involved two-minute observations of activities of health workers in a community health program.

- **Panel of experts**—another method that is used to study the delivery process of a service is to ask experts in the area of that service to make recommendations about the process. These experts may use various methods (quantitative or qualitative) to gather information, and supplement it with their own knowledge. They then share their experiences and assessments with each other in order to come up with recommendations.

There are several methods of evaluation to choose from, however, you must keep in mind that use of multiple methods may provide more detailed and possibly better information though their use should depend upon the resources at your disposal and the purpose of your evaluation. Your skills as an evaluator lie in selecting a method (or methods) that best suits the purpose of evaluation within the given resources.

Impact/outcome evaluation

Impact or outcome evaluation is one of the most widely practised types of evaluation. It is used to assess what changes can be attributed to the introduction of a particular intervention, program or policy. It establishes causality between an intervention and its impact, and estimates the magnitude of this change(s). It plays a central role in decision making by practitioners, managers, administrators and planners who wish to determine whether or not an intervention has achieved its desired objectives in order to make an informed decision about its continuation, termination or alteration. Many funding organisations base their decisions about further funding for programs on impact evaluations. Specifically, an outcome evaluation is for the purpose of:

- establishing causal links between intervention inputs and outcomes;
- measuring the magnitude of these outcomes;
- determining whether a program or intervention has achieved its intended goals;
- finding out the unintended effects, if any, of an intervention;
- comparing the impacts of an intervention with an alternative one in order to choose the more effective of the two.

As you are aware, in any cause-and-effect relationship, in addition to the cause there are many other factors that can affect the relationship. (For details see Chapter 7.) Just to refresh your memory:

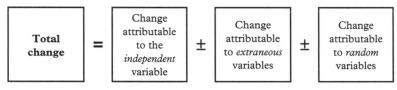

In relation to a program or intervention, this is:

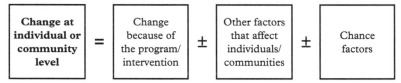

This ***theory of causality*** is of particular relevance to impact assessment studies. In determining the impact of an intervention, it is important to realise that the changes produced by an intervention may not be solely because of the intervention. Sometimes, other factors (extraneous variables) may play a more important role than the intervention in bringing about changes in the dependent variable. When you evaluate the effectiveness of an intervention, without comparing it to that of a control group, your findings will include the effects of extraneous variables. If you want to separate out the respective contributions of extraneous variable and the intervention, you need to use a control study design.

There are many designs from which you can choose in conducting an impact assessment. Impact assessment studies range from descriptive ones—in which you describe people's experiences and perceptions of the effectiveness of an intervention—to random-control-blind experiments. Again, your choice of a particular design is dependent upon the purpose of the evaluation and resources available. Some of the commonly used designs are:

- **After-only design**—though technically inappropriate, this design is a commonly used design in evaluation studies. This design measures the impact of a program or intervention (after it has occurred) without having a baseline. The effectiveness of the intervention is judged on the basis of the current picture of the state of evaluation indicators. It relies on such indicators as:

—number of users of the service;

—number of dropouts from the service;

—satisfaction of clients with the service;

—stories/experiences of clients that changed them;

—assessment made by experts in the area;

—the opinions of service providers.

It is on the basis of findings about these outcome indicators that a decision about continuation, termination or alterations in an intervention is made. One of the major drawbacks of this design is that it does not measure change that can be attributed to the intervention as such, since (as mentioned) it has neither a baseline nor a control group to compare results with. However, it provides the current picture in relation to the outcome indicators. This design is therefore inappropriate when you are interested in studying the impact of an intervention *per se*.

- **Before-and-after design**—the before-and-after design is technically sound and appropriate for measuring the impact of an intervention. There are two ways of establishing the baseline. One way is where the baseline is determined before the introduction of an intervention, which requires advance planning; and the other is where the baseline is established retrospectively, either from previous service records or through recall by clients of their situation before the introduction of the intervention. Retrospective construction of the baseline may produce less accurate data than the after data collection and hence may not be comparable. However, in the absence of anything better, it does provide some basis of comparison.

  As you may recall, one of the drawbacks of this design is that the change measured includes change brought about by extraneous and change variables. Hence, this design, though acceptable and better than the after-only design, still has a technical problem in terms of evaluation studies. Also, it is more expensive than the after-only design.

- **Experimental-control design**—the before-and-after study, with a control group, is probably the closest to a technically correct design for impact assessment of an intervention. One of the biggest strengths of this design is that it enables you to isolate the impact of independent and extraneous variables. However, it adds the problem of comparability between control and experimental groups. Sometimes this problem of comparability can be overcome by forming the groups through randomisation. Unfortunately, complexity in its execution and increased cost restrict the use of this design for the average evaluation study. Also, in many situations it may not be possible to find or construct a suitable control group.

- **Comparative study design**—comparative designs are used when evaluating two or more interventions. For comparative studies you can follow any of the above designs; that is, you can have a comparative study using either *after-only*, *before-and-after* or *experimental-control* design.

- **Reflexive control design**—to overcome the problem of comparability in different groups, sometimes researchers treat data collected during the non-intervention period to represent a control group, and information collected after the introduction of the intervention as if it pertained to an experimental group (Figure 18.5).

Figure 18.5   Reflexive control design

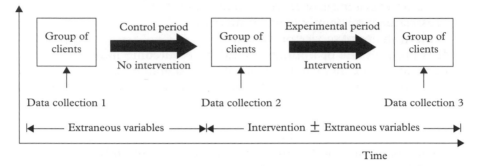

In the reflexive control design, comparison between *data collection 2* and *data collection 1* provides information for the control group, while, comparison between *data collection 3* and *data collection 2* provides data for the experimental group. One of the main advantages of this design is that you do not need to ensure the comparability of two groups. However, if there are rapid changes in the study population over time, and if the outcome variables are likely to be affected significantly, use of this design could be problematic.

- **Interrupted time-series design**—in this design you study a group of people before and after the introduction of an intervention. It is like the before-and-after design, except that you have multiple data collections at different time intervals to constitute an aggregated before-and-after picture (Figure 18.6). The design is based upon the assumption that one set of data is not sufficient to establish, with a reasonable degree of certainty and accuracy, the before-and-after situations.

Figure 18.6   Interrupted time-series design

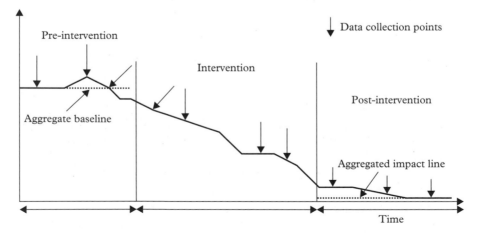

- **Replicated cross-sectional design**—the replicated cross-sectional design studies clients at different stages of an intervention, and is appropriate for those interventions that take new clients on a continuous or periodic basis. See Figure 18.7. This design is based on the assumption that those who are currently at the termination stage of an intervention are similar in terms of the nature and extent of the problem to those who are currently at the intake stage.

  In order to ascertain the change that can be attributed to an intervention, a sample at the intake and termination stages of the program is selected, so that information can be collected pertaining to pre-situations and post-situations with respect to the problem for which the intervention is being sought. To evaluate the pattern of impact, sometimes researchers collect data at one or more intermediary stages.

Figure 18.7   Replicated cross-section design

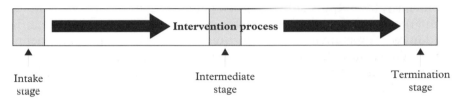

Intake
stage

Intermediate
stage

Termination
stage

You select a sample from different stages of an intervention

These designs vary in sophistication and so do the evaluation instruments. Choice of design is difficult and (as mentioned earlier) it depends upon the purpose and resources available. Another difficulty is to decide when, during the intervention process, to undertake the evaluation. How do you know that the intervention has made its impact? One major difficulty in evaluating social programs revolves around the question: Was the change the product of the intervention or did it come from a consumer's relationship with a service provider? Many social programs are accepted because of the confidence consumers develop in a service provider. In evaluation studies you need to keep in mind the importance of a service provider in bringing about change in individuals.

Cost-benefit/cost-effectiveness evaluation

While knowledge about the process of service delivery and its outcomes is highly useful for an efficient and effective program, in some cases it is critical to be informed about how intervention costs compare with outcomes. In today's world, which is characterised by scarce resources and economic rationalism, it is important to justify a program in relation to its cost. Cost-benefit analysis provides a framework for relating costs to benefits in terms of a common unit of measurement, monetary or otherwise. Specifically, cost-benefit/cost-effectiveness analysis is important because it helps to:

- put limited resources to optimal use;

- decide between two equally effective interventions which one to replicate on a larger scale.

Cost-benefit analysis follows an input/output model, the quality of which depends upon the ability to accurately identify and measure all intervention inputs and outputs. Compared to technical interventions, such as those within engineering, social interventions are more difficult to subject to cost-benefit analysis. This is primarily because of the difficulties in accurately identifying and measuring inputs and outputs, and then converting them to a common monetary unit. Some of the problems in applying cost-benefit analysis to social programs are outlined below:

- What constitutes an input for an intervention? There are direct and indirect inputs. Identifying these can sometimes be very difficult. Even if you have been able to identify them, the next problem is putting a price tag on each of them.
- Similarly, the outputs or benefits of an intervention need to be identified and measured. Like inputs, benefits can also be direct and indirect. In addition, a program may have short-term as well also long-term benefits. How do you cost the various benefits of a program? Another complexity is the need to consider benefits from the perspectives of different stakeholders.
- The main problem in cost-benefit analysis is the difficulty in converting inputs as well as outputs to a common unit. In social programs, it often becomes difficult to even identify outputs let alone measure and then convert them to a common unit of measurement.

Types of evaluation from a *philosophical* perspective

From a philosophical perspective, there are no specific models for, or methods of, evaluation. You use the same methods and model but the required information is gathered from different people or aspects depending upon the philosophy that you subscribe to. Daniel Stufflebeam and Anthony J. Shinkfield's book *Systematic Evaluation: A Self-Instructional Guide to Theory and Practice* is an excellent source to acquaint you with these perspectives. The types of evaluation, on the basis of the philosophies mentioned here, are dealt with in detail in this book. It is beyond the scope of this book to summarise them, but it is highly recommended that you refer to their book to have some appreciation of these perspectives. These perspectives range from advocating consumer opinion as a measure of success or failure at one end to attainment of the goals with statistical verification on the other. They also range from a unifocal approach to evaluation to a holistic one. On the basis of these perspectives, there are four types of evaluation. Again, we would like to remind you that this classification and the classification developed on the basis of the *focus of evaluation* are not mutually exclusive.

Goal-centred/objective-oriented evaluation

This approach is based upon the philosophy that the success or failure of an intervention should be based upon the extent of congruence between the objectives of an intervention and its actual outcomes. This approach studies outcomes to determine the achievement of objectives, and congruence between the two is regarded as the sole determinant of success or failure. One of the main criticisms of the objective-oriented model is that it assesses the effectiveness of a program without explaining the reasons for it.

Basically, the process of evaluation involves, first, identification of the desired goals of an intervention and, second, the use of a process to measure their success or failure. Again, you can use either qualitative or quantitative methods to achieve this.

Consumer-oriented/client-centred evaluation

The core of this philosophy rests on the assumption that assessment of the value or merit of an intervention—including its effectiveness, outcomes, impact and relevance—should be judged from the perspective of the consumer. Consumers, according to this philosophy, are the best judges of a program.

Client-centred evaluations, again, may use qualitative or quantitative methods to find out how clients feel about various aspects of an intervention. You can even use a mix of the two to find out consumers' perceptions and opinions.

Improvement-oriented evaluation

The basic philosophy behind improvement-oriented evaluation is that an evaluation should foster improvement. 'Not to prove but to improve' seems to be central theme of such evaluations. The focus is to study the context in order to help improve an intervention content—the process rather than outcomes.

Again, a multiplicity of methods can be used to undertake such evaluation.

Holistic/illuminative evaluation

The primary concern of illuminative evaluation is description and interpretation, rather than measurement and prediction. It fits with the social-anthropological paradigm, acknowledging as it does historical, cultural and social factors when evaluating an intervention. The aim is to study a program in all its aspects: how it operates, how it is influenced by various contexts, how it is applied, how those directly involved view its strengths and weaknesses, and what are the experiences of those who are affected by it. In summary, it tries to illuminate a complex array of questions, issues and factors, and to identify procedures that give both desirable and undesirable results. So a holistic evaluation tries to understand issues relating to an intervention from many perspectives: it seeks to view the performance of a program in its totality.

An evaluation can be conducted from any one of the above philosophical perspectives. To us, these are perspectives rather than evaluation models; but, some use them as types of evaluation. The aim of this section has been to acquaint you with some of these perspectives.

Undertaking an evaluation: the process

Like the research methodology model, which forms the basis of this book, the evaluation process is also based upon certain operational steps. It is important for you to remember that the order in the write-up of these steps is primarily to make it easier for you to understand the process. Once you are familiar with these steps, their order can be changed.

Step 1: Determining the purpose of evaluation

In a research study you formulate your research problem before developing a methodology. In an evaluation study, too, you need to identify the purpose of undertaking it and develop your objectives before venturing into it. It is important to seek answers to questions such as: 'Why do I want to do this evaluation?' and 'For what purpose would I use the findings?' Specifically, you need to consider the following matters, and to identify their relevance and application to your situation. Is the evaluation being undertaken to do the following?

- Identify and solve problems in the delivery process of a service.
- Increase efficiency of the service delivery manner.
- Determine the impacts of the intervention.
- Train staff for better performance.
- Work out an optimal workload for staff.
- Find out about client satisfaction with the service.
- Seek further funding.
- Justify the continuation of the program.
- Resolve issues so as to improve the quality of the service.
- Test out different intervention strategies.
- Choose between the interventions.
- Estimate the cost of providing the service.

It is important that you identify the purpose of your evaluation and find answers to your reasons for undertaking it with active involvement and participation of the various stakeholders. It is also important that all stakeholders—clients, service providers, service managers, funding organisations and you, as an evaluator—agree with aims of the evaluation. Make sure that all stakeholders also agree that the findings of the evaluation will not be used for any purpose other than those agreed upon. This agreement is important in ensuring that the findings will be acceptable to all, and for developing confidence among those who are to provide the required information do so freely. If your respondents are sceptical about the evaluation, you will not obtain reliable information from them.

Having decided the purpose of your evaluation, the next step is to develop a set of objectives that will guide it.

Step 2: Developing objectives or evaluation questions

As in a research project, you need to develop evaluation questions, which will become the foundation for the evaluation. Well-articulated objectives bring clarity and focus to the whole evaluation process. They also reduce the chances of disagreement later among various parties.

Some organisations may simply ask you 'to evaluate the program', whereas others may be much more specific. The same may be the situation if you are involved in evaluating your own intervention. If you have been given specific objectives or you are in a situation where you are clear about the objectives, you do not need to go through this step. However, if the brief is broad, or you are not clear about the objectives in your own situation, you need to construct for yourself and others a 'meaning' of *evaluation.*

As you know, evaluation can mean different things to different people. To serve the purpose of evaluation from the perspectives of different stakeholders, it is important to *involve all stakeholders in the development of evaluation objectives, and to seek their agreement with them.* You need to follow the same process as for a research study (Chapter 4). The examples in Figure 18.8 may help you to understand more about objective formulation.

Figure 18.8   Developing evaluation objectives: examples

Recently the author was asked to undertake two evaluations. For one, the brief was 'To evaluate the principle of community responsiveness in the delivery of health in . . . (name of the state)', and for the other it was 'To evaluate . . . (name of the model) service delivery model in . . . (name of the region)'.

Evaluation One

For the first evaluation, after having initial discussions with various stakeholders, it was discovered that understanding of the principle of 'community responsiveness' was extremely vague and varied among different people. Also, there were neither any instructions about how to achieve community responsiveness nor any training program for the purpose. A few people, responsible for ensuring the implementation of the principle, had no idea about its implementation. Our first question was: 'Can we evaluate something about which those responsible for implementation are not clear, and for which there is no specific strategy in place?' The obvious answer was 'no'. We discussed with the sponsors of the evaluation questions what they

(*continues on next page*)

had in mind when asking us for the evaluation. On the basis of our discussion with them and our understanding of their reasons for requesting the evaluation, we proposed that the evaluation be carried out in two phases. For the first phase, the aim of the evaluation should be to define 'community responsiveness', identify/develop/explore operational strategies to achieve it, and identify the indicators of its success or otherwise. During the second phase, an evaluation to measure the impact of implementation of the community responsiveness strategies was proposed. Our proposal was accepted. We developed the following objectives in consultation with the various stakeholders.

Evaluation of the principle of community responsiveness in health

Phase One

Main objective:
To develop a model for implementing the principle of community responsiveness in the delivery of health care in . . . (name of the state).

Specific objectives:

1 To find out how the principle of community responsiveness is understood by health planners, administrators, managers, service providers and consumers, and to develop an operational definition of the term for the department.
2 To identify, with the participation of stakeholders, strategies to implement the concept of community responsiveness in the delivery of health services.
3 To develop a set of indicators to evaluate the effectiveness of the strategies used to achieve community responsiveness.
4 To identify appropriate methodologies that are acceptable to stakeholders for measuring effectiveness indicators.

Phase Two

Main objective:
To evaluate the effectiveness of the strategies used to achieve the principle of community responsiveness in the delivery of health services.

Subobjectives:

1 To determine the impact of community responsiveness strategies on community participation in decision making about health issues affecting the community.
2 To find out the opinions of the various stakeholders on the degree to which the provision of community responsiveness in the delivery of health services has been/is being observed.
3 To find out the extent of involvement of the community in decision making in issues concerning the community and its attitude towards involvement.

(*Continues on next page*)

Evaluation Two

Now, let us take the second study. In this case the service delivery model was well-developed and the evaluation brief was clear in terms of its expectations; that is, the objective was to evaluate the model's effectiveness. Before starting the evaluation, the following objectives were developed in consultation with the steering committee, which had representatives from all stakeholder groups.

Remember, it is important that your objectives be unambiguous, clear and specific, and that they are written using verbs that express your operational intentions.

The . . . Model

Main objective:
To evaluate the effectiveness of the . . . (name of the model) developed by . . . (name of the office).
Subobjectives:
1 To identify the strengths and weaknesses of the model as perceived by various stakeholders.
2 To find out the attitudes of consumers, service providers and managers, and relevant community agencies towards the model.
3 To determine the extent of reduction, if any, in the number of children in the care of the department since the introduction of the model.
4 To determine the impact of the model on the number of Child Concern Reports and Child Maltreatment Allegations.
5 To assess the ability of the model to build the capacity of consumers and service providers to deal with problems in the area of child protection.
6 To recommend strategies to overcome problems, if any, with the model.
7 To estimate the cost of delivering services in accordance with the model to a family.

Step 3: Converting concepts into indicators into variables

In evaluation, as well as in other research studies, often we use concepts to describe our intentions. For example, we say that we are seeking to evaluate outcomes, effectiveness, impact or satisfaction. The meaning ascribed to such words, may be clear to you but may differ markedly from the understanding of others. This is because these terms involve subjective impressions. They need operational definitions in terms of their measurement in order to develop a uniform understanding. When you use concepts the next problem you need to deal with is the development of a 'meaning' for each concept that describes them appropriately for the contexts in which they are being applied. The meaning of a concept in a specific situation is arrived at by developing indicators. To develop indicators, you must answer questions such as: 'What does this concept mean?', 'When can I say that the program is effective, or has brought about a change, or consumers or service providers are satisfied?' and 'On what basis should I conclude that an intervention has been effective?' Answers to such questions become your *indicators* and their measurement and assessment become the basis of judgement about effectiveness, impact or satisfaction. Indicators are specific, observable, measurable characteristics or changes that can be attributed to the program or intervention.

A critical challenge to an evaluator in outcome measurement is identifying and deciding what indicators to use in order to assess how well the program being evaluated has done regarding an outcome. Remember that not all changes or impacts of a program may be reflected by one indicator. In many situations you need to have multiple indicators to make an assessment of the success or failure of a program. Figure 18.9 shows the process of converting concepts into questions that you ask of your respondents.

Figure 18.9   Converting concepts into variables into questions in evaluation studies

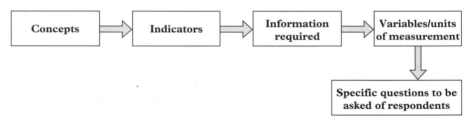

Some indicators are easy to measure, whereas others may be difficult. For example, an indicator such as the number of program users is easy to measure, whereas a program's impact on self-esteem is more difficult to measure.

In order to assess the impact of an intervention, different types of effectiveness indicators can be used. These indicators may be either qualitative or quantitative, and their measurement may range from subjective-descriptive impressions to objective-measurable-discrete changes. If you are inclined more towards qualitative studies, you may use in-depth interviewing, observation or focus groups to establish whether or not there have been changes in perceptions, attitudes or behaviour among the recipients of a program with respect to these indicators. In this case, changes are as perceived by your respondents: there is, as such, no measurement involved. On the other hand, if you prefer a quantitative approach, you may use various methods to measure change in the indicators using *interval* or *ratio* scales. In all the designs that we have discussed above in outcome evaluation, you may use qualitative or quantitative indicators to measure outcomes.

Now let us take an example to illustrate the process of converting concepts to questions. Suppose you are working in a department concerned with protection of children and are testing a new model of service delivery.

Let us further assume that your model is to achieve greater participation and involvement of children, their families and non-statutory organisations working in the community in decision making about children. Your assumption is that with their involvement and participation in developing the proposed intervention strategies, higher compliance will result, which, in turn, will result in the achievement of the desired goals.

As part of your evaluation of the model, you may choose a number of the indicators such as the impact on the:

- number of children under the care of the department/agency;
- number of children returned to the family or the community for care;
- number of reported cases of 'Child Maltreatment Allegations';
- number of reported cases of 'Child Concern Reports';
- extent of involvement of the family and community agencies in the decision-making process about a child.

You may also choose indicators such as the attitude of:
- children, where appropriate, and family members towards their involvement in the decision-making process;
- service providers and service managers towards the usefulness of the model;
- non-statutory organisations towards their participation in the decision-making process;
- various stakeholders towards the ability of the model to build the capacity of consumers of the service for self-management;
- family members towards their involvement in the decision-making process.

The scales used in the measurement determine whether an indicator will be considered as a 'soft' or 'hard'. Attitude towards an issue can be measured using well-advanced attitudinal scales or by simply asking a respondent to give his/her opinion. The first method will yield a hard indicator while the second will provide a soft. Similarly, change in the number of children, if asked as an opinion question, will be treated as a soft indicator.

Figure 18.10 summarise the process of converting concepts into questions, using the example described above. Once you have understood the logic behind this operationalisation, you will find it easier to apply in other similar situations.

Step 4: Developing evaluation methodology

As with a non-evaluative study, you need to identify the design that best suits the objectives of your evaluation, keeping in mind the resources at your disposal. In most evaluation studies the emphasis is on 'constructing' a comparative picture, before and after the introduction of an intervention, in relation to the indicators you have selected. On the basis of your knowledge about study designs and the designs discussed in this chapter, you propose one that is most suitable for your situation. Also, as part of

Figure 18.10 An example of converting concepts into questions

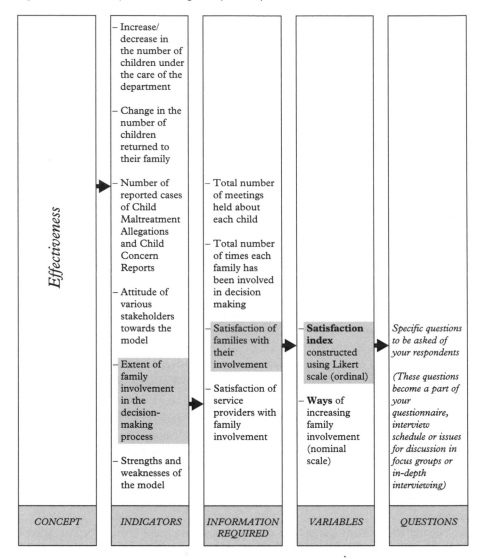

evaluation methodology, do not forget to consider other aspects of the process such as:

- From whom will you collect the required information?
- How will you identify your respondents?
- Are you going to select a sample of respondents? If yes, how and how large will it be?
- How will you make initial contact with your potential respondents?
- How will you seek the informed consent of your respondents for their participation in the evaluation?
- How will the needed information be collected?
- How will you take care of the ethical issues confronting your evaluation?
- How will you maintain the anonymity of the information obtained?

- What is the relevance of the evaluation for your respondents or others in a similar situation?

You need to consider all these aspects before you start collecting data.

Step 5: Collecting data

As in a research study, data collection is the most important and time-consuming phase. As you know, the quality of evaluation findings is entirely dependent upon the data collected. Hence, the importance of data collection cannot be overemphasised. Whether quantitative or qualitative methods are used for data collection, it is essential to ensure that quality is maintained in the process.

You can have a highly structured evaluation, placing a great emphasis on indicators and their measurement, or you can opt for an unstructured and flexible inquiry: as mentioned earlier, the decision is dependent upon the purpose of your evaluation. For exploratory purposes, flexibility and a lack of structure is an asset; whereas, if the purpose is to formulate a policy, measure the impact of an intervention or to work out the cost of an intervention, a greater structure and standarisation and less flexibility are important.

Step 6: Analysing data

As with research in general, the way you can analyse the data depends upon the way it was collected and the purpose for which you are going to use the findings. For policy decisions and decisions about program termination or continuation, you need to ascertain the magnitude of change, based on a reasonable sample size. Hence, your data need to be subjected to a statistical framework of analysis. However, if you are evaluating a process or procedure, you can use an interpretive frame of analysis.

Step 7: Writing an evaluation report

As you know, the quality of your work and the impact of your findings are greatly dependent upon how well you communicate them to your readers. Your report is the only basis of judgement for an average reader. Hence, you need to pay extra attention to your writing.

As for a research report, there are different writing styles. In the author's opinion you should communicate your findings under headings that reflect the objectives of your evaluation. We prefer that the findings be accompanied by recommendations pertaining to them. Your report should also have an executive summary of your findings and recommendations.

Step 8: Sharing findings with stakeholders

A very important aspect of any evaluation is the sharing of the findings with the various groups of stakeholders. It is a good idea to convene a group comprising all stakeholders to communicate what your evaluation has found. Be open about your findings and resist pressure from any interest group. Objectively and honestly communicate what your evaluation has found. It is of utmost importance that you adhere to ethical principles and the professional code of conduct.

As you have seen, the process of a research study and that of an evaluation is almost the same. The only difference is the use of certain models in the measurement of the effectiveness of an intervention. It is therefore important for you to know about research methodology before undertaking an evaluation.

Involving stakeholders in evaluation

Most evaluations have a number of stakeholders, ranging from consumers to experts in the area, including service providers and managers. It is important that all categories of stakeholder be involved at all stages of an evaluation. Failure to involve any group may hinder success in completion of the evaluation and seriously affect confidence in your findings. It is therefore important that you identify all stakeholders and seek their involvement and participation in the evaluation. This ensures that they feel a part of the evaluation process, which, in turn, markedly enhances the probability of them accepting the findings. The following steps outline a process for involving stakeholders in an evaluation study.

Step 1　**Identifying stakeholders**. First of all talk with managers, planners, program administrators, service providers and the consumers of the program, either individually or collectively, and identify who they think are the direct and indirect stakeholders. Having collected this information, share it with all groups of stakeholders to see if anyone has been left out. Prepare a list of all stakeholders making sure it is acceptable to all significant ones. If there are any disagreements, it is important to resolve them.

Step 2　**Involving stakeholders**. In order to develop a common perspective with respect to various aspects of the evaluation, it is important that different categories of stakeholder be actively involved in the whole process of evaluation from the identification of their concerns to the sharing of its findings. In particular, it is important to involve them in developing a framework for evaluation, selecting the evaluation indicators, and developing procedures and tools for their measurement.

Step 3　**Developing a common perspective among stakeholders towards the evaluation**. Different stakeholders may have different understandings of the word 'evaluation'. Some may have a very definite opinion about it and how it should be carried out while others may not have any conception. Different stakeholders may also have different opinions about the relevance of a particular piece of information for answering an evaluation question. Or they may have different interests. To make evaluation meaningful to the majority of stakeholders, it is important that their perspectives and understandings of evaluation be understood and that a common perspective on the evaluation be arrived at during the planning stage.

Step 4 **Resolving conflicts of interest**. As an evaluator, if you find that stakeholders have strong opinions and there is a conflict of interest among them with respect to any aspect of the evaluation, it is extremely important to resolve it. However, you have to be very careful in resolving differences, and must not give the impression that you are favouring any particular subgroup.

Step 5 **Identifying the information stakeholders need from the proposed evaluation**. Identify, from each group of stakeholders, the information they think is important to meet their needs and the objectives of the evaluation.

Step 6 **Forming a steering committee**. For routine consultation, the sharing of ideas and day-to-day decision making, it is important that you ask the stakeholders to elect a steering committee with whom you, as the evaluator, can consult and interact. In addition to providing you with a forum for consultation and guidance, such a committee gives stakeholders a continuous sense of involvement in the evaluation.

Ethics in evaluation

Being ethical is the core requirement of an evaluation. If for some reason you cannot be ethical, do not undertake the evaluation, as you will end up doing harm of indescribable proportion to others, and that is unethical. Whenever you undertake an evaluation, keep in mind that different stakeholders may have different interests in the evaluation. Although, as a good evaluator, you may have involved all of them in the planning and conduct of the evaluation, it is possible that sometimes, when findings are not in someone's interest, a stakeholder will challenge you. It is of the utmost importance that you stand firm on the findings and do not surrender to any pressure from anyone. Surrendering to such pressure is unethical. It is for this reason also that you need to be very competent in research and evaluation methodologies.

In order to influence an intervention, as a sequel to your evaluation, the following are important:

- Your use of research methodology should be sound so that you can defend it if subjected to professional scrutiny. Use of inappropriate methodologies is unethical.
- You involve *all* stakeholders in the planning and execution of the evaluation. At the same time avoid being influenced by any interest group to the extent of altering the observed facts.
- You follow all the rules of ethical practice in undertaking the evaluation. Honesty, objectivity in intentions and practice, a sound platform of

professional knowledge, proper use of information and so on are well-known indicators of ethical practice. (Refer to Chapter 14 for details.)

• You should be honest and firm about the findings of the evaluation. Do not change your findings under the influence of anyone. It is unethical not to report your findings objectively.

SUMMARY

In this chapter some of the aspects of evaluation research are discussed, in brief, in order to make you aware of them, rather than to provide you with a detailed knowledge base. It is highly recommended that you read some books on evaluation research. This chapter highlights the relationship between research methodology *per se* and its application to evaluation in practice. Evaluation skills are built on the knowledge and skills of research methodology: an evaluator has to be a good researcher.

In this chapter we look at some of the definitions of 'evaluation' and identify its characteristics. The chapter examines the reasons for undertaking an evaluation. The intervention-development-evaluation process is discussed in detail, exploring the relationship between program development and its evaluation. Evaluation studies are classified from two perspectives: the *focus of evaluation* and the *philosophical basis* that underpins them. The typology of evaluation studies is developed from these perspectives. The chapter describes the four different types of evaluation from the perspective of their focus: *program/intervention planning evaluation*, *process/monitoring evaluation*, *impact/outcome evaluation* and *cost-benefit/cost-effectiveness evaluation*. From the perspective of the philosophies that underpin these evaluations, again, four types of evaluation are identified: *goal-centred/objective evaluation*, *consumer-oriented/client-centred evaluation*, *improvement-oriented evaluation* and *holistic evaluation*. The evaluation process is discussed step by step. Considerable discussion centres on how to convert concepts into indicators into variables, enabling the formulation of questions for respondents that will elicit the required information. How to involve stakeholders in an evaluation process is discussed, again, step by step. Finally, the chapter points out some of the ethical issues in evaluation.

APPENDIX

Developing a research project—
a set of exercises for beginners

Application is the essence of knowledge. However, there always remains a gap between theoretical knowledge and its application. It is only with practice that this gap can be narrowed. A beginner attempting to apply theoretical knowledge needs direction and guidance. This set of exercises has been developed with this belief. The exercises are based upon the operational steps in the research process and can be applied to the development of any research project or, more correctly, a research project can be developed while working through these exercises.

The main aim of these exercises is to provide a broad framework for developing the operational steps. For each operational step, there is at least one exercise. Within each exercise, questions are provided to stimulate awareness of issues relevant to the steps, to help you to think through procedures and to provide a framework for the development of an outline for your study.

Answers to these questions and awareness of the issues that the exercises outline will put you in a position to complete the framework suggested for writing a research proposal (Chapter 13), and these will constitute the core of your research proposal.

It is important for a beginner to work through these exercises with considerable thought and care.

Exercise A: Formulating a research problem

Selecting a research problem is one of the most important aspects of social research. Thinking through a research problem with care can prevent a tremendous wastage of human and financial resources. A research problem should be clearly stated and be specific in nature. The feasibility of the study in terms of the availability of technical expertise, finances and time, and in terms of its relevance, should be considered thoroughly at the problem-formulation stage. In studies that attempt to establish a causal relationship or an association, the accuracy of the measurement of independent (cause) and dependent (effect) variables is of crucial importance and, hence, should be given serious consideration. If you have already selected a problem, you need not go through this process.

Start by identifying a broad area you are interested in. For example: a health, education or treatment program; migration; patient care; community health; community needs; foster care; or the relationship between unemployment and street crime. Chapter 4 of this book will help you to work through this exercise.

Step I   Select a broad area of study that interests you from within your academic discipline. ⎯⎯⎯⎯⎯⎯⎯⎯⎯⎯⎯⎯⎯⎯⎯⎯⎯⎯⎯

Having selected an area, 'dissect' it in order to identify its subareas. For example, say your broad area of interest is migration. Some aspects or subareas of migration are:

- A socioeconomic–demographic profile of immigrants
- Reasons for immigration
- Problems of immigrants
- Services provided to immigrants
- Attitudes of immigrants towards migration
- Attitudes of host communities towards immigrants
- The extent of acculturation and assimilation
- Racial discrimination in the host country

Perhaps you are interested in studying a public health program. Dissect it as finely as possible in order to identify the aspects that could be studied. List them as they come to you. For example:

- A socioeconomic–demographic profile of the target group
- The morbidity and mortality patterns in a community
- The extent and nature of program utilisation
- The effects of a program on a community
- The effectiveness of a particular health promotion strategy

Or your interest may be in studying delinquents. Some aspects of delinquency are:

- Delinquency as related to unemployment, broken homes or urbanisation
- A profile of delinquents
- Reasons for delinquency
- Various therapeutic strategies

Step II 'Dissect' your broad area of study into subareas as discretely as possible. Have a one-person brainstorming session.

1 _____

2 _____

3 _____

4 _____

5 _____

To investigate all these subareas is neither advisable nor feasible. Select only those subareas that would be possible to study within the constraints of time, finance and expertise at your disposal. One way to select your subarea is to start with a process of elimination: delete those areas you are not very interested in. Towards the end it may become difficult but you need to keep eliminating until you have selected a subarea that can be managed within your constraints. Even one subarea can provide you with a valid and exhaustive study.

Step III From the above subareas, select a subarea or subareas in which you would like to conduct your study.

1 _____

2 _____

3 _____

Step IV Within each chosen subarea, what research questions do you hope to answer? Be as specific as possible. (You can select one or as many subareas as you want.)

Subarea	Specific research questions to be answered	
1	(a)	_____
	(b)	_____
	(c)	_____
	(d)	_____
	(e)	_____

2 (a) _____
   (b) _____
   (c) _____
   (d) _____
   (e) _____

3 (a) _____
   (b) _____
   (c) _____
   (d) _____
   (e) _____

The research questions to be answered through the study become the basis of your objectives. Use action-oriented words in the formulation of objectives. The main difference between research questions and objectives is the way they are written. Questions are worded in question form and objectives are statements referring to the achievement of a task.

Your main objective should indicate the overall focus of your study and the subobjectives, its specific aspects. Subobjectives should be numerically listed. They should be worded clearly and unambiguously. Make sure each objective contains only one aspect of the study.

Step V On the basis of your research questions, formulate the main objective and the subobjectives of your study.

Main objective (the main focus of your study):

_____

_____

_____

Subobjectives (specific aspects of your study):

1 _____

_____

2 _____

_____

3 _____

_____

4 _____

_____

5 _____

_____

Step VI Carefully consider the following aspects of your study.

Task	What is involved	Time needed	Approx. cost	Technical expertise needed	Gaps in knowledge and skills
Literature review					
Instrument construction					
Data collection					
Data analysis					
Draft report					
Final report					

> Now you have developed the objectives of your study. Take some time to think about them. Be clear about what tasks are involved, what time is realistically required and what skills you need to develop in order to conduct your study. Consider these areas carefully.

Step VII Double-check:

- Are you really interested in the study?
  Yes ☐ No ☐ Uncertain ☐

- Do you agree with the objectives of the study?
  Yes ☐ No ☐ Uncertain ☐

- Are you certain you want to pursue the study?
  Yes ☐ No ☐ Uncertain ☐

- Do you have adequate resources?
  Yes ☐ No ☐ Uncertain ☐

- Do you have access to an appropriate study population?
  Yes ☐ No ☐ Uncertain ☐

If your answer to any of these questions is either 'no' or 'uncertain', re-examine the aspect carefully and make the appropriate changes.

What, in your opinion, is the relevance of this study to theory and practice? How will your study contribute to the existing body of knowledge, help the practitioners in your profession and assist in program development and policy formulation?

Relevance to theory: _____

_____

_____

_____

Relevance to practice: _____

_____

_____

_____

Exercise B: Identifying variables

In the process of formulating a research problem, knowledge about variables plays an important role. Concepts are highly subjective as their understanding varies from person to person and, as such, they may not be measurable. Any concept, perception or imagination that can be measured on any one of the four measurement scales (nominal, ordinal, internal or ratio), is called a variable. It is important for concepts used in a study to be operationalised in measurable terms so that the extent of variation in a study population's understanding of them is reduced, if not eliminated.

Think how you will operationalise any concepts used in the objectives, research questions or hypotheses formulated: what are their indicators and how will they be measured?

The following table suggests how you might operationalise the concept of 'effectiveness', in relation to a health education program on AIDS. It lists the indicators of effectiveness, sets out the variables that measure the indicators, and describes the unit of measurement for the variables.

Concept	Indicator	Variable(s)	Unit of measurement
Effectiveness	*Awareness* of AIDS	Extent of change in:	Change in the *proportion* of the population, before and after the health education program, with respect to:
	Knowledge about AIDS	Awareness Knowledge Practice	Awareness of, and knowledge about, different aspects of AIDS
	Use of contraceptives (*practice*)		Use of contraceptives for safe sex

This exercise is designed to help you operationalise the major concepts used in your study. Refer to Chapter 5 for a discussion of variables.

Step I   Operationalise your concepts.

Objectives/research questions/hypotheses	Major concepts	Indicators	Variables	Unit of measurement

It is essential to develop a working or operational definition of your study population. For example, who would you consider to be a patient, an immigrant, a youth, a psychologist, a teacher, a delinquent or a Christian? Working definitions play a crucial role in avoiding ambiguities in the selection of a sample and help you to narrow your study population.

Step II Operationally define your study population.

_____

_____

_____

_____

Exercise C: Constructing hypotheses

As discussed, some believe that one must have a hypothesis to undertake an investigation; however, in the author's opinion, hypotheses, although they bring clarity, specificity and focus to a research problem, are not essential for a study. You can conduct a valid investigation without constructing a single formal hypothesis. On the other hand, you can construct as many hypotheses as you think appropriate. In epidemiological studies, to narrow the field of investigation, one must construct a hypothesis as to the probable cause of the condition to be investigated.

A hypothesis is a hunch, assumption, suspicion, assertion or idea about a phenomenon, relationship or situation, which you intend to investigate in order to find out if you are right. If it proves to be right, your assumption was correct; hence, you prove that your hypothesis was true. Otherwise, you conclude your hypothesis to be false.

Disproving a hypothesis is as important as, or more important than, proving it. As a hypothesis is usually constructed on the basis of what is commonly believed to be right, your disproving it might lead to something new that has been ignored by previous researchers.

A hypothesis should be conceptually simple, clear and specific, and be capable of verification and being expressed operationally.

There is a specific way of writing a hypothesis, with which you need to be familiar (refer to Chapter 6).

Step I   Construct your hypothesis or hypotheses for each subobjective/ research question.

Objectives/research questions	Hypotheses to be tested
	1
	2
	3
	1
	2
	3
	1
	2
	3

Exercise D: Conceptualising a study design

All the previous exercises have been developed to help you decide *what* you want to find out *about*. The next step is to decide *how* to investigate. This includes deciding on a plan, procedures and methods. The details of your plan, procedures and methods become the core of your study design.

A study design describes the design *per se* and details the logistical procedures required to obtain information from the study population. It provides you with an overall plan for undertaking your study.

The issues raised in this exercise will help you to conceptualise your study design. Chapter 8 details the various types of study design.

Step I   Answer the following questions about your study.

1   Is the design that you propose to adopt to conduct your study cross-sectional, longitudinal, experimental or comparative in nature?

_____

_____

_____

_____

_____

2   Why did you select this design?

_____

_____

_____

3   What, in your opinion, are the strengths of this design?

_____

_____

_____

4   What are the limitations of this design?

_____

_____

_____

5   Who constitutes your study population?

_____

_____

6   Will you be able to identify each respondent?

Yes ☐   No ☐

6(a) If yes, how will they be identified?

_____

_____

_____

6(b) If no, how do you plan to get in touch with them?

_____

_____

_____

_____

7 Do you plan to select a sample?

Yes ☐   No ☐

7(a) In either case, explain the reasons for your decision.

_____

_____

_____

8 How will you collect data from your respondents (e.g. interview, questionnaire)?

_____

_____

8(a) Why did you select this method of data collection?

_____

_____

8(b) What, in your opinion, are its strengths and weaknesses?

Strengths:

_____

_____

Weaknesses:

_____

_____

8(c) If you are interviewing, where will the interviews be held?

_____

8(d) If you are using mailed questionnaires:
　　　(i) From where will you obtain the addresses of potential respondents?

_____

_____

(ii) Are you planning to enclose a self-addressed stamped envelope with the questionnaires?

Yes ☐   No ☐

(iii) In the case of a low response rate, will you send a reminder?

Yes ☐   No ☐

(iv) If there are queries, how should respondents get in touch with you?

_____

_____

Step II On the basis of the above information, describe your study design. (For further guidance, consult Chapter 8.)

_____

_____

_____

_____

_____

_____

_____

_____

_____

_____

_____

_____

_____

Exercise E: Developing a research instrument

The construction of a research instrument is the first practical step in operationalising your study. It is the most important aspect of your research as it constitutes the input; the output (the findings and conclusions) is entirely dependent upon it. Items in a research instrument are questions asked of respondents. Responses become the raw data that are processed. The famous saying about computers 'garbage in garbage out' also applies to research. To a large extent, the validity of the findings depends upon the quality of the raw data which, in turn, depends upon the research instrument you have used. If the latter is valid and reliable, the findings should also be valid and reliable.

The quality of a research instrument largely depends upon your experience in research. It is important for a beginner to follow the suggested steps outlined in Chapter 9.

The wording of your questions should be simple and without ambiguities. Do *not* ask leading questions or questions based upon presumptions. Double-barrelled questions should also be avoided.

The pre-test of a research instrument is an integral part of instrument construction. As a rule, the pre-test should not be carried out on your sample but on a similar population.

Step I   Formulate questions by examining your subobjectives/research questions/hypotheses; by specifying what information you require to address them; by identifying the required variables; and by formulating questions to obtain the required information.

Step II   Write down these questions on a piece of paper, giving particular attention to the following:

- the wording of questions;
- the order of questions;
- the relevance of each question.

Specific objectives/ research questions/ hypotheses	Specifically what information do you require?	Identify the required variables	Formulate questions

Step III   If you are developing a questionnaire, incorporate interactive statements at appropriate places.

Step IV   After developing the first draft of your research instrument answer the questions yourself; that is, interview yourself. If you are unable to answer a question, re-examine it.

Step V   Once you are satisfied with the research instrument, select a few respondents from a population similar to the one you are going to study and pre-test it. The purpose of the pre-test/field-test is not to obtain information but to uncover problems with the instrument. If the instrument is an interview schedule, interview the pre-test respondents to find out if they understand the questions. If a question is not understood, find out what the respondent did not understand. If the same problem is identified by others, change the wording. If your instrument is a questionnaire, ask the pre-test respondents to go through the questions with the aim of identifying any questions that are difficult to understand. It may be necessary to change the wording of questions with which pre-test respondents have difficulties.

Step VI   When you are sure that the instrument is free from ambiguities and other problems, finalise it.

Step VII   Having developed the instrument, take a piece of paper and draw two columns. In one column write each subobjective, research question and hypothesis separately, and in the other, write the question number(s) that provide information for these objectives, research questions or hypotheses. In other words, make each question match the objective for which it provides information. If a question cannot be linked to a specific objective, research question or hypothesis, examine why it was included.

Step VIII   Prepare the final draft of your research instrument.

Step IX   If you plan to use a computer for data analysis, you may provide space on the research instrument for coding the data.

Exercise F: Selecting a sample

The accuracy of your research results also depends upon the way in which you select your sample. The basic objective of any sampling design is to minimise, within the limitation of cost, any difference between the values obtained from your sample and those prevalent in the population.

The underlying premise in sampling is that if a relatively small number of units is scientifically selected, it can provide, with a sufficiently high degree of probability, a true reflection of the sampling population that is being studied.

Sampling theory is guided by two principles:

- the avoidance of bias in the selection of a sample;
- the attainment of maximum precision for a given outlay of resources.

You can select a probability or a non-probability sample. Both have advantages and disadvantages and both are appropriate for certain situations. But whatever sampling design you choose, make sure you take steps to avoid introducing bias.

For details on sampling designs, refer to Chapter 12.

Step I   Answer the following about your sampling design.

1 What is the total size of your study population?

☐ _____   Unknown

2 Do you want to select a sample?

Yes ☐   No ☐

2(a) If yes, what is your sample size? _____

3 How will you select your sample?

_____

_____

_____

4 Why did you select this design? (What are its strengths?)

_____

_____

_____

5 In your opinion, what are the limitations of this design?

_____

_____

_____

_____

Step II On the basis of the answers to the above questions, write about
your sampling design as described in Chapter 13, 'Writing a
research proposal'.

_____

_____

_____

_____

_____

_____

_____

Exercise G: Data analysis and developing a frame of analysis

In general terms describe the strategy you plan to use for data analysis. Specify whether the data will be analysed manually or by computer. For computer analysis you need to identify the program you plan to use.

You should also specify the type of analysis you plan to carry out—that is, frequency distributions, cross-tabulations, regression analysis or analysis of variance. It is also important to plan which variables will be subjected to which type of statistical procedure.

If you have used certain concepts in your study, how will these concepts be operationalised? For example, if you were measuring the effectiveness of a health program, how would the responses to the various questions be combined to ascertain effectiveness? Keep in mind that when you actually carry out data analysis, you may develop new ideas on how to improve the analysis of data. Refer to Chapter 15 for details.

Step I   Think through the following issues:

1   If you are planning to use a computer for data analysis, what software will you use?

_____

2   Which variables will you subject to frequency distribution analysis?

_____

_____

_____

_____

_____

3   Which variables will be cross-tabulated?

_____

_____

_____

_____

_____

4 Which variables will be subjected to which statistical procedures (e.g. regression analysis, ANOVA, factor analysis)?

_____

_____

_____

_____

5 How do you plan to construct the major variables (e.g. satisfaction index, effectiveness)?

_____

_____

_____

_____

Exercise H: Developing an outline of your chapters

Although each operational step is important, in a way writing the report is the most crucial as it tells others about the outcome of your study: it is the outcome of the hard work you have put into your study and is the only thing visible to readers. Hence, you could lose even the most valuable work if your report is not well-written.

The quality of your report depends upon many things: your writing skills; the clarity of your thoughts and their logical expression; your knowledge of the subject; and your experience in research writing.

Developing an outline for the structure of the report is extremely useful. As a beginner it is important that you think through carefully the contents of your report, organise them around the main themes of your study, and ensure that the various aspects of a theme are well-integrated and follow a logical progression.

This exercise is designed to help you to organise your thoughts with respect to writing your research report. You should, as far as possible, attempt to place the various aspects of your report under chapter headings, even if these are very tentative. However, for this exercise just develop headings for your chapters. When you actually start writing, the contents of each chapter can be developed and adjusted in greater detail. Consult Chapter 17 for more details.

1 What are the main themes of your study?

_____

_____

_____

_____

_____

_____

2 Develop chapter headings under which the above themes will be organised in writing your report.

_____

_____

_____

_____

_____

_____

REFERENCES

Ackroyd, Stephen & John Hughes, 1992, *Data Collection in Context*, New York, Longman.

Alkin, Marvin C. & Lewis C. Solomon (ed.), 1983, *The Costs of Evaluation*, Beverly Hills, Sage Publications.

Alwin, Duane F. (ed.), 1978, *Survey Design and Analysis—Current Issues*, Beverly Hills, California, Sage Publications.

Babbie, Earl, 1989, *The Practice of Social Research*, Belmont, California, Wadesworth Publishing Company.

Babbie, Earl, 1990, *Survey Research Methods* (2nd ed.), Belmont, California, Wadesworth Publishing Company.

Bailey, Kenneth D., 1978, *Methods of Social Research* (3rd ed.) New York, The Free Press.

Barton, Ruth, 1988, *Understanding Social Statistics—An Introduction to Descriptive Statistics*, Perth Editorial/Publication Unit, Division of Arts, Education and Social Sciences, Curtin University of Technology.

Bernard H. Russell, 1994, *Research Methods in Anthropology: qualitative and quantitative approaches* (2nd ed.), Thousand Oaks, Sage Publications.

Black, James A. & Dean J. Champion, 1976, *Methods and Issues in Social Research*, New York, John Wiley & Sons, Inc.

Bogdan, Robert & Sari Knopp Biklen, 1992, *Qualitative Research for Education: An introduction to theory and methods* (2nd ed.), Boston, Allyn & Bacon.

Bradburn, M. Norman & Seymour Sudman, 1979, *Improving Interview Method and Questionnaire Design*, London, Jossey-Bass Publishers.

Brinberg, David & Joseph E. McGreth, 1985, *Validity and the Research Process*, Beverly Hills, Sage Publications.

Bulmer, Martin (ed.), 1977, *Sociological Research Methods—An Introduction*, London, The MacMillian Press Ltd.

Burns, Robert B., 1994, *Introduction to Research Methods* (2nd ed.), Melbourne, Longman Cheshire.

Butcher, Judith, 1981, *Copy-Editing, The Cambridge Handbook for Editors, Authors and Publishers* (2nd ed.), Cambridge, Cambridge University Press.

Carr, Wilfred & Steven Kemmis, 1986, *Becoming Critical: education, knowledge and action research*, Melbourne, Vic., Deakin University.

Chicago Manual of Style, The (14th ed.), 1993, Chicago and London, The University of Chicago Press.

Cohen, Morris R. & Ernest Nagel, 1966, *An Introduction to Logic and Scientific Methods*, London, Routledge and Kegan Paul Ltd.

Collins Dictionary of the English Language, 1979, Sydney, Collins.

Cozby, C. Paul, 1985, *Methods in Behavioral Research*, London, Mayfield Publication Company.

de Vas, D.A., 1985, *Survey in Social Research*, Sydney, Allen & Unwin.

Dixon, Beverly & Gary Bouma, 1984, *The Research Process*, Melbourne, Oxford University Press.

Duncan, Otis Dudley, 1984, *Notes on Social Measurement—Historical and Critical*, New York, Russell Sage Foundation.

Festinger, Leon & Daniel Katz (eds), 1966, *Research Methods in Behavioral Sciences*, New York, Holt, Rinehart and Winston.

Grinnell, Richard Jr (ed.), 1988, *Social Work Research and Evaluation* (3rd ed.), Itasca, Illinois, F.E. Peacock Publishers.

Grinnell, Richard Jr (ed.), 1993, *Social Work, Research and Evaluation* (4th ed.), Itasca, Illinois, F.E. Peacock Publishers.

Hakim, Catherine, 1987, *Research Design—Strategies and Choices in the Design of Social Research*, London, Allen & Unwin.

Hawe, Penelope, Deirdre Degeling & Jane Hall, 1992, *Evaluating Health Promotion*, Sydney, Maclennan+Petty.

Hessler, Richard M., 1992, *Social Research Methods*, New York, West Publishing Company.

Kerlinger, Fred N., 1973, *Foundations of Behavioral Research* (2nd ed.), Holt, Rinehart and Winston, Inc.

Kerlinger, Fred N., 1979, *Behavioral Research—A Conceptual Approach*, Sydney, Holt, Rinehart and Winston.

Kerlinger, Fred N., 1986, *Foundations of Behavioral Research* (3rd ed.) New York, Holt, Rinehart and Winston.

Leary, Mark R., 1995, *Introduction to Behavioral Research Methods* (2nd ed.), Pacific Grove California, Brooks/Cole.

Longyear, Marie (ed.), 1983, *The McGraw-Hill Style Manual, A Concise Guide for Writers and Editors*, New York, McGraw-Hill Book Company.

Lundberg, George A., 1942, *Social Research—A Study in Methods of Gathering Data* (2nd ed.), New York, Longmans, Green & Co.

Martin, David W., 1985, *Doing Psychological Experiments* (2nd ed.), Monterey, California, Brooks/Cole Publishing Company.

Minium, Edward W., 1978, *Statistical Reasoning in Psychology and Education* (2nd ed.), New York, John Wiley & Sons.

Moser, C.A. & G. Kalton, 1989, *Survey Methods in Social Investigation* (2nd ed.), Eldershot, England, Gower.

Nachmias, David & Clara Nachmias, 1987, *Research Methods in Social Sciences*, New York, St Martin's Press.

Patton, Michael Quinn, 1990, *Qualitative Evaluation and Research Methods*, Newbury Park, California, Sage Publications.

Poincaré, 1952, *Science and Hypothesis*, New York, Dover Publications.

Powers, Gerald T., Thomas M. Meenaghan & Beverley G. Twoomey, 1985, *Practice Focused Research: Integrating Human Practice and Research*, Englewood Cliffs, NJ, Prentice Hall.

Rohlf, F. James & Robert R. Sokal, 1969, *Statistical Tables*, San Francisco, W.H. Freeman and Company.

Rossi, Peter H. & Howard E. Freeman, 1993, *Evaluation: A Systematic Approach*, Newbury Park, California, Sage Publications.

Rossi, Peter H., Howard E. Freeman & Mark W. Lipsey, 1999, *Evaluation: A systematic Approach* (6th ed.), Thousand Oaks, Sage Publications.

Rutman, Leonard (ed.), 1977, *Evaluation Research Methods: a basic guide*, Beverly Hills, Sage Publications.

Rutman, Leonard, 1980, *Planning Useful Evaluations: availability assessment*, Beverly Hills, Sage Publications.

Rutman, Leonard, 1984, *Evaluation Research Methods: A Basic Guide* (2nd ed.), Beverly Hills, Sage Publications.

Sandefur, Gary D., Howard E. Freeman & Peter H. Rossi, 1986, *Workbook for Evaluation: A Systematic Approach* (3rd ed.), Beverly Hills, Sage Publications.

Schinke, Steven P. & Lewayne, Gilchrist, 1993, 'Arrics in Research' in R.M. Grinnell (ed.), *Social Work, Research and Evaluation* (4th ed.), Itasca, Illinois, F.E. Peacock Publishers.

Selltiz, Jahoda, Morton, Deutsch & Stuart Cook, 1962, *Research Methods in Social Relations* (revised), New York, Holt, Rinehart and Winston.

Siegel, Sidney, 1956, *Nonparametric Statistics for the Behavioral Sciences*, Sydney, McGraw-Hill Book Company Inc.

Simon, Julian L., 1969, *Basic Research Methods in Social Sciences—The Art of Empirical Investigation*, New York, Random House.

Smith, Herman W., 1991, *Strategies of Social Research* (3rd ed.), Orlando, FL, Holt, Rinehart and Winston.

Steven, S.S., 1951, 'Mathematics, Measurement, and Psychophysics' in S.S. Steven (ed.), *Handbook of Experimental Psychology*, New York, Wiley.

Stufflebeam, Daniel L. & Anthony J. Shinkfield, 1985, *Systematic Evaluation: A Self-Instructional Guide to Theory and Practice*, Boston, Kluwer-Nizhoff Publishing.

Taylor Steven J. & Robert Bogdan, 1998, *Introduction to Qualitative Research Methods: A guidebook and resource* (3rd ed.), New York, Wiley.

Thyer, Bruce A., 1993, 'Single-systems Research Design' in R.M. Grinnell (ed.), *Social Work, Research and Evaluation* (4th ed.), Itasca Illinois, F.E. Peacock Publishers.

Webster's Third International Dictionary, 1976, G. & C. Company, Springfield, Mass.

Yegidis, Bonnie & Robert Weinback, 1991, *Research Methods for Social Workers*, New York, Longman.

Young, Pauline V., 1966, *Scientific Social Survey Research* (4th ed.), Englewood Cliffs, Prentice Hall Inc.

INDEX

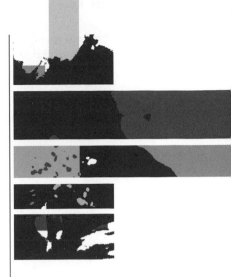